REGULATING CORPOR[illegible]
INTERNATIONAL [illegible]

The significance of Nicholas Lord's book lies in its analysis of the complexities and dynamics of translating international conventions into domestic legislation and then implementing them effectively at a country level. In doing so, it brings to the anti-corruption discourse at both academic and policy-maker levels, a wider perspective in terms of substantive and evidenced understanding of the rhetoric and realities of anti-corruption initiatives and agendas within country contexts.

Alan Doig, Northumbria University, UK

Nicholas Lord shows in this conceptually innovative and thoroughly researched comparative study just why efforts to counter transnational corporate bribery - unquantifiable but assumed to be widespread - rarely get beyond the symbolic. Encouraging self-regulation and reaching negotiated settlements with offenders is usually as good as it gets.

Peter Gill, University of Liverpool, UK

This excellent book is that rare thing - a readable and detailed examination of the dilemmas that contemporary societies - especially the UK and Germany - face in dealing with corporations operating transnationally in international commerce that use bribery to win or maintain contracts in overseas jurisdictions, often poor countries that most NGO campaigns focus on. Nick Lord persuasively argues that historical traditions have left a contemporary legacy that complicates international co-operation in prosecuting transnational and complexly organised corporate crimes. With well researched case studies, he shows that these historical traditions help us understand the limitations of criminal sanctioning by sovereign actors as an enforcement mechanism for controlling illicit corporate behaviour. He thoughtfully broadens out these case studies to discuss the overlap of regulatory and criminal justice in a context ignored in most recent work on preventive justice.

Michael Levi, Cardiff University, UK

Law, Crime and Culture

Series editors:
Professor Susanne Karstedt, University of Leeds, UK;
Professor Ralf Rogowski, University of Warwick, Coventry, UK; and
Professor Dirk Tänzler, University of Konstanz, Germany

The Law, Crime and Culture series explores an increasingly important and topical area of interdisciplinary research, covering a broad range of themes from understandings of social and legal order in individual cultures to intersections of criminological, legal and cultural inquiry. The series promotes cross-disciplinary and comparative research and the series editors actively welcome submissions on the many and varied topics related to crime, social control, and legal culture across the world.

Previously Published in this Series:

The Social Construction of Corruption in Europe
Edited by Dirk Tänzler, Konstadinos Maras and Angelos Giannakopoulos
978-1-4094-0297-8

Regulating Corporate Bribery in International Business

Anti-corruption in the UK and Germany

Nicholas Lord
University of Manchester, UK

Routledge
Taylor & Francis Group
LONDON AND NEW YORK

First published 2014 by Ashgate Publishing

Published 2016 by Routledge
2 Park Square, Milton Park, Abingdon, Oxfordshire OX14 4RN
711 Third Avenue, New York, NY 10017, USA

First issued in paperback 2016

Routledge is an imprint of the Taylor & Francis Group, an informa business

British Library Cataloguing in Publication Data
A catalogue record for this book is available from the British Library

The Library of Congress has cataloged the printed edition as follows:
Lord, Nicholas, author.
Regulating corporate bribery in international business : anti-corruption in the UK and Germany / by Nicholas Lord.
pages cm. – (Series: law, crime and culture)
Includes bibliographical references and index.
ISBN 978-1-4094-7055-7 (hardback) 1. Corporations–Corrupt practices–Great Britain. 2. Corporations–Corrupt practices–Germany. 3. Bribery–Great Britain. 4. Bribery–Germany. 5. Corpora-tions–Corrupt practices–Prevention. 6. International trade–Corrupt practices–Prevention.
I. Title.
KJE8643.L67 2014
345.41'02323–dc23

2014011138

ISBN 13: 978-1-138-63770-2 (pbk)
ISBN 13: 978-1-4094-7055-7 (hbk)

Contents

List of Figures and Tables

Figures

Tables

List of Abbreviations

ABPI	Association of the British Pharmaceutical Industry
ACOBA	Advisory Committee on Business Appointments
AG	*Aktiengesellschaft* (Public Limited Company) when following German company name, for example 'Siemens AG'
BaFin	*Bundesanstalt für Finanzdiesntleistungsaufsicht* (Federal Financial Supervisory Authority)
CJA	Criminal Justice Act
CoE	Council of Europe
CPS	Crown Prosecution Service
DoJ	Department of Justice
DPA	Deferred prosecution agreement
EC	European Commission
EU	European Union
FCPA	US Foreign Corrupt Practices Act 1977
FSA	Financial Services Authority
FT	Financial Times
FTSE	Financial Times and London Stock Exchange
GCC	German Criminal Code
GRECO	Group of States against Corruption
ICC	International Chamber of Commerce
MDB	Multi-lateral development bank
MLA	Mutual Legal Assistance
MNC	Multi-national Corporation
MoU	Memorandum of Understanding
MP	Member of Parliament
NASDAQ	originally the National Association of Securities Dealers Automated Quotations (a US stock exchange)
NCA	National Crime Agency

NPA	Non-prosecution agreement
OECD	Organisation for Economic Cooperation and Development
OLAF	European Anti-Fraud Office
OWiG	*Gesetz über Ordnungswidrigkeiten* (Administrative Offences Act)
PACI	Partnering Against Corruption Initiative
PIDA	Public Interest Disclosure Act 1998
POCA	Proceeds of Crime Act 2002
PwC	PricewaterhouseCoopers
QC	Queen's Counsel
SEC	Securities and Exchange Commission
SFO	Serious Fraud Office
SME	Small and medium enterprises
SOCA	Serious Organised Crime Agency
SOCPA	Serious Organised Crime and Police Act 2005
StPO	*Strafprozeßordnung* (German Code of Criminal Procedure)
TEL	Tetraethyl lead
TI	Transparency International
UK	United Kingdom
UKBA	UK Bribery Act 2010
UN	United Nations
UNCAC	UN Convention against Corruption 2003
US	United States

Acknowledgements

This research could not have been conducted without the support, cooperation and guidance of a number of individuals and organisations.

The greatest of thanks go to colleagues Michael Levi and Adam Edwards, for their support and advice throughout the research project and for comments on the manuscript. Thanks also to Susanne Karstedt and Trevor Jones for feedback on an early version of the manuscript.

Thanks must also go to all those individuals and organisations in the UK, Germany, France and Switzerland that participated in the research, in particular the UK Serious Fraud Office and the prosecutor's offices and police departments in the two German *Bundesländer*. Without these participants, the research could not have been conducted.

Thanks also to my parents and to Helen for their endless support.

I would also like to acknowledge the funding provided by the Economic and Social Research Council (ESRC) that facilitated the completion of this research.

Nicholas Lord
September, 2014

To my parents, for everything, but specifically for encouraging me to pursue my own interests which led to an extended stay in education; and to Helen, for always being there and for her continuous support during the researching and writing of this book.

Chapter 1
Introduction

> [C]orporations have committed crimes against one or more of the following classes of victims: consumers, competitors, stockholders and other investors, inventors, and employees, as well as against the state in the form of tax frauds and bribery of public employees. These crimes are not discrete and inadvertent violations of technical regulations. They are deliberate and have a consistent unity … the criminality of the corporations, like that of professional thieves, is persistent: a large proportion of the offenders are recidivists (Sutherland, 1983: 227).

This book is about the 'regulation' of corporations that use bribery in international business transactions to win or maintain business contracts and business interests in overseas jurisdictions (shortened to *transnational corporate bribery* throughout this book). Such bribery involves at least two willing or consenting actors who may either *actively* offer, promise to give or give, or *passively* request, agree to receive or accept, bribes and inducements. (The bribe receiver may of course be more 'active' in demanding bribes but such distinctions are made in law.) The direction of these bribes is from corporations to foreign public officials in the context of a corporation's overseas business. (Of course, 'private to private' bribery (that is, commercial bribery) also occurs, but the focus of this book is on 'private to public' bribery.) These bribes take myriad forms, from cash payments (potentially of £billions) through to indirect hospitalities (including shopping trips, tickets for sports events and so on) to non-monetary favours such as the provision of prostitutes or employment for self or social network. There is intent behind such bribes and this is usually to ensure the commission or omission of certain acts that breach the duties of *public* officials for organisational gains (that is, for the benefit of the corporate entity). These include the awarding or continuance of multi-million pound contracts for the corporation, though inevitably individual gains usually also accompany this.

One of the most prominent and recognisable of scandals emanates from the UK – that of BAE Systems, the UK's largest arms manufacturer. In 1985, the UK and Saudi Arabian governments signed the contract for the initial al-Yamamah I arms deal (al-Yamamah II followed in 1988) where it was agreed that the UK would provide 72 Tornado and 30 Hawk aircraft, amongst other defence equipment, in return for oil (up to 600,000 barrels a day) – BAE was appointed to be the prime contractor to deliver the deal and it is estimated to have been worth around £43bn. However, to facilitate the deal, BAE was alleged to have paid more than £6bn in bribes and inducements. The finances for the bribes were generated by inflating the prices of the defence equipment in order for 'kickbacks' to be provided. Such kickbacks, or bribes, included extravagant travel expenses, shopping trips, prostitutes, a private jet and cash payments, amongst others, to Saudi Arabian officials.

A Serious Fraud Office[1] (SFO) investigation into the alleged bribery was halted in 2006 following government pressure where the UK Prime Minister at the time, Tony Blair, alluded to national security fears. It was asserted that Saudi Arabia had threatened to withdraw counter-terrorism assistance and intelligence should the investigation continue. Economic interests were also endangered as Saudi Arabia threatened to withdraw from a £10bn deal to buy Eurofighter Typhoons. However, this was an impermissible rationale, since halting an investigation for economic reasons would contravene international conventions (Chapter 4). Scrutiny of BAE by interested parties also led to investigations into bribes given by BAE Systems to the Czech Republic, Romania, Qatar, Chile and Tanzania to secure sales of their defence equipment. This culminated in 2010 when the SFO agreed a 'plea-bargain' with BAE in relation to accusations of substantial bribery in Tanzania, although BAE admitted only to relatively minor accounting offences and not bribery. As part of this deal, where BAE paid a £500k fine plus an *ex gratia* payment of £29.5m to Tanzania, it was agreed that all SFO investigations into BAE would be terminated and that the SFO would not investigate or prosecute any member of BAE for any conduct (disclosed or not) preceding 5 February 2010. The sentencing judge, Mr Justice Bean, expressed several concerns over the settlement that had been agreed with BAE.[2]

The BAE case is just one of an increasing number to be investigated, all of which demonstrate how large commercial 'non-criminal' enterprises are being implicated in substantive overseas bribery scandals. These include large-scale cases involving multi-national corporations (MNCs) such as Siemens, GlaxoSmithKline, Ferrostaal, Oxford Publishing, Innospec, Hewlett-Packard and MAN Group, amongst others – this list is becoming more extensive as international pressure to investigate and prosecute such cases increases. These have received extensive publicity in the business press, and variable publicity in mainstream newspapers, radio and television.

Hence, as in the words of Edwin Sutherland (1883–1950) above, 'corporations have committed crimes'. Sutherland's ground-breaking work identified corporations as recidivist offenders and in doing so his work challenged the views of early criminologists concerned with the individual and sociological pathologies of lower class offenders (Croall, 2001: 2). It remains legally[3] and normatively contested whether a corporation (that is, legal person) itself can *commit* a crime and thus bear responsibility, or whether it is the individuals (that is, natural persons)

1 The lead authority for transnational corporate bribery in England and Wales, and Northern Ireland – see Chapter 5.

2 http://www.judiciary.gov.uk/Resources/JCO/Documents/Judgments/r-v-bae-sentencing-remarks.pdf <Accessed 10/11/2013>.

3 For example, corporate criminal liability exists in some jurisdictions (such as the UK) but not others (such as Germany) – see Chapter 4.

within the corporation that ought to be culpable. However, within the vision set out by Sutherland, it is plain that the organisational cultures and structures of corporations create conditions in the context of international business within which bribery can take place: the difficulties are to judge the extent to which such facilitating conditions are deliberate or not, and whether this can be demonstrated in a court or to a regulator to the standard of proof required.

As business transactions become more transnational in nature, both increased white-collar crime opportunities and the possibility of externalising risk and thus evading prosecution for those involved in bribery have been created (Gibbs et al., 2010). For example, corporations using third parties and intermediaries in overseas jurisdictions to bribe to win or maintain contracts distances this conduct from those who ought to be held accountable. The global marketplace also intensifies the impacts of white-collar crimes and risky transactions as we have seen with the global economic crisis and subprime mortgage lending (Gibbs et al., 2010: 544). How nation-states go about dealing with such 'corporate offenders' within this international context in relation to overseas bribery forms a key focus of this book.

While the nature of the offender is contested, to some extent, so are the impacts of bribery and corruption. Some would accept such bribery as the cost of development or the unavoidable interdependence between licit and illicit commerce in 'grey' markets (for example, legitimate corporations acquiescing to overseas, cultural demands/expectations for bribes to be given to facilitate business). For example, the comments of Prince Bandar bin Sultan, the former Saudi Arabian ambassador to the United States, and significant player in the Al-Yamamah arms deal, support such a position:

> But the way I answer the corruption charges is this. In the last 30 years, we have made – we have implemented a development program that was approximately – close to $400 billion worth. You could not have done all of that for less than, let's say, $350 billion. Now, if you tell me that building this whole country and spending $350 billion out of $400 billion, that we had a – misused or get corrupted with $50 billion, I'll tell you, 'Yes'. But I'll take that any time. But more important, who are you to tell me this? I mean, I see every time all the scandals here, or in England, or in Europe. What I'm trying to tell you is, so what? We did not invent corruption (Prince Bandar bin Sultan, quote from PBS Frontline Documentary, Black Money, 2009).

Others would argue that corruption and bribery have devastating political, social, economic and environmental harms and consequences (Chapter 2; see also Rose-Ackermann, 1997; Delaney, 2007; Transparency International, 2013), in particular for developing countries where much corporate bribery is directed (though in what proportion is unknown):

> Corruption is an insidious plague that has a wide range of corrosive effects on societies. It undermines democracy and the rule of law, leads to violations of

> human rights, distorts markets, erodes the quality of life and allows organized crime, terrorism and other threats to human security to flourish. This evil phenomenon is found in all countries – big and small, rich and poor – but it is in the developing world that its effects are most destructive. Corruption hurts the poor disproportionately by diverting funds intended for development, undermining a Government's ability to provide basic services, feeding inequality and injustice and discouraging foreign aid and investment. Corruption is a key element in economic underperformance and a major obstacle to poverty alleviation and development (Kofi Annan, former UN Secretary-General, in the foreword to the United Nations Convention against Corruption (UNCAC) 2003, 2004: iii).

It is this latter perspective that views corruption as a harmful and 'bad' activity (as opposed to a means to an end, that is, corruption not being inherently harmful *per se*) that has shaped the anti-bribery and anti-corruption agenda, in particular through the creation of international conventions which aim to harmonise legal (and normative) understandings of bribery and corruption across jurisdictions. Since the creation of the Organisation for Economic Cooperation and Development's (OECD) Anti-Bribery Convention 1997 and subsequent pressure for nation-states to conform, such corporate bribery in international business has been placed on the agenda of national governments. Sovereign states that do not have an active enforcement stance against transnational bribery are facing intense criticism from (i) international and intergovernmental organisations such as the OECD and the United Nations (UN) and (ii) international anti-corruption bodies including non-governmental organisations such as Transparency International (TI). International measures such as the OECD Anti-Bribery Convention, the UN conventions and numerous regional (for example, European Union and Council of Europe) level conventions provide anti-corruption frameworks within which to address these crimes – these often incorporate monitoring and evaluation mechanisms (for example, the Group of States against Corruption (GRECO) and the OECD Working Group on Bribery) to review the efficacy of national anti-bribery and corruption policies and enforcement practices, though serious measurement and conceptual issues remain.

Corruption and corporate bribery, then, are 'serious business' and the associated moral-social-economic-political-environmental harms have led concerned parties to seek criminal justice and other control mechanisms. But implementing international frameworks at the national criminal justice level is not straightforward. For example, while countries sign and ratify international frameworks, some jurisdictions often possess insufficient infrastructures and resources to enforce them (Shover and Hochstetler, 2006: 107). State corruption may also reduce enforcement while powerful nations may have the ability to influence the creation of international treaties and therefore protect their business activities by resisting criminalisation or refusing to ratify treaties (Michalowski and Bitten, 2005). There is no widely accepted or effective transnational law-making and law enforcement body or mechanism, though models of transnational regulation and standard-setting have been proposed (see for example Braithwaite and Drahos, 2000; Djelic and Sahlin-Andersson, 2006; Abbot and Snidal, 2013). Enforcement authorities, however, generally remain constrained by different domestic operational frameworks and jurisdictional boundaries. It is here that a key contradiction becomes evident: in short, *national* authorities are pressured to respond to *trans*-national corporate bribery using *inter*-national frameworks for enforcement that are distanced from context and the cultural and internal/external pressures faced at the operational level.

At the national level, the particular nature of transnational corporate bribery creates substantial difficulties for enforcement responses: the social practices, relations and processes that characterise such bribery are organised across jurisdictional boundaries (for example, via intermediaries or third parties; money laundering) and are often ambiguous or made to seem so (for example, exchange of legitimate services); it is clandestine and often involves consenting actors (for example, as both parties benefit from the corrupt transaction); there is a lack of identifiable consequences (for example, few direct victims or harms); and the state faces problems of knowledge and power when attempting to access corporate subsystems (that is, internal cultures and processes) (see Gill, 2000; Mayntz, 1993).

This problem of transnational corporate bribery and its control have received insubstantial empirical attention within the elite criminological academic community and remains under-researched, under-theorised and under-conceptualised – a simple analysis of the content of major criminological journals over the period 2000 to 2013 reinforces this.[4] In this timeframe, the *British Journal of Criminology* contained only *two* publications related to transnational corporate bribery that were directly relevant to the substantive focus of this book. These were an analysis of the crimes of neo-liberal rule in occupied Iraq (Whyte, 2007) and a comparative study of corruption derived from a public lecture (Zimring and Johnson, 2005). In contrast, the journal contained 315 separate publications on the subject of 'murder' and 207 on the subject of 'burglary' over the same period. Likewise, the leading American journal *Criminology* contained 0 (zero) publications on the subject of transnational corporate bribery: while a number of hits for 'corruption' were available, these focused primarily on police corruption and low-level corruption. This trend is reflected in a number of other leading criminological journals.[5]

4 It is not known how many articles on transnational corruption were submitted to elite journals in this period. Authors may have also been (directly or indirectly) deterred from submitting to such journals and opted to submit elsewhere (or not at all).

5 The content of six leading criminological journals between 2000 and 2013 was analysed. The titles, abstracts and full texts of all publications in this timeframe were searched for key words and phrases such as 'corporate bribery', 'corporate corruption', 'transnational bribery' and 'foreign bribery' and so on. Any publications found were then analysed methodically to determine their relevance and use to this research.

Both in the official narratives of international organisations and their conventions and in the narratives of criminological theory, the problem of controlling *trans*-nationally organised corporate bribery has not been sufficiently analysed or theorised. Criminological insights have been preoccupied with problems of white-collar and corporate crime (so variously defined) *within* (rather than across) nation-states. This book therefore imports concepts from regulation theory to understand and frame the emerging control responses in what is a broad regulatory landscape. Furthermore, this study provides comparative, empirical insights into this relatively invisible area of criminological interest to aid our understanding of enforcement responses (such as criminal prosecution and civil sanctioning), self-regulatory responses (such as, business initiatives and private-private regulation) and hybrid responses (such as self-reporting, and self-investigation)to transnational corporate bribery in addition to making major contributions to wider conceptual and substantive concerns regarding policing and regulation at the transnational level. The study also makes a contribution to an area of public policy that is evolving quickly at a time when there is major pressure on public finances resulting in significant austerity measures. High-cost, labour-intensive criminal law enforcement is part of this debate and the inclusion in this research of alternative responses to the control of transnational corporate bribery, and criminal behaviour more broadly, is timely given this macro-social context and concern with public funding.

In the course of this book, I hope to present a framework that rethinks and questions the nature of regulation and regulatory theory. There is often a tendency to think of regulation in its narrow conception, focusing on the formal institutions of regulation (for example, state regulators) and where focus has been placed on non-state institutions there remains a preoccupation with regulatory mechanisms that are created with the primary intention to control behaviour (for example, formal, direct policy responses). But behaviour change may also come about as a secondary effect of mechanisms created for other primary purposes (such as for profit creation) and therefore have a more indirect impact.

With this in mind, a broad and inclusive definition of 'regulation' is used (Chapter 3) and is characterised by a landscape that incorporates a diverse array of state (for example, investigatory and prosecutorial agencies) and non-state (for example, private sector enterprises, non-governmental and intergovernmental organisations) 'regulatory' actors that are involved in the direct and indirect negotiation of regulation. Regulation in this sense may be considered as a social relationship between the 'regulator' and 'regulatee' where compliance outcomes and behaviour changes are accomplished and negotiated through the interactions of these social actors over time. In this context, analytical focus can be shifted away from a sole concern with *formal* regulatory institutions (and their strategies) and from narrow conceptions of regulation towards understanding the broader processes, practices and relations that shape behaviour within corporations and markets. Viewing the regulatory landscape at the level of populations, as opposed to the level of individual corporations *per se*, enables analysis of the mixture of responses that are manufactured or emerge more organically and which may be direct or indirect in their influence, but together serve to regulate the markets within which corporations operate.

Thinking in these terms enables conceptual and theoretical development in relation to how behaviour in corporations is regulated and changed. However, it is important to note that the role of state and non-state 'regulators' that aim to regulate transnational corporate bribery remain a fundamental part of the regulatory landscape, and the argument here is not that responsibility for regulation ought to be shifted away from these actors – the public authorities and concerned non-state actors should (and do) retain a primary role in regulation, and for this reason the book returns to address the formal policy responses of the state.

Framing the Research

The above issues raise significant questions that shape the empirical inquiry in this book:

- In what ways are nation-states, under pressure from international organisations, reframing transnational corporate bribery as a key public policy issue and attempting to control it?
- In light of this international pressure, to what extent are enforcement frameworks and policy responses at the national level diverging or converging?
- How is 'the problem' being defined, responded to and 'regulated' in different jurisdictions and what can be learned from comparing and contrasting these responses?
- How do we determine when responses to bribery and corruption are 'adequate' or 'enough'?

These questions imply an analysis of the qualitative aspects of control and regulation. It is important to understand the necessary and contingent social practices, processes and relations that constitute the regulatory responses of investigators, prosecutors and other (anti-corruption) actors at the operational level. The social settings of regulation and the relationships developed (for example, between regulators and regulatees) also add to this complex landscape. This qualitative approach was underpinned by a comparative research design – the need for comparison is implied in the problem of trans-national (as contrasted with domestic) crime and control. Much can be learned from comparing the responses of authorities and regulatory landscapes in theoretically comparable jurisdictions.

Due to several key intellectual similarities and differences, comparative analysis of the UK[6] and Germany is particularly suitable as both jurisdictions are

6 Although the 'UK' is used, this refers specifically to England and Wales, and Northern Ireland – Scotland is not included here as it constitutes a separate jurisdiction in relation to transnational corporate bribery (and other offences).

sufficiently involved in the regulation of transnational corporate bribery to have modes of regulation to analyse. For example, data taken from the Transparency International (TI) (2012) Progress Report indicate that in the period since the OECD Convention came into force up until the end of 2011, Germany had concluded (either through criminal prosecution, civil action or judicial investigation) 176 cases (of which over 16 were 'major') while the UK had concluded 23 cases (all of which were 'major') up until August 2012. Despite the significant difference in figures, the enforcement numbers of major cases and individual prosecutions have become more similar (the UK concluded its first case in 2008). The subsequent TI (2013) report introduced a new classification methodology whereby countries are ranked based on a points system for the most recent four-year enforcement period (as opposed to the collation of cumulative raw numbers – see Chapter 8). Under both systems, the UK and Germany are categorised as 'active enforcers' of the OECD Convention.[7]

Furthermore, there are notable similarities and differences in the UK and German institutional and legal settings – this is useful for demonstrating how the key arguments in this book apply across more than one jurisdiction and are not due to the idiosyncrasies of one or another jurisdiction. For example, both the UK and Germany are key economic players, both being members of the G8 and both having the largest share of world exports in the EU. (This is significant given the focus on *transnational* corruption.) Significantly, the anti-corruption enforcement systems of the two jurisdictions differ in structure. The UK may be considered a centralised system while the German system is decentralised. Furthermore, *corporate* criminal liability exists in the UK but not in Germany, in accordance with the long-standing philosophical principles of German law.

The empirical insights and quotes in this book are based upon a mixture of formal and informal research methods located within a critical realist methodological framework. Accessing elites, particularly when the population of the available sample is itself small, is challenging, but I was able to gain access to key organisations and individuals in the UK and Germany. I conducted 20 *formal* semi-structured interviews primarily with UK and German investigators and prosecutors in their own languages. In the UK, due to the centralised nature of anti-corruption enforcement, there is only one main state agency with national jurisdiction (excluding Scotland); this is the Serious Fraud Office (SFO), and thus the available sample was small (although other agencies provide assistance; see Chapter 5). However, I was able to access and sample investigators and prosecutors in the SFO across different levels of operational and strategic involvement. In Germany the anti-corruption system is decentralised and primary responsibility is located with regional state prosecutors and police, and there are no specialist anti-corruption agencies. I accessed key state actors in two active *Bundesländer*

7 'Active enforcement' is assessed using arbitrary thresholds and considers share of world exports along with number of investigations, cases and convictions of overseas bribery during a four-year period.

who subsequently acted as gatekeepers to prosecutorial and investigatory agencies and departments. I carried out interviews with those at the operational and strategic level of responsible policing and prosecutorial authorities. All interviews discussed the policy responses in the two jurisdictions and at the international level with specific focus on detection, investigation, prosecution and prevention and their location within the cultural, institutional and legal contexts of both countries.

I also conducted formal interviews with representatives of two intergovernmental organisations and a leading non-governmental organisation that are highly influential in the response to transnational corporate corruption and bribery. UK and German lawyers with extensive prosecutorial/defence experience of white-collar crimes and country-specific experts were also interviewed. Interviews discussed both formal, state policy responses but also the changing nature of the regulatory landscape and the emergence of non-state responses.

Gaining formal access to commercial organisations to research their anti-bribery and anti-corruption responses without conceding some ownership over the research findings and without being restricted in subsequent dissemination was not possible. Accessing the closed environments of the private sector therefore had to be undertaken indirectly and *informally*. I accessed actors involved with anti-bribery and corruption compliance within corporations at several anti-corruption events and conferences in which I participated. Here I was able to observe and interact with key anti-corruption actors. In many cases discreet conversations were held with these actors to gain insights into self-regulatory responses within corporations, their perceptions and understandings of state responses and how they were aiming to comply with legal frameworks, and interact and negotiate with responsible authorities. I also participated in a number of interactive online webcasts where industry and legal experts discussed varying aspects of bribery and corruption and where observers could submit questions in real time. In addition, conversations and email exchanges with those working for companies seeking to profit through the provision of anti-corruption services were conducted. Conversations with these actors demonstrated the nature of the services and products that they were providing and how they encourage corporate compliance.

Finally, I continuously conducted extensive bilingual document analysis of laws and statutes, international and regional conventions, internal and open source reports and documents from enforcement authorities and state departments, reports produced by international, intergovernmental and non-governmental organisations, corporate policies, media articles, court proceedings and Hansards, private sector publications and court documents.

Key Thesis of the Book

In answering the above questions, this book aims to demonstrate how the emerging responses in the UK and Germany can be understood in terms of a mixture of enforcement, self-regulatory and hybrid mechanisms. However, only some level of regulation can be achieved through these mechanisms though establishing how much regulation is achieved is difficult: there are little valid 'before and after' data on the impacts of control mechanisms, which presents difficulties in determining 'what works'.

Thus, the overriding argument is that despite significant differences (for example, centralised or decentralised systems, existence of corporate criminal liability, legal cultures), both UK and German anti-corruption authorities[8] (i) face similar difficulties in enforcement as they are limited by their national jurisdictional boundaries and face several procedural, evidential, legal, financial and structural obstacles but (ii) are converging towards similar prosecution policies (for example, the negotiation of civil settlements for corporations). However, in both cases, while the emergence of hybrid and self-regulatory mechanisms supplement the formal enforcement and regulatory responses of the state, there is an assumption that this mixture of enforcement, self-regulatory and innovative hybrid mechanisms is sufficient to regulate transnational corporate bribery. In reality this is not the case. Instead, the key argument of this book is that while these mechanisms are aiding the response and gaining some level of regulation, several obstacles mean they are likely to be insufficient, leading to (iii) the default position of accommodation by state agencies, even where the will to enforce the law is high.

Structure of the Book

To demonstrate these arguments, the book is structured as follows. This first chapter, by way of introduction, has served to introduce the reader to the purpose of the book and now goes on to review more specifically its key ideas. In Chapter 2, attention shifts to the problem of transnational corporate bribery. First, the concept of transnational corporate bribery is defined. Second, the question of why we need to regulate transnational corporate bribery is addressed. Third, to ground the research problem for the reader, two cases are presented, those of Innospec Ltd and Siemens AG – these cases have been selected partly because they were extensively discussed by respondents given their prominence at the time and given that many of the respondents had some direct role in the investigation, prosecution or evaluation of the cases. These cases highlight certain transnational problems that are evident for those responsible for responding to such bribery cases across jurisdictions. This discussion provides the reader with an understanding of the problem and why it needs to be controlled and regulated – readers with substantial knowledge of these two cases may choose to move to the next chapter.

Chapter 3 conceptualises the regulatory framework within which this research is located. Shifts from 'policing' to 'regulation' and from 'old' to 'new' governance

8 Although the term 'anti-corruption authority' is used throughout this book, it should be noted that in both the UK and Germany no formal anti-corruption agency exists. Instead, the investigation and prosecution of corruption and bribery is carried out by several responsible agencies and departments (See Chapter 5). The term, however, is used generally to denote all such anti-corruption bodies.

models are analysed and critiqued, and their application to *transnational* problems considered. The book draws upon a theoretical framework from Edwards and Gill (2002) for understanding the regulation of populations of actors in licit and illicit markets. The framework proposes a theoretical mixture of enforcement and non-enforcement responses in relation to transnational organised crime. The approach shifts focus away from a preoccupation with individual offenders and with formal regulatory institutions *per se* towards a focus on populations of offenders and the 'markets' within which they operate and within which criminal activities occur. Transnational corporate bribery is inherently a market phenomenon in that it involves licit corporations operating in licit markets but involves illicit activities that are dependent on 'grey' markets where much transnational commerce is directed (for example, where bribery may be culturally but not legally acceptable). This chapter utilises the framework to analyse and provide empirical insights into those mechanisms that are emerging within the regulatory landscape of transnational corporate bribery.

A fundamental part of any regulatory framework is the law. Chapter 4 demonstrates that at the international and interregional levels, organisations such as the OECD and the UN, in reflection of their 'moral entrepreneurship', have created legal conventions outlining undesired bribery and corruption offences and related provisions that must be implemented at the national level once signed and ratified. Similarly, at the regional level, the EU and Council of Europe (CoE) have produced conventions and requirements of Member States in relation to anti-bribery and corruption. These international and regional conventions and legal instruments significantly shape anti-corruption legislation at the national level leading to a significant degree of convergence (although Germany is yet to ratify the UNCAC). However, significant differences remain – corporate criminal liability exists in the UK but not Germany, for example. These differences can co-exist within the 'functional equivalence' approach of international conventions and their monitoring and evaluating bodies (for example, GRECO and the OECD's Working Group on Bribery), implying harmonisation of legal mechanisms to control corruption and bribery is not required within all states. Instead, it is considered more important that the 'goals' of the conventions are met rather than that the 'means' used to implement anti-corruption enforcement are being harmonised.

The policy initiatives of intergovernmental and regional organisations and bodies have therefore influenced regulation in the form of available legal mechanisms and in the UK and Germany there exist extensive legal provisions for responding to transnational bribery. However, these policy initiatives hold less influence over the extent to which the law is enforced and the ways in which states negotiate with corporations, particularly in relation to self-regulatory mechanisms. For example, aspects of the regulatory strategies of UK and Germany anti-corruption authorities demonstrate convergence in the decisions to utilise civil solutions rather than criminal sanctions, albeit convergence in prosecution policy is shaped by several antecedent factors. Cultural and legal frameworks that emerged long before the policy initiatives of intergovernmental and regional organisations, as well as procedural, evidential, financial and structural obstacles all shape and influence policy responses.

Chapter 5 begins to map out the regulatory landscape and the extent to which the laws analysed in Chapter 4 are enforced. More specifically, the focus of Chapter 5 is on how responsible anti-corruption authorities and actors located at the *national* level detect and investigate such *transnational* corporate bribery within the context of the two contrasting enforcement systems of the UK (centralised) and Germany (decentralised), and the strengths and limitations within each system and the structural obstacles that exist. The centralised and decentralised enforcement structures are presented and the key practices of detection and investigation and associated differences and similarities discussed – the associated evidential difficulties to such investigations are outlined. Within these practices the significant role of discretion is analysed along with the impact that such discretion has on the legitimacy of enforcement responses. The key argument is that whether centralised or decentralised, and whether guided by flexible or rigid legal frameworks, formal and informal practices of discretion lead to legal and operational tensions that reduce the legitimacy (as defined in Chapter 5) of enforcement responses.

Chapter 6 builds upon the analysis of enforcement processes in Chapter 5 by devoting detailed analysis to the prosecution policies of the two jurisdictions. It is through analysis of prosecution policy that enforcement responses are best understood. UK and German prosecutors and investigators, though socialised into the centrality of criminal law to their professional work and values, understand the difficulties of criminal law enforcement and seek to explore the available 'tools' at their disposal. The chapter analyses these mechanisms within the UK and German enforcement frameworks and outlines a shift beyond traditional law enforcement practices (that is, pursuing criminal prosecution) towards the expanding use of *non-criminal* alternatives that fall within the remit of state agencies and authorities.

The chapter initially analyses the use of, and strengths and limitations of, criminal prosecution in the UK and Germany, giving special attention to debarment, or the 'corporate death penalty' as it has otherwise been termed – legal, procedural, financial obstacles to enforcement are explored in addition to the structural and evidential problems outlined in Chapter 5. Consequently, there is an increasing use of non-criminal alternatives, in particular the use of civil mechanisms aimed at ensuring changes in corporate culture. The key argument of the chapter is that investigators and prosecutors in the UK and Germany are aiming to 'negotiate' regulation via a varied set of enforcement mechanisms shifting away from criminal prosecution towards non-criminal forms of enforced self-regulation, characterised by financial civil settlements and hybrid enforcement mechanisms including 'self-reporting', 'self-cleaning', 'monitoring' and forms of reintegrative shaming.

Given the obstacles to enforcement responses as detailed in Chapters 5 and 6, the key argument in Chapter 7 is as follows: informational asymmetries mean that criminal and regulatory enforcement alone are unlikely to substantially reduce transnational bribery as only some level of regulation can be gained, and therefore need to be supplemented by self-regulatory mechanisms. The chapter conceptualises these self-regulatory practices, arguing that they may be thought of as a spectrum between a more manufactured (that is, high state intervention) and a more organic (that is, minimal or no state intervention) nature. Analytically, these mechanisms emanate from the micro- (for example, individual corporations), meso- (for example, individual markets) and macro- (for example, multi-sector/ transnational initiatives) levels and originate within three main 'domains' (state, commercial and intergovernmental/non-governmental organisations). The mechanisms involve both state and non-state 'regulatory' actors, reflect varying levels of formality (for example, mandatory-voluntary), can be specific or general and may be direct and/or indirect in their influence.

Analysis of the above enforcement, self-regulatory and hybrid mechanisms raises the question of how we know these responses are 'adequate' or 'enough'. Chapter 8 addresses the issue of how we might go about understanding 'regulatory performance'. Gaining an understanding of when particular sorts of enforcement responses are sufficient and adequate, both in the instant case and taking all enforcement responses together, is problematic. We can only properly assess levels and impacts of state and non-state activity against transnational corporate bribery and their adequacy when we understand the levels (for example, extent and scope) and organisation of such crimes. Determining relative to what variables levels of enforcement and (self-)regulation are understood and how we can develop an appropriate 'threshold' against which levels of enforcement and (self-)regulation can be compared is the key issue in this chapter.

If understanding regulatory performance is a serious problem at the national level, it is a far more difficult problem transnationally, where consistent data on both the harms and enforcement practices are unobtainable. Chapter 8 considers what is and ought to be understood by 'regulatory' performance, going on to analyse the need to understand extent and scope for performance measures to have value. Available data to inform extent and consider current performance measures are explored and it is argued that as we can only ever understand *some* level of the problem, current performance measures cannot provide valid indicators of levels of enforcement. Instead, research and policing strategies that aim to understand the *organisation* of transnational corporate bribery and the corresponding impact of intervention, disruption and prevention strategies provides a more useful indicator of 'regulatory performance' – potential data sources and models for understanding 'regulatory performance' to this end are presented.

Finally in Chapter 9, by way of conclusion, the assumption that the enforcement, self-regulatory and hybrid mechanisms emerging in the regulatory landscape provide sufficient means for dealing with transnational corporate bribery is critically interrogated. Much corporate bribery currently goes undetected and is therefore unknown beyond the direct parties, while investigators and prosecutors in the UK and Germany have no comprehensive plausible estimations of the scope and the extent of the transnational corporate bribery problem beyond the cases that are reported to them or come to their attention in the course of other investigations.

These cases are centrally recorded in both the UK and Germany and represent the scope and extent of the problem as understood by the enforcement authorities.

Enforcement data collated by intergovernmental organisations such as the OECD as part of the requirements of their Convention and international organisations such as TI provide the most wide-ranging understanding of the extent and scope of corruption. But such data use raw numbers rather than the proportion of estimated cases dealt with which presents problems for understanding levels of enforcement as well as for comparative understandings between jurisdictions. Nonetheless, these data are used to provide a threshold against which enforcement numbers can be measured as demonstrated in the reports of TI, for example, that use the number of investigations and prosecutions as indicators of how 'active' a state is in enforcing the law. Organisations such as TI also attempt to supplement such understandings of extent and scope and provide an insight into how much greater the problem is by using perception studies, but such figures are beset by various methodological limitations.

The key issue is that even these (relatively conservative) estimations outweigh the UK's and Germany's capacities for enforcement, even more so in times of austerity – the difficulties in criminally prosecuting corporations, the shift towards civil settlements and negotiation, the need to use resources effectively, the evidential burdens of transnational investigations, the unknown or anecdotal impact of self-regulatory practices and so on inhibit the policy responses of the UK and Germany to address transnational corporate bribery. Consequently, while the mixture of enforcement, hybrid and self-regulatory mechanisms are aiding the response and gaining some level of regulation, the default position is one of 'accommodation' by state agencies, even where the will to enforce the law is high.

Chapter 2
What is 'Transnational Corporate Bribery' and Why Do We Need to Regulate It?

Introduction

This chapter aims to define in more detail the concept of 'transnational corporate bribery', exploring how it is understood and applied in this book. Bribery is considered the main tool of corruption and is the main focus of international conventions aimed at tackling corruption (Chapter 4). In this book, the terms bribery and corruption are often used interchangeably, transnational corporate bribery being a form of corruption.[1] The chapter begins by framing transnational corporate bribery in relation to understandings of the broader concepts of corruption and bribery from different disciplines, drawing out key analytical issues, before narrowing the definition to transnational corporate bribery specifically. But the question of why transnational corporate bribery needs to be regulated requires discussion. To answer this, the chapter identifies the perceived social, economic and political harms of such activities as identified by key international organisations, amongst others. Finally, to further ground the nature of transnational corporate bribery for the reader, two cases, Innospec from the UK and Siemens from Germany, are analysed.

Defining Corruption and Bribery

Definitions of corruption are numerous. They vary in terms of analytical focus and can be located within various academic disciplines (for an overview see Shihata, 1997) such as political science (see Doig, 1984, 2003; Doig and Theobald, 1999; Montinola and Jackman, 2002; Gerring and Thacker, 2004; Goodin, 2010), economics (see Rose-Ackermann, 1999; Lambsdorff, 2007), law (see George et al., 2000) and sociology (Deflem, 1995). It is of little use here to analyse such definitions other than to say that they are often broad and inclusive but possess notable commonalities, some of which are identified below.

1 Analytical distinctions could of course be made between the concepts of bribery and corruption, a necessary relation of the former being the involvement of two actors, where the latter could involve an individual only.

Within the field of political science, for example, Joseph Nye[2] (1967: 419) offered an early definition, seeing it as 'behaviour which deviates from the formal duties of a public role because of private-regarding (personal, close family, private clique) pecuniary or status gain; or violates rules against the exercise of certain types of private-regarding influence'. This definition addresses the key distinction between *private* and *public* roles which has continued to be of significance and results in a focus on public officials, as can be seen in more operational definitions (see below). A more socio-legal definition is offered by Deflem (1995: 243) who defines corruption as a 'colonisation of social relations in which two or more actors undertake an exchange relation by way of a successful transfer of the steering media of money or power, thereby sidestepping the legally prescribed procedure to regulate the relation'. This second definition highlights the key role of the *necessary* social relations that characterise corrupt exchanges as understood within normative frameworks (that is, socially constructed laws). The nature of such relationships is also emphasised by Doig (2006: 116):

> … corruption relates to the abuse or misuse of a 'normal' relationship, whether genuine or contrived, by either or both parties. Further, the decision or action (or absence of either) by one in favour of the other also requires deception of others and collusion between the two parties involved.

This definition identifies the key issue of abuse *and* misuse of such relations which involve acts *or* omissions. These key analytical aspects are fundamental to the carrying out of transnational corporate bribery.

Beyond academia, anti-corruption and bribery conventions (see Chapter 4) do not define corruption, instead establishing the offences for a range of corrupt behaviour (OECD, 2008a: 22), therefore providing content definitions rather than analytical definitions. Thus, the conventions define international standards for the criminalisation of corruption by prescribing specific offences that may be located under the umbrella of 'corruption'. This is also applicable to legislation at the national level: from a criminal law perspective, broad definitions result in few prosecutions and convictions. In terms of policy, however, international definitions of corruption are more common, with one frequently cited operational definition from leading global non-governmental organisation TI stating:

> Corruption is operationally defined as the misuse of entrusted power for private gain. TI further differentiates between 'according to rule' corruption and 'against the rule' corruption. Facilitation payments, where a bribe is paid to receive preferential treatment for something that the bribe receiver is required to do by law, constitute the former. The latter, on the other hand, is

2 Interesting to note is that Nye's work is also frequently used as an argument to support the notion that corruption can be of use for a country's economy.

> a bribe paid to obtain services the bribe receiver is prohibited from providing (TI website).[3]

This definition covers a broad range of corrupt activities. As the OECD (2008a: 22) indicates, the definition is useful as a reference for policy development and awareness-raising as well as for elaborating anti-corruption strategies, action plans and corruption prevention measures. Thus, in addition to the above academic conceptualisations, there is also often a need for operational definitions that can be of use in real social settings. Each country has its own laws and regulations aimed at tackling corporate bribery and corruption and the country-specific legal situations in the UK and Germany are discussed in Chapter 4. Generally speaking, however, bribery has been defined in terms of:

> The offering, promising, giving, accepting or soliciting of an advantage as an inducement for an action which is illegal, unethical or a breach of trust. Inducements can take the form of gifts, loans, fees, rewards or other advantages (taxes, services, donations, etc.) (TI, 2009b: 5).

So defined, bribery poses difficulties for state agencies given these agencies and actors are largely concerned with illegal acts, as opposed to 'unethical' acts. Legal but immoral or unethical actions that fall into the grey area of bribery and corruption are also the concern of non-governmental organisations and other third sector organisations. Moral definitions (that is, broader than the law so as to include legal but undesirable acts) of corruption and bribery may allow freedom from more narrow and restrictive definitions but it is legal definitions that are of operational importance for anti-corruption agencies. These definitions of bribery direct us towards the necessary and contingent key actors, relations, processes, objects and employment settings that exist during the processes of transnational corporate bribery.

It is important however to be wary of such singular and abstract concepts such as 'bribery' and 'corruption' which can reflect political, academic or operational aspirations for theoretical or rhetorical purposes, or in other words, their *constructed* rather than obvious and objective qualities. Analytically, it is of more use to focus on the processes involved in bribery, focusing on aspects such as how the finances to bribe are obtained, how potential bribe receivers are identified and so on (see Chapter 8; also Levi, 2007: 779 more generally). Furthermore, the concept of bribery may have different meanings in different social and legal cultures. The extent to which culturally specific constructs of bribery can be stretched into other cultural contexts without losing their meaning is key and poses a significant problem for policy entrepreneurs developing international conventions that aim to standardise the understanding of bribery

3 http://archive.transparency.org/news_room/faq/corruption_faq#faqcorr1 <Accessed 10/11/2013>.

and norms for 'its' control. However, the concept of bribery can be understood through processes and practices that can be labelled as bribery, such as the use of hospitality to secure business contracts and therefore market advantage. Such practices and their intentions may be understood in the UK and Germany independent of the concept of 'bribery' while international conventions leading to policy convergence (Chapter 4) may allow greater cross-cultural 'elasticity' (see Edwards and Gill, 2002) of concepts of bribery.

Defining Transnational Corporate Bribery

Transnational corporate bribery, as understood in this book, involves at least two willing/consenting (active, for example, offering/promising/demanding, or passive, for example, accepting/soliciting) actors and different forms of inducements ranging from cash bribes (potentially totalling £billions) to more indirect hospitalities (for example, tickets for sports events; shopping excursions and so on) or non-monetary favours (for example, provision of prostitutes and so on). The intention is to ensure the commission or omission of certain acts that breach the duties of *public* officials (broad legal definition – see Chapter 4) for organisational (but usually accompanied by individual) gain in the context of international business transactions (for example, a senior politician accepting/demanding a bribe from a corporation to facilitate the organisation winning a business contract in their country). The commission and/or omission of such acts are prohibited under national and international laws.

In other words, the book is focused on *corporate* bribery, that is to say, bribery involving individuals within corporations carried out for the benefit of the corporation in the context of business – as in law, a distinction may be made between 'legal' persons (that is, corporate entities) and 'natural' persons (that is, individuals). However, the focus excludes bribes paid by corporations domestically and instead focuses on *transnational* bribery, explicitly incorporating *multi*-national corporations. The research therefore examines corporations that operate at the international level across at least two jurisdictions in terms of their business activities and which are governed by national *and* international laws.

Other forms of corruption and transnational corruption do of course take place, but for conceptual and empirical purposes, it is the control and regulation of transnational corporate bribery that is examined. Table 2.1 outlines the key elements of corporate bribery of public and private officials whereby bribery may occur domestically and/or transnationally and may be 'active' and/or 'passive' (Chapter 4). Bribery may occur between private and public actors (that is, public bribery) and/or between private actors (that is, commercial bribery) – the empirical focus in this book is on 'public bribery'. Such bribery remains the main focus of international and non-governmental organisations. Bribes may be given or offered, or accepted or solicited, but always have the intention to induce illegal or unethical (non-)action.

Table 2.1 Corporate bribery of public and private officials

Form of bribery	Origin of bribe	Recipient of bribe	Transnational or domestic?	Active or passive?
Public bribery (private-public)	Corporation (i.e. board member, employee, subsidiary, intermediary, agent, etc.).	Public official (i.e. foreign or domestic state representatives e.g. politician, state owned firms, police officer, etc.).	Both	Both
Commercial bribery (private-private)	Corporation (i.e. board member, employee, subsidiary, intermediary, agent, etc.).	Private official (i.e. corporate competitor, vendors/ contractors, etc.).	Both	Both

Why Do We Need to Regulate Transnational Corporate Bribery?

A number of common assertions are made about the harms of corruption, often by intergovernmental and non-governmental organisations, as well as other 'moral entrepreneurs' (for example, charities, activists), as we saw with the statement from Kofi Annan in Chapter 1 referring to the 'corrosive effects' of corruption on societies. Such arguments may use or even be based on empirical findings, but also often reflect informed morality (that is, normative judgements). In any case, certain consequences of corruption are consistently noted by academics and anti-corruption organisations. Rose-Ackerman (1997: 42–6) encapsulates these consequences when she identifies six key impacts of corruption which are still relevant in contemporary cases:

- inefficient government contracting and privatisations;
- use of delays and red tape to induce payoffs;
- inefficient use of corrupt payments (for example, payoffs diverted into illegal activities);
- inequities in reference to the distribution of gains and losses;
- damaged political legitimacy; and,
- slowed growth whereby the benefits of development are distributed unequally.

Similarly, Delaney (2007: 419) notes diminished economic development and growth; increased social inequality; and further distrust of government as significant consequences. Furthermore, Transparency International points to the significant political, economic, social and environmental impacts that corruption may lead to (see below). In sum, the following statement from Rose-Ackerman (1997: 42) remains relevant:

> … [c]orruption can produce inefficiency and unfairness. It can undermine the political legitimacy of the state. Corruption is also evidence that deeper problems exist in the state's dealings with the private sector. The most severe costs are not the bribes themselves but the underlying distortions they reveal – distortions that may have been created by officials to generate payoffs.

Due to these harms, many social actors and organisations have recognised the need to reduce corruption and bribery, and placed its control on the political agenda. Transnational corporate bribery penetrates much of society, at the micro- (for example, individual officials), meso- (for example, pervasive corruption in institutions) and macro- (for example, industry sectors and markets, and economic systems) levels. The consequences of bribery in international legal markets can be seen in various areas. TI notes that corruption has significant *political*, *economic*, *social* and *environmental* impacts[4] – politically, corruption creates a major obstacle to democracy and the rule of law. The rule of law is significantly shaped not only by the presence and introduction of formal rules and regulation, but also cultural and institutional safeguards and supports (Krygier, 1999: 71). Once corruption enters into these areas, the rule of law may become disrupted: Shihata (1997: 456), while discussing the legal literature on corruption, makes clear that lawyers largely agree, that where corruption is commonplace, 'the rule of law … is substituted for by the rule of whoever has the influence or the ability and willingness to pay … [and] … they are particularly concerned when corruption reaches the ranks of the judiciary and distorts the system of justice'. The misuse of such offices and institutions in democratic systems in the pursuit of private gain can therefore result in a lack of legitimacy. As Rose-Ackerman (1997: 45) notes, 'systemic corruption undermines the legitimacy of governments, especially democracies. Citizens may come to believe that the government is simply for sale to the highest bidder. Corruption undermines claims that government is substituting democratic values for decisions based on ability to pay'. For TI, this causes substantial harm in established democracies, even more so in emerging democracies, and such corruption prevents the development of accountable political leadership and creates wide-ranging distrust of political leaders and authorities.[5] As Cragg (1998: 654) suggests, 'respect for the law is an obvious casualty' as well as 'public confidence in the law and in legal institutions'. Windsor and Getz (2000: 757) go as far to suggest that '[t]he immediate effects of corruption include the destruction of democratic institutions'. Such literature, however, inform us largely only about the level and consequences of corruption in countries and governments that receive the bribes, and not about the countries and governments where the bribes originate.

4 TI discussion of 'costs of corruption', available at: http://www.transparency.org/whoweare/organisation/faqs_on_corruption#costsOfCorruption <Accessed 10/11/2013>.

5 See TI discussion of 'costs of corruption'.

Economically, corruption depletes national wealth, hinders the development of fair market structures and distorts competition which consequently deters investment.[6] As Mauro (1997: 6–7) notes, 'empirical evidence suggests that corruption lowers investment and retards economic growth to a significant extent'. Mauro further states that corruption can lead to talent being misallocated as financial incentives lure talented and educated individuals to lucrative rather than productive work (although the same could be said about most sectors, for example, the movement of graduates to the financial services rather than the manufacturing sector in the UK). Aid in developing countries may also be disrupted or misused and tax revenue may be lost which can lead to adverse budgetary consequences. The misallocation of public procurement contracts, for example, may lead to lower quality infrastructure and public services. The composition of government expenditure may also be distorted if bribe extortion is placed ahead of public welfare. For example, corruption is often responsible for scarce public resources being channelled to uneconomic high-profile projects, such as dams, power plants, pipelines and refineries, instead of fundamental infrastructure projects such as schools, hospitals and roads, as well as the supplying of water and power to rural areas[7] – although foreign aid agencies may also be responsible as such capital projects are favoured ways of using aid. Such corruption in public investments can significantly harm growth (see Tanzi and Davoodi, 1998). Corruption, however, is not constrained to public contracts and the construction industry, although much corruption seems to be located here, most specifically in the industrial sector of 'public work contracts and construction' which is considered the sector where most bribes are paid (see TI (2011a) Bribe Payers Index).

Corruption, then, can impact on investment. Smarzynska and Wei (2000) examined the impact of the level of corruption in a given host country upon a foreign direct investor's choice of investing through a joint venture or through a wholly owned subsidiary. Corruption decreases transparency at the local level and therefore increases the value of using local partners to avoid local bureaucracy. On the other hand, corruption reduces the probability of disputes between foreign and domestic partners being fairly adjudicated and decreases the level of effective protection for an investor's intangible assets. Their empirical tests found that corruption reduces inward foreign investment and shifts ownership structures towards joint ventures. US companies, however, were more likely to retain full ownership in corrupt countries but not less likely to undertake foreign direct investment in them (whether this is because these corporates are more ethically and socially responsible, or because they come under the jurisdiction of stringent legal frameworks and enforcement regimes is not known). The private sector therefore also suffers as a result of the above corruption as '[a] corrupt system does not reward the producer of the best and cheapest product, but instead rewards

6 See TI discussion of 'costs of corruption'.

7 See TI discussion of 'costs of corruption'.

the producer who pays the largest bribe; the rational producer, therefore, will shift resources away from quality and toward the bribe payment' (Nichols, 2000: 631). Consequently, ethical companies may miss out on contracts, and this distorts the markets.

Socially, corruption can undermine people's trust in the political system, in its institutions and in its leadership, which can lead to frustration and apathy amongst the public and therefore a weak civil society.[8] It is this that TI considers to be the most damaging impact of all: a weak civil society 'clears the way for despots as well as democratically elected yet unscrupulous leaders to turn national assets into personal wealth'.[9] As a result, 'persistent corruption erodes social equality. The poor are further disadvantaged, as efficient infrastructure is forgone to line the pockets of government officials' (Delaney, 2007: 420–421). Within such cultures, the demanding of and paying of bribes becomes the norm which may lead those unwilling to comply to emigrate, therefore leaving the country without its most able and honest citizens. Environmentally, corruption can cause great degradation through the lack of, or non-enforcement of, environmental regulations, and legislation has historically enabled the North to export its polluting industry to the South, while exploitation of natural resources by domestic and international agents has led to ravaged natural environments.[10] Such environmentally devastating projects received funding preference due to being easy targets for siphoning off public money for private gain.

The discussion of the costs of corruption by TI is clearly emotive and symbolic, and certainly one-sided in its approach. Neither does TI specify what levels and forms of corruption have these consequences – it is the aggregate or particular acts of corruption, not most corruption (by volume), that can have significant consequences. However, the supplementary literature above provides empirical support for some of these arguments. The problem of transnational corporate bribery penetrates much of society, at the micro-, meso- and macro-levels, and creates difficulties for the control agencies responsible for investigation and prosecution. For example, how can a German prosecutor investigate the impacts of a bribe given by a German company to a state official in a small African town to maintain a business contract? How can a UK regulator follow the 'cash-flow' of a bribe that was sent to the receiver via multiple international bank accounts and 'shell-firms'? It is such difficulties that influence regulatory responses as discussed in Chapters 5, 6 and 7.

Quantifying the Costs of Corruption

Is it possible to quantify the costs of corruption? As TI succinctly notes, and goes on to argue through three key points,[11] '[t]he short answer is "no"'. First,

8 See TI's discussion of 'costs of corruption'.

9 See TI's discussion of 'costs of corruption'.

10 See TI's discussion of 'costs of corruption'.

11 TI discussion on 'quantifying the costs of corruption' available at: http://archive.transparency.org/news_room/faq/corruption_faq#faqcorr5 <Accessed 10/11/2013>.

payments of bribes are not publicly recorded; therefore the amount paid to corrupt officials annually is unknown. (The costs of controlling and investigating such corruption for governmental agencies and private corporations further adds to this complexity.). Second, bribes take a number of forms, not only monetary. Favours, services, presents and so on, are used. Third, at most, the correlation between levels of corruption and phenomena such as democratisation, economic development or environmental degradation may be researched, but the social costs are even less quantifiable. The cost of the loss of talented individuals such as acclaimed scientists or entrepreneurs to a country cannot be calculated while estimated social costs in financial terms are inadequate to reflect certain social impacts such as illiteracy or inadequate medical care. Thus, as TI notes, '[a] general scepticism, vis-á-vis any attempt at quantifying the costs of corruption is thus warranted'.[12]

Due to these harms and the arguments of key players internationally (whether based on evidence or morality), who are influential in shaping legal frameworks and enforcement practices given their significant powers of persuasion and intense lobbying of governments, many social actors and organisations have identified a need to reduce corruption and bribery, and placed its control on the political agenda. Consequently, corruption and bribery are controlled and regulated by sovereign states that sign and ratify such frameworks.

Grounding the Research Problem

As a means of grounding the problem further and introducing the reader to the organisation and nature of transnational corporate bribery, it is useful to present some real-life, contemporary examples which aid in fleshing out the content-less abstractions of concepts such as 'corruption', 'bribery' and 'transnational corporate bribery'. Two cases will be analysed: Innospec Ltd. that was investigated and prosecuted in the UK; and Siemens AG that is the largest case so far to be prosecuted in Germany. These cases are presented as the interviewed investigators and prosecutors in the UK and Germany frequently drew upon their involvement of these cases to demonstrate and substantiate their arguments and provided case details to contextualise their examples.

Innospec Ltd[13]

Innospec pleaded guilty on 18 March 2010 at Southwark Crown Court to bribing employees of Pertamina (an Indonesian state owned petroleum refinery) as well as other Indonesian government officials in order to secure sales of a fuel additive, TEL (tetraethyl lead). Innospec, based in Cheshire, UK, is a subsidiary

12 See TI's discussion of 'quantifying the costs of corruption'.

13 SFO press release available at: http://www.sfo.gov.uk/press-room/press-release-archive/press-releases-2010/innospec-limited-prosecuted-for-corruption-by-the-sfo.aspx <Accessed 10/11/2013>.

of Innospec Inc., a NASDAQ[14] listed company based in the United States and a manufacturer of the lead-based, anti-knock, fuel additive TEL. TEL cannot be sold in Europe or the US for motor vehicles on health and environmental grounds but the company continued to produce and sell TEL where it remained lawful, for example in countries such as Indonesia. The 'directing minds' of Innospec engaged in systematic and large-scale corruption of senior government officials (Judiciary of England and Wales, 2010). They appointed agents in Indonesia to act on their behalf in seeking to win or continue contracts to supply TEL, and between 14 February 2002 and 31 December 2006 (the indictment period) the company paid US $11.7m to its agents. These commissions enabled agents to pay bribes to staff at Pertamina and other public officials at higher regulatory or ministerial levels who were in a position to favour the company by purchasing and influencing orders of TEL. These payments therefore ensured that Pertamina favoured TEL over other unleaded alternatives. The agents acted under the instruction of the company who also authorised the commission fees paid by them. The company accepted that it was aware that a proportion of the commission funds would be used to pay bribes. The company also created 'ad hoc' funds that assisted specific or 'one-off' arrangements with particularly influential individuals within Pertamina or at a political level. One particular fund was structured to protect the interests of the lead-based additives industry but was in actual fact no more than a slush fund to corrupt senior officials in various ministries with the intention of blocking legislative moves to ban or enforce the ban on TEL on environmental grounds and/or seeking a higher level buy-in to continued yearly supplies of TEL to Pertamina. This impact can be seen through the fact that while the Indonesian government's intention to go lead-free was initially conceived in 1999, it was not actually realised until 2006.

Legal Proceedings

The SFO involvement in the Innospec case came following a referral from the US Department of Justice (DoJ) in October 2007 who at that time was investigating Innospec Inc. following the report from the UN Independent Inquiry Committee into the Oil for Food Programme on 27 October 2005. The SFO accepted the corruption case for investigation on 23 May 2008. Following this, the company disclosed to the SFO evidence that the company had sought to influence decision-makers in public contracts for the purchase of TEL in Indonesia between 1999 and 2006. As the SFO press release on this case states, the company provided the SFO with a high level of cooperation throughout the investigation.

The Attorney General gave consent to the SFO to bring these proceedings on 2 November 2009.[15] Innospec was summonsed on 24 February 2010 on the charge

14 The NASDAQ Stock Exchange is a US stock exchange. NASDAQ originally stood for the 'National Association of Securities Dealers Automated Quotations'.

15 The new UK Bribery Act 2010 enables the Director of the SFO to bring prosecutions without the consent of the Attorney General.

of conspiring with certain of its directors, executives, employees and agents to give or agree to give corruption payments contrary to Section 1 of the Criminal Law Act 1977 and Section 1 of the Prevention of Corruption Act 1906. After two preliminary hearings, the case was listed for plea and sentence on 18 March 2010.

Sentence

Innospec agreed that it would be subject to financial penalties and the SFO carried out an investigation in tandem with the Securities and Exchange Commission (SEC) in the US into the company's ability to pay. This investigation concluded that the amount available to the UK was US $12.7m. The company also agreed to pay the costs of a monitor, to be acceptable in both the UK and US, for up to three years. In the US, a criminal fine of US $14.1m was paid to the DoJ in relation to the UN Oil for Food programme while parent company Innospec Inc. paid a fine of US $11.2m in profits to the SEC and $2.2m to the Office of Foreign Assets Control in line with the Foreign Corruption Practices Act 1977 (FCPA) for violating anti-bribery and books and records provisions relating to conduct in Iraq.

Court Judgement

On 26 March 2010 the Crown Court Judgement of Lord Justice Thomas on the case was issued. A number of key points were made by Lord Justice Thomas. He objected to the agreeing of a settlement between the authorities and Innospec and felt forced to accept and limit the fine, as agreed through the SFO and SEC investigation, due to certain unique circumstances. First, the US courts had already agreed the plea agreement made in the US. This reflects the *negotiated justice* approach evident in the US where plea-bargains leading to civil/criminal settlements and the use of non-prosecution and deferred prosecution agreements are common. Second, Innospec had pleaded guilty, fully cooperated and provided evidence that would be of significant assistance to the prosecution of others. Third, according to sentencing judge Lord Justice Thomas, sentencing Innospec to a larger fine would have resulted in its insolvency and therefore 'affected the innocent employees of the company, caused considerable difficulties for the pension liabilities of the company and been detrimental to the agreed "clean up" programme the company has in place in the UK' (Judiciary of England and Wales, 2010: 12). Thus, economic and public interest considerations were made (although under the OECD Convention certain economic considerations should not influence the decision to prosecute: see Chapter 4). Fourth, the prospect of a 'global settlement' as described above had already been announced to the markets. What was made clear by Lord Justice Thomas was that he felt the fine was inadequate to reflect the level of criminality. In other words, corruption (especially where the directing minds of the company played a significant role) requires criminal sanctions, and that such 'plea agreements' should not begin to erode the fundamental constitutional principle of judicial sentencing in the UK. He concluded that '… the Director of the SFO had no power to enter into the arrangements and made and no such agreements should be made again' (Judiciary of England and Wales, 2010: 13). Commenting on this guidance from Lord Justice Thomas, the then SFO Director Richard Alderman stated:

> This has been a ground-breaking case involving a global settlement that the SFO has brought to the English courts. I am deeply grateful to Lord Justice Thomas for the detailed guidance he has given on all the complex issues involved. This is a very important decision which will guide the SFO in our approach to these matters in future (SFO website press release, 2010).[16]

These issues of plea-bargaining, agreeing settlements, the potential for deferred prosecution agreements, and so on, have remained a significant issue in the prosecution policy of the UK (see Chapter 6).

Key Issues

This case reflects a number of current issues in relation to the regulatory approach and prosecution policy of the SFO as well as tensions with adjudication and these are touched upon in the two quotes from UK investigators and prosecutors below:

> Innospec was limited to its own facts because the settlement as it was with the SFO and other US body, was limited by their ability to pay … ours was about $12.7 million, had it been any higher than that the company would have gone bust and no one would have got anything (UK Investigator/Prosecutor Interview 114).

> I could see the Innospec thing being closed down now that they have got the company out of the way – too hard, too costly to do the individuals … If a company comes in, reports it's non-endemic, senior management are not making a personal benefit out of it and if senior management were involved they have been got rid of then it's a case for a civil confiscation order. If a company is a bit more endemic but still cleared things out, that sort of thing, then it's a plea agreement like Innospec (Former UK Investigator/Prosecutor Interview 113).

These quotes, along with the above information and comments of Lord Justice Thomas, raise some significant questions. First, the case indicates a predilection in the UK towards the use of *civil* agreements and settlements as opposed to *criminal* sanctions. Whether the use of criminal prosecution (which can lead to debarment of corporations – the 'corporate death penalty' – and of individuals) is being legitimately limited by finite resources (cost and difficulty) and other economic considerations (for example, the ability to pay a fine; can't afford to destroy companies as providers of tax and employment) needs considering. Second, the above questions raise the issue of whether the moral underpinning of legislation and of prosecutorial policy is being weakened or if criminal acts can be dealt with through non-criminal sanctions. Do civil sanctions therefore reflect the

16 Quote from: http://www.sfo.gov.uk/press-room/press-release-archive/press-releases-2010/innospec-judgment.aspx <Accessed 10/11/2013>.

level of criminality and what does this mean for regulation? Likewise, questions are raised over whether a company that produces and sells a substance banned for motor vehicles in Europe and the US should even be allowed to continue its trade in other countries. Third, tensions between the courts and enforcement authorities as indicated above puts the regulatory approach in doubt and raises the question of whether the investigators and prosecutors with the specialist knowledge and expertise in this area should be able to 'negotiate justice' and 'self-adjudicate' as per the US model and whether the role of the courts needs to adapt. For example, should leniency for full cooperation and/or self-reporting be applied to criminal acts of corruption and are all individuals and companies therefore being treated equally before the law? These issues are addressed in Chapters 5, 6 and 7.

Siemens AG

Siemens has been the subject of multiple bribery scandals in various countries. The subsequent investigations resulted in prosecutions and sanctions in various jurisdictions including Germany, the US, Italy, Russia, Nigeria and Libya, and indicated an estimated €1.3bn[17] in bribes was paid. Numerous diverse scandals have emerged. For example, in one investigation in 2004 a Milan court banned Siemens from selling gas turbines to the Italian public administration for one year for its part in an Italian corruption scandal.[18] Further investigations were also initiated in Switzerland, Greece and Lichtenstein. It is the cases in Germany and the US, however, which have received most attention. Towards the end of 2006 five Siemens executives were arrested by German authorities on charges of bribery and embezzlement. The allegations involved the payment of up to €420m into secret bank accounts (mainly Swiss and Austrian) over seven years to facilitate the paying of bribes to win overseas contracts. Since then, other individuals have been investigated and convicted. In a separate investigation, German authorities examined allegations of illegal payments including one six-figure payment to Saddam Hussein's Iraqi government in order to secure energy and medical equipment contracts in the UN Oil-for-Food programme.

The Corrupt Activities

The payment of bribes by Siemens to win and maintain overseas contracts involved various offences. A report[19] from the US DoJ, who investigated the case under the

17 See *The Guardian: 'Siemens boss admits setting up slush funds'*, 27/05/2008. Available at: http://www.guardian.co.uk/business/2008/may/27/technology.europe <Accessed 10/11/2013>.

18 In the above-mentioned Italian case involving Enelpower, the Darmstadt Regional Court sentenced two former Siemens employees to suspended sentences and order Siemens to disgorge €38m in profits. In 2009, these convictions were partially overturned and partially upheld.

19 Report available at: http://www.justice.gov/opa/documents/siemens-ag-info.pdf <Accessed 10/11/2013>.

extra-jurisdictional reach of the US FCPA, outlined numerous breaches with regards two counts related to 'internal controls' and 'books and records'. All the offences took place from around March 2001 until at least November 2006. The report states that Siemens knowingly circumvented and knowingly failed to implement a system of internal accounting controls. That is to say, that Siemens: (a) knowingly failed to implement sufficient anti-bribery compliance policies and procedures; (b) knowingly failed to implement sufficient controls over third-party bank accounts and the use of cash; (c) knowingly failed to appropriately investigate and respond to allegations of corrupt payments; (d) knowingly failed to discipline employees involved in making corrupt payments; (e) knowingly failed to establish a sufficiently empowered and competent Corporate Compliance Office; (f) knowingly failed to report to the Audit Committee substantiated allegations of corrupt payments around the world; (g) limited the quantity and scope of audits of payments to purported business consultants; (h) created and utilised certain mechanisms for making and concealing approximately $1,361,500,000 in payments to third parties; (i) engaged former Siemens employees as purported business consultants to act as conduits for corrupt payments; (j) continued to use off-books accounts for corrupt payments even after compliance risks associated with such accounts were raised at the highest levels of management; (k) used removable Post-It notes to affix signatures to approval forms authorising payments to conceal the identity of the signers and obscure the audit trail; (l) allowed third-party payments to be made based on a single signature in contravention of Siemens' 'four eyes principle', which required authorization of payments by two Siemens managers; (m) changed the name of purported business consulting agreements to 'agency agreements' or similar titles to avoid detection and conceal non-compliance with the 2005 business consulting agreement guidelines; (n) knowingly failed to exercise due diligence to prevent and detect criminal conduct; (o) knowingly included within substantial authority personnel individuals whom Siemens knew had engaged in illegal activities and other conduct inconsistent with an effective compliance and ethics program; (p) knowingly failed to take reasonable steps to ensure Siemens' compliance and ethics program was followed, including monitoring and internal audits to detect criminal conduct; (q) knowingly failed to evaluate regularly the effectiveness of Siemens' compliance and ethics program; (r) knowingly failed to have and publicise a system whereby employees and agents could report or seek guidance regarding potential or actual criminal conduct without fear of retaliation; (s) knowingly failed to provide appropriate incentives to perform in accordance with the compliance and ethics program; and, (t) knowingly entered into purported business consulting agreements with no basis, and without performing any due diligence, sometimes after Siemens had won the relevant project.

In relation to the books and records, the report makes clear that Siemens knowingly falsified and caused to be falsified books, records and accounts required to, in reasonable detail, accurately and fairly reflect the transactions and dispositions of Siemens. That is to say, Siemens: (a) used off-books accounts as a way to conceal corrupt payments; (b) entered into purported business consulting agreements with no basis, sometimes after Siemens had won the relevant project; (c) justified payments to purported business consultants based on false invoices; (d) mischaracterised bribes in the corporate books and records as consulting fees and other seemingly legitimate expenses; (e) accumulated profit reserves as liabilities in internal balance sheet accounts and then used them to make corrupt payments through business consultants as needed; (f) used removable Post-It notes to affix signatures to approval forms authorising payments to conceal the identity of the signers and obscure the audit trail; and (g) drafted and backdated sham business consulting agreements to justify third-party payments; and (h) falsely described kickbacks paid to the Iraqi government in connection with the Oil for Food Program in its corporate books and records as commission payments to agents.

Sanctions

In October 2007, a Munich district court imposed a €201m penalty on Siemens in connection to charges against the Communications Group for bribery in Nigeria, Russia and Libya. The court's decision related to the involvement of a former manager of the Communications Group, who, acting in concert with others, committed bribery of foreign public officials in 77 cases in the period 2001–04 in order to obtain contracts on behalf of Siemens. The court based the level of the fine on the unlawfully obtained economic advantages that Siemens derived from the illegal acts of the former employee. The fine incorporated a €200m disgorgement of profits and €1m administrative fine.[20] In addition to these fines, the Munich prosecutors also pursued a number of individual prosecutions such as those against Siemens' former Chief Executive Officer, Chair and members of the Supervisory and Managing Boards for failures in their supervisory duties. Siemens itself also brought a claim for damages against members of the Managing Board's Executive Committee (see TI, 2009a: 28). In July 2008, Reinhard Siekaczek, a mid-level manager, was the first former employee to be convicted. He set up a slush fund and front companies that were used to siphon off €48.8m to fund 'consultancy' fees. Siekaczek was sentenced to two years' probation and a fine of €108,000.[21] In December 2009, six former Siemens executives agreed to pay almost €20m in compensation for their parts in the bribery. Most notably, Heinrich Von Pierer, who was Siemens' chairman from 1992 until 2005, paid €5m in compensation, but still defended himself against the allegations.[22] Siemens also accepted a

20 A Siemens press release from 2007 details these proceedings. Available at: http://www.siemens.com/press/pool/de/events/jahrespk2007/legal-proceedings-q4–2007-e.pdf <Accessed 10/11/2013>.

21 See *Spiegel Online: 'Former manager convicted of corruption'*, 28/07/2008, available at: http://www.spiegel.de/international/business/0,1518,568504,00.html <Accessed 10/11/2013>.

22 See *The Independent: 'Siemens bribery deal close'*, 03/12/2009, available at: http://www.independent.co.uk/news/business/news/siemens-bribery-deal-close-1833088.html <Accessed 10/11/2013>.

settlement with German tax authorities for the Communications Group which involved payments of over €179m plus interest in back taxes. In December 2008, a further civil settlement was agreed when the Munich prosecutors terminated other proceedings against the company. This involved Siemens agreeing to pay a fine of €250,000 as well as disgorge profits of €394,750,000.

In December 2008 in the US, in response to DoJ charges of transnational bribery, Siemens pleaded guilty to the above-mentioned internal controls, books and record provisions violations. Three of its subsidiaries, Siemens S.A. Argentina, Siemens Bangladesh Limited and Siemens S.A. Venezuela, also pleaded guilty to FCPA violations. The SEC similarly agreed a settlement of books and records charges related to allegations of the payment of over US $1.4bn in bribes to government officials in Asia, Africa, the Middle East and the Americas. Siemens agreed to pay a criminal fine of US $448.5m to the DoJ and a disgorgement of profits of $350m to the SEC. Its three subsidiaries each paid US $500,000. In addition to the monetary settlements, Siemens agreed to appoint a compliance monitor. The US charges against Siemens AG included charges in relation to books and records violations by its subsidiaries in France and Turkey, amongst others, involved in the UN Oil-for-Food Programme. The fines imposed on Siemens by the US authorities were almost 20 times the previous record fines in an FCPA case. This involved Baker Hughes that was fined $44m in April 2007 (see TI, 2009a: 54).

In total, Siemens paid €2.5bn in fines and settlements, which includes €850m that was spent on lawyers' and accountants' fees to Debevoise and Plimpton, Deloitte and PricewaterhouseCoopers, amongst others.[23]

Key Issues

The Siemens case represents a number of further significant issues, some which can be seen in the Innospec case, but additional issues also. First is the issue of corporate criminal liability and the non-existence of this in Germany – although corporations can be sanctioned under *Ordnungswidrigkeitengesetz* (Administrative Law – see Chapter 4). This concern is acknowledged in the following passage from an interview with a German Public Prosecutor:

> Of course it would without a doubt be better, I think, if and when you have a proper corporate criminal law, simply for the following reason. For example, imagine the administrative law resolution, not the notice, but the resolution that was given to Siemens for the Communications Group via the County Court; there is a resolution of a court and there is a notice, which we did. The resolution is limited to, for a start to the Communications Group at Siemens and that is a total sum of €201 million that was imposed; why €201m? €200m was the

23 See *The Guardian: 'Record US fine ends Siemens bribery scandal'*, 16/12/2008, available at: http://www.guardian.co.uk/business/2008/dec/16/regulation-siemens-scandal-bribery <Accessed 10/11/2013>.

> disgorged profit and €1m was basically the fine, the real penalty. That is of course the maximum penalty by law (German Prosecutor Interview 211).

As this quote indicates, in Germany corporations can receive no criminal prosecution but a maximum administrative fine of €1m. Unlimited profits can be confiscated, however. The issue of whether a lack of corporate criminal liability impacts upon the regulation of transnational corporate bribery is therefore significant. For example, a lack of criminal law threat may impact on the level of cooperation of corporations and this lack of criminal law may in itself have a significant symbolic meaning. As the Siemens case indicates, a number of individuals were successfully prosecuted, but can this lack of corporate criminal liability increase pressure on prosecutors and courts to get successful prosecutions of individuals? Likewise, the company itself may create 'scapegoats' such as Reinhard Siekaczek for its wrongdoing. Furthermore, once we move beyond the criminal law issue, the question of whether confiscations offer a suitable enforcement mechanism arises.

The Siemens case also outlines the transnationality of overseas corporate bribery, given the global investigations and settlements that are increasingly being reached in these cases. For example, the US and German authorities worked closely together on the Siemens case, but what impact do differing legal frameworks, cultures and approaches have on such cases? How are sovereigns and nation-states moving beyond their traditional law enforcement frameworks to enact transnational investigations and utilise a varied set of enforcement mechanisms? These questions are addressed in the following chapters.

Comparing the Cases

Some key enforcement mechanisms can be seen in both cases. In the Innospec case, the SFO adopted a mixture of sanctions that included a fine made up of a criminal fine, civil settlement and confiscation, as well as the imposition of a monitor in the company to observe future behaviour for up to three years. The company took steps to restructure and remove involved individuals itself and implemented an enhanced compliance programme: this represents a form of enforced self-regulation triggered by the prospect of criminal prosecution. As Innospec gave an early guilty plea, it was also entitled to a credit well in excess of 50 per cent and cooperated fully in the investigation which aided in mitigation: this represents a form of legal incentive. In October 2011 three former executives were charged with corruption.[24]

24 SFO press releases available at: http://www.sfo.gov.uk/press-room/press-release-archive/press-releases-2011/innospec-ltd-two-more-executives-charged-with-corruption.aspx and http://www.sfo.gov.uk/press-room/press-release-archive/press-releases-2011/innospec-ltd--former-executive-in-court-on-fraud-and-corruption-charges.aspx <Accessed 10/11/2013>.

In Germany, Siemens faced an administrative fine and disgorgement of profits, with no *corporate criminal* sanctioning possible due to German law. Individuals were criminally prosecuted and required to pay compensation. A compliance monitor was also put in place to observe Siemens' future conduct and report to the US authorities. As in the Innospec case, Siemens also implemented extensive changes in its compliance regime prior to settlements being agreed, and now markets its compliance programme as a 'recognized leader in terms of integrity':[25] this latter example highlights the potential of market-based incentives (that is, increasing profit and share prices through actively selling the company's compliance programme) to change behaviour that represents a form of market self-regulation. Other regulatory mechanisms are also evident such as the use of civil enforcement mechanisms, the enforcement of improved compliance in Siemens by the state, and the allocation of a state monitor. This admixture of enforcement and self-regulatory practices is discussed in Chapters 6 and 7 respectively.

Conclusion

The concept of transnational corporate bribery as understood and applied in this book has now been defined. As demonstrated in the discussion above, the concern is with corporations operating transnationally in international commerce that use bribery to win or maintain contracts in overseas jurisdictions, often in developing countries where bribery is culturally accepted or expected and where anti-corruption responses are under-developed. The definition incorporated both 'active' and 'passive' elements of bribery, a distinction that is made in UK and Germany law also (Chapter 4). The empirical focus is upon 'public' as opposed to 'commercial' bribery with international focus often being placed on the bribery of foreign *public* officials. The cases of Innospec and Siemens, as detailed above, highlight the sheer complexity and transnationality of transnational corporate bribery given that such large corporations operate in multiple jurisdictions and in high-level business transactions. These cases contextualise and ground the nature of the research problem and provide the overarching setting for the subsequent analysis of 'regulatory' responses.

However, as argued both by (inter)national governmental and non-governmental organisations, and academic scholars, there are moral, social, political, economic and environmental harms that reinforce why it is important to regulate corruption and transnational corporate bribery. Assertions made about the harms of corruption may be based on empirical findings, but often also reflect informed morality (although determining how 'informed' such 'informed morality' is, is a difficult

25 See an external presentation from Siemens entitled 'Siemens Compliance Program – Track Record and Challenges' available at: http://www.siemens.com/sustainability/pool/collectiveaction/ourlearnings/pdf/Siemens_ComplianceProgram_EN.pdf <Accessed 10/11/2013>.

methodological question). But there are significant impacts of corruption that can undermine state legitimacy in the context of diminished economic development and growth, increases in social inequalities and societal distrust in governments, amongst others. These consequences are often most salient in jurisdictions far away from the location of parent corporations, and responsible authorities in Western liberal democracies, such as the UK and Germany, are now under intense pressure and scrutiny to respond. The extent to which these two jurisdictions are able to do so is the key focus of this book.

Chapter 3
Conceptualising the 'Regulatory' Framework: Policing as Regulation

Introduction

Both in the official narratives of international organisations and their conventions[1] and in the narratives of criminological theory, the problem of controlling *trans*nationally organised corporate bribery has not been sufficiently analysed or theorised with criminological insights largely being preoccupied with problems of white-collar and corporate crime (so variously defined) *within* (rather than across) nation-states (see Chapter 1). This book therefore draws upon literature and theory from the area of regulation and applies this thinking to transnational corporate bribery. This chapter begins by identifying the problems to policing that are created by the complex nature of transnational corporate bribery and transnational crimes more broadly. These challenges, in addition to limitations of the state to police or regulate crime within their national boundaries, have led contemporary theories of regulation to propose shifts away from 'old governance' (for example, traditional policing practices) towards models of 'new governance' (for example, practices of steering and responsibilisation). Such models are discussed and applied to transnational corporate bribery and the limitations of such models identified. The particular nature of transnational corporate bribery creates substantial difficulties for such regulation theory. Thus, the chapter concludes by developing an analytical framework within which the regulation of transnational corporate bribery can be located.

In particular, this book draws upon a theoretical framework by Gill (2000, 2002) and Edwards and Gill (2002) for understanding the regulation of *populations* of actors in licit and illicit markets. The framework proposes a theoretical mixture of enforcement and non-enforcement responses (in relation to transnational organised crime but of use in the current context also). As the remainder of this book demonstrates, and as contemporary discussion on regulation indicates, regulation may be interpreted broadly enabling a shift away from formal, regulatory institutions towards understanding the variety of state and non-state actors, and direct and indirect mechanisms of control. In this sense, the approach shifts focus away from a preoccupation with offenders towards a focus on the 'markets' within which they operate and within which criminal activities occur.

1 For example, the Organisation for Economic Cooperation and Development and the United Nations.

Controlling Corporate Bribery in International Business Transactions: the Challenges of Policing

Business transactions are increasingly transnational in nature, a factor that has opened up increased opportunities for white-collar crimes and the possibility of externalising risk (Gibbs et al., 2010: 544) and thus evading prosecution for those involved in bribery. For example, corporations using third parties and intermediaries in overseas jurisdictions to bribe to win or maintain contracts results in the disassociation of the risks from those who ought to be held accountable – although the UK Bribery Act 2010 is one policy that aims to reduce the legally acceptable explanations should bribes come to light (Chapter 4).

According to Passas (1999), cross-border crime is the product of 'criminogenic asymmetries' which incorporate conflicts, mismatches and inequalities in the spheres of politics, culture, the economy and the law which are intensified through globalisation. While models of transnational regulation and standard-setting have been proposed (see below and Braithwaite and Drahos, 2000; Djelic and Sahlin-Andersson, 2006; Abbot and Snidal, 2013), there remains no widely accepted or effective transnational law-making and law enforcement body or mechanism. Enforcement authorities generally remain constrained by different domestic operational frameworks and jurisdictional boundaries. The intense legal debates about extradition to the US of British businesspeople (for example, the NatWest Three) and hackers (for example, Gary McKinnon) illustrate the tensions created regarding the extraterritorial reach of the law. Additionally, the global marketplace intensifies the impacts of white-collar crimes and risky transactions as we have seen with the global economic crisis and subprime mortgage lending (Gibbs et al., 2010: 544). Thus, the difficulties for states attempting to regulate the behaviour of transnational corporations also include a host of political concerns and economic interests (Rothe, 2010: 561; Snider and Bittle, 2011). It is within this context and in response to transnational corporate bribery that national authorities are pressured to respond to transnational corporate bribery using international frameworks for enforcement that are distanced from context and the cultural and internal/external pressures faced at the operational level. A key contradiction is therefore evident.

Attempts at global regulation often encounter inconsistencies in the legal requirements between and across jurisdictions and international treaties aimed at harmonising regulation are generally not mandatory (Passas, 2002). Countries are therefore not obliged to ratify relevant treaties and if ratified, the resources required to enforce might not be available (Chayes et al., 1998). This can be seen with Germany, which has signed but at the time of writing is yet to ratify the United Nations Convention against Corruption (Chapter 4). In some instances, multinational corporations may even be able to operate within 'transnational loopholes' (Rothe, 2010: 561, citing Michalowski and Kramer, 1987) (for example, using overseas subsidiaries to conduct business using bribery in jurisdictions where accountability to the parent company would be difficult to ascertain). However, not all transnational corporations are criminogenic in nature but criminal activity is more likely to occur under favourable conditions which 'lure' individuals and corporations: this is particularly so if they are predisposed to such behaviour and if there is a lack of self-constraint and credible oversight (Gibbs et al., 2010). Thus, lure, predisposition, temptation and non-credible oversight combined with the nature of international transactions pose significant challenges for regulation and enforcement (Gibbs et al., 2010: 549–50): this does, however, present a somewhat conflicting theoretical explanation with elements of rational choice, determinism, self-control and opportunity theories mixed together, but understanding the conditions under which bribery may take place is useful for informing preventative and repressive regulatory approaches.

It has further been argued that powerful nations may also have the ability to influence the creation of international treaties and therefore protect their business activities by resisting criminalisation or refusing to ratify treaties (Michalowski and Bitten, 2005). Developing countries may also be unable to enforce laws and treaties due to insufficient infrastructures and resources (Shover and Hochstetler, 2006). Policing and controlling transnational crimes at the international level, while providing useful international conventions and agreements, is hampered by difficulties in enforcement. Anti-corruption enforcement is national, and the investigation and prosecution of transnational corporate bribery can only be realised through Mutual Legal Assistance (Chapter 5). The scope of national laws in the UK and US enable a larger reach, with any company or business based in or formally passing funds through these countries liable for investigation and prosecution. However, the anonymity involved in international business transactions via numerous financial institutions and through difficult to access jurisdictions causes great difficulties for regulation (Elliot, 2009). Likewise, distant relationships between agents and clients, and differing laws in different countries, not to mention the high level of secrecy and privacy or lack of direct victims to report, also create major problems. Thus, the nature of global business transactions creates a significant barrier to effective regulation and enforcement (Gibbs et al., 2010: 550). Although the work of Gibbs et al. (2010) focuses on the global trade in electronic waste, the solution they offer is of relevance for the emerging regulatory landscape of corporate bribery in international business transactions. They suggest rather than the promulgation of rules, the use of 'smart' (Gunningham and Grabosky, 1998) or 'responsive' (Ayres and Braithwaite, 1992) regulation through a combination of prevention, third-party regulation and state intervention may promote more effective practices. Such theoretical developments provide the foundation upon which much contemporary regulatory theory is based (see below).

Limitations of the State? Power, Knowledge and Legitimacy

The challenges faced in policing transnational crimes due to their cross-border nature, as outlined above, form only one area of complexity. A second set of difficulties refers to the ability of the state to manage and control transnational corporate crimes. Academic debates over state capacities to respond to corporate crimes, and crimes more generally, have led many to the argument that even in advanced developed countries the sovereign state is no longer solely able to provide security, law and order and crime control within its territorial boundaries (Garland, 2001) and this has been accompanied by subsequent shifts towards a focus on the 'responsibilisation' of non-state agencies and actors (Garland, 2001; O'Malley, 1992). As Garland (1996: 452) stated, '[t]his involves the central government seeking to act upon crime not in a direct fashion through state agencies (police, courts, prisons, social work, etc.) but instead by acting indirectly, seeking to activate action on the part of non-state agencies and organizations'. Such a transformation can be seen in analyses of 'post-Keynesian policing' whereby the focus on community policing highlights the extent to which the public are seen as 'competent and skilled agents' who are able 'to govern themselves in ways approved by the appropriate experts (police, insurance companies, criminologists)' (O'Malley and Palmer, 1996: 146). But such responsibilisation strategies are a one-way process reflecting the intentions of the state to manufacture (self-)regulation but (self-)regulatory practices may also emerge independent of state influence (Chapter 7).

Later research has similarly indicated that 'in the absence of effective national and intergovernmental regulation to ameliorate global environmental and social problems, "private" alternatives have proliferated, including self-regulation, corporate social responsibility, and public-private partnerships' (Bernstein and Cashore, 2007: 347). As Braithwaite (2008: 1, 3) notes, '[g]overnance is a wider set of control activities than government' whereby modes of 'networked governance' enable a 'shift in both the private and public sector … to post-Fordist steering or more volatile systems that are partially contracted out and partly contracted in to shifting collaborative groups that compete for growth with outsiders and insiders'. For Braithwaite (2008: 2), within the context of such regulatory capitalism, states and companies that fail to adapt to the networked economy and networked governance respectively are unable to dominate global markets and global governance. The key theme within such frameworks is that crime control and prevention is not, and cannot be, the responsibility of the state alone, and that private agencies and individuals must recognise their responsibility and be persuaded to change their practices in order to reduce criminal opportunities and strengthen informal social control. In this model of 'governance-at-a-distance', the state maintains all its traditional functions while simultaneously taking on a new set of coordinating and activating roles, thus leaving the 'centralised state machine' more powerful and with extended capacity but also eroding the idea of the state as the 'public's representative and primary protector' (Garland, 1996: 454). Thus, traditional understandings of the roles of 'sovereigns' and 'states' in relation to crime control have been substituted by concepts of 'governance' that involve a 'process of co-ordination, steering, influencing and balancing' the interactions of public and private groups' (Kooiman, 1993: 255). This also reflects Foucauldian notions of 'governmentality', whereby governance through institutions and varying social practices can be viewed as mechanisms for exercising power over individuals (see Foucault, 1991).

While Garland (1996, 2001) outlined this shift, the work of Gill (2002: 527–8) aids in explaining how the shift can be understood through the knowledge and power problems facing states. Social and economic subsystems in a complex and economic world are highly impenetrable, meaning states and outsiders cannot learn how they work. Where information is required from social and economic subsystems in order to control and/or regulate them, the regulatees have some important tactical powers, though they may be punished if they are found to have withheld information they are legally obliged to disclose (see for example the News International case[2] as well as countless corporate crime cases). There are therefore no possibilities for the state to obtain the information independent of those who are to be regulated. If this knowledge problem can be solved, the 'power' problem arises: state agencies and authorities often do not possess sufficient powers and instruments of policy with which to influence the processes of the subsystems (Mayntz, 1993: 13–16). As Mayntz notes:

> The assertion basically is that the state, because of the inherent short-comings of its traditional instruments, is not able (any more) to solve the economic and social problems it has identified. Since the state is not able to steer social development in a preferred direction, in order to prevent unwanted developments it is either necessary to look for alternative instruments or to lower the aspirations of central-state control (Mayntz, 1993: 10).

While knowledge and power problems apply to *legal* social and economic activities, they apply in greater force when the state aims to control *illegal* social activities (Gill, 2002: 529, emphasis in original). If the state has difficulty monitoring or gaining access to information from large corporations about their legal operations (for example, tax avoidance or to maintain competitive advantage and so on), it is likely this difficulty is even greater when corporations protect information about their illegal operations (for example, disguising the giving of bribes overseas).

Notwithstanding, some commentators propose that state capacities for enforcement *do* exist where under-enforcement can be addressed through changes in political will, proactive inspectorial strategies and increased resources (see Slapper and Tombs, 1999: 186; see also Almond, 2013; Pearce and Tombs, 1998; Tombs and Whyte, 2007). This is because 'many corporate crimes tend not to be one-off acts of commission, but are actually ongoing states or conditions' (Slapper and Tombs, 1999: 185). For example, the maintenance of false records and collusive relationships, amongst others, would be such 'states' that would be detected through proactive approaches supported by increased resources.

---

2 See article in *The Guardian* (20/07/2011): '*News International "deliberately" blocked investigation*', available at: http://www.guardian.co.uk/media/2011/jul/20/news-international-deliberately-blocked-investigation <Accessed 10/11/2013>.

From this latter perspective, inadequacies in enforcement are often explained through state complicity (although when a lack of concern or action becomes complicit is not clear) in the production of corporate crime (that is, state failures to implement/enforce effective legal regimes; states being actively complicit in their relationships with the corporate sector and so on) (Tombs 2011: 70). However, even where political will and resources may be evident, the 'real' obstacles posed by such transnational problems to state authorities hinder enforcement (Chapters 5 and 6). Nevertheless, such approaches argue that 'deterrence as a principle informing enforcement activity and the sanctioning of corporate crime has considerable potential' (Slapper and Tombs, 1999: 187). For such scholars,

> ... effective forms of deterrence constitute a condition of existence for law-abiding behaviour on the part of organisations or corporations; that is, the existence of a likelihood of detection and credible sanctions following successful prosecution makes it possible for corporations to obey the law, and thus is central to effective *regulation* (Slapper and Tombs, 1999: 188, emphasis in original).

These above arguments are central to debates about the adoption of enforcement (particularly criminal and civil sanctioning) or the promotion of self-regulation as a means of changing behaviour. These polemical approaches have been referred to as models of 'deterrence' as opposed to models of 'compliance' (Reiss, 1984) and were traditionally characterised by debates advocating criminal prosecution as a fundamental part of responses (see Pearce and Tombs, 1998; Slapper and Tombs, 1999) or advocating criminal prosecution be used as a last resort (Hawkins, 1998; Clarke, 1990). Of course, most analysts accept contemporary models of 'new governance' (see below), where the question of 'when to punish; when to persuade', incorporating aspects of both compliance and deterrence is considered (Ayres and Braithwaite, 1992: 21).

Both compliance and deterrence approaches can utilise criminal and civil penalties but the regulatory (that is, compliance) approach can be distinguished from criminal law in two ways: 'it targets those engaged in specialised activities and its underlying purpose is said to be different in that regulation is concerned to mould or encourage behaviour rather than to condemn it' (Wells, 2011: 15). As indicated above, and also in line with the thesis of Wells (2011: 15), such binary distinctions are debateable and 'the lines between regulatory and criminal procedures are becoming more tangled and blurred'. Such debates do raise the issue of what the role of the criminal law and criminal prosecution ought to be given evidence of their impacts are unclear. Levi (2010), for example, states that there is no hard evidence of the relative and absolute impacts of civil and criminal sanctions on tax offenders. He does suggest, however, that 'increased prosecution might be justified for purposes of moral retribution as well as perceived social fairness' (Levi, 2010: 493). He states:

> The use of the criminal sanction has a moral component. Governments criminalise acts on the basis that they are morally wrong and deserve public

> sanction – not just as a pragmatic technique for controlling the behaviour more effectively (Levi, 2010: 507).

The role of morality or the context of public norms and attitudes towards tax noncompliance in this instance, and not just deterrence, is important. Arguments for the use of criminal as opposed to non-criminal proceedings for these reasons, however, 'needs to be interspersed with a suite of other sanctioning mechanisms that have political support and that are embedded in the public's understanding of how justice can be delivered in the domain of tax noncompliance' (Braithwaite, 2010: 515). Increased prosecutions, however, may be necessary for fairness and may also positively impact upon voluntary compliance (Leighton, 2010: 529) although this raises significant questions as to the meaning of fairness and fairness for who and for what.

However, the issue of morality raises another dimension to this debate. Whether governments criminalise acts on the basis that they are morally wrong (*mala in se*), or on the basis that some factions of society *believe* or *perceive* them to be morally wrong, is debateable. Take the BAE Systems investigation, for example. Had the government truly believed such payments to be morally wrong, would it have interfered with and stopped the SFO investigation? Perhaps, then, it is a case of what is 'economically right' (or right in terms of national security), rather than 'morally wrong'. Or maybe some things are morally wrong some of the time, to some people. Furthermore, the 'moral' state of society and the economy may even provide frameworks within which individuals can justify their morally dubious or illegal behaviour (see Karstedt and Farrall, 2006).

Conceptualising the Problem: Policing vs. Regulation

> Even though law enforcement remains an area in which states still seek to act as 'sovereigns', an examination of what police do suggests that, here too, there are distinct signs of 'steering' – an activity more normally associated with regulation (Gill, 2002: 524).

Criminology is often concerned and preoccupied with notions of 'policing' and 'law enforcement' but the usefulness of such concepts for understanding transnational corporate bribery is limited. In other words, the key question here is to what extent traditional notions of 'policing', as part of the state's apparatus, provide a useful framework for understanding the control of corporate bribery. Literatures utilising the concepts of 'policing' and/or 'regulation' are largely separate, implying some form of distinction between the two types of activities, although more can be gained from viewing the two as essentially similar, rather than essentially different (Gill, 2002: 524). In other words, the similarities between policing and regulation are more analytically significant than their differences.

As Gill (2002: 524–6) notes, the enforcement behaviour of police has traditionally been associated with the criminal prosecution of offenders, with prosecution being seen as a 'result' (see for example Reiner, 2010). Conversely, non-police agencies, or regulators, seek compliance via alternative measures, with prosecution being seen as unproductive and a last resort (see Hawkins, 1998: 295). This reflects the ideological/strategic distinction that criminal law seeks to punish anti-social conduct rather than encourage certain purposive activities (Baldwin et al., 1998: 3) and this is shaped by internal cultures and 'working rules' (see Dixon, 1997: 7–8) or 'social practices' (Lange, 1999: 549–50).

Kagan (1984) reinforced these differences by outlining the differing social functions of police and regulators in relation to their mandates, and the types of offences and offenders they deal with, but acknowledged that some commonalities are evident, especially in some forms of policing more than others. Such decades-old research may not reflect contemporary policing, however, where more non-traditional methods, such as the use of community approaches, regulatory, disruption and non-justice system approaches and private sector involvement in relation to the prevention of organised crime, have been developed (see Levi and Maguire, 2004). Likewise, new policing models concerned with combating harms and threats, not just law enforcement, have emerged as can be seen in the radical Dutch model of organised crime prevention and the UK's Serious Organised Crime Agency (SOCA) (now National Crime Agency (NCA)) (Edwards and Levi, 2008).

Thus, some have found this distinction between policing and regulation unconvincing (Baldwin et al., 1998; Gill, 2002). For example, the significance of discretion in light of an inability to adopt full-blown enforcement approaches has long since been acknowledged (Goldstein, 1960). As Gill (2002) notes, further studies of policing have indicated that individuals are able to negotiate their way out of prosecution dependent on their acceptance of wrongdoing and the authority of the police to use compliance techniques such as warning and cautioning: thus, 'prosecution is no more the "normal" outcome of policing than it is of regulation' (Gill, 2002: 526).

Rather than concepts of 'policing' in its traditional sense, it is beneficial to understand the response to transnational corporate bribery in relation to concepts of 'steering', 'governance' and/or 'regulation' (see Kooiman, 1993; Gill, 2002). In the specific context of corporate crime, this shift has been acknowledged by Wells (2011: 13) who states 'enforcement of criminal law against corporate crime increasingly uses classic regulatory techniques of negotiation and settlement'. This shift, however, has been influenced by the power and knowledge problems of the state along with the limitations of the sovereign to deal with crime control. By broadening the understanding of 'policing' beyond criminal law enforcement to incorporate other mechanisms for controlling, regulating, and changing the behaviour of populations, it is possible to gain richer insights into various levels of formal and informal, and direct and indirect forms of control in relation to corporate bribery in overseas commerce. Consequently, this research imports analytical concepts and theories from the related field of 'regulation' and it is towards these concepts and theories that this chapter now turns.

What is 'Regulation'?

The concept of regulation, while appearing to be easily understood, is often discussed in the literature with varied meanings. As noted by Baldwin and Cave (1999: 1–2), '[r]egulation is spoken of as if an identifiable and discrete mode of governmental activity, yet the term has been defined in a number of ways'. They therefore suggest it is useful to think of the word regulation being used in four different senses. First, it may be considered as a *specific set of commands* where regulation involves the promulgation of a binding set of rules to be applied by a devoted body (Chapter 5 and 6). Second, as *deliberate state influence* where regulation is considered broadly and includes all state actions designed to influence industrial or social behaviour (Chapter 5 and 6). This would include command-based regimes but also other modes of influence such as those based on the use of economic incentives. Third, as *all forms of social control or influence* where all mechanisms affecting behaviour, whether state-derived or from other sources, are considered regulatory (Chapter 7). Fourth, while regulation is often considered restrictive and preventive, the influence of regulation may also be *enabling or facilitative* such as in the regulation of broadcasting operations. Many of these components of regulation (but not all) can be seen in the following definition provided by Scott (2001: 331), who states:

> We can think of regulation as any process or set of processes by which norms are established, the behaviour of those subject to the norms monitored or fed back into the regime, and for which there are mechanisms for holding the behaviour of regulated actors within the acceptable limits of the regime (whether by enforcement action or by some other mechanism).

This definition usefully directs us to the need to broaden our understanding of policing beyond criminal law enforcement to incorporate other mechanisms for regulating the behaviour of individuals, but also populations. It touches upon the potential for informal responses and there is a normative and prescriptive focus to the definition. Thus, regulation can be thought of broadly, encompassing a wide array of social mechanisms from state agencies through institutional discipline and control as in the Foucauldian sense, to individual self-control and responsibilisation as per Garland (2001). On the other hand, it can be viewed narrowly as in a traditional understanding of the regulation of a particular sector such as financial services.

The concept of regulation, then, can be used to cover a broad range of processes and actions (or non-actions) which aim to provide a framework within which companies and individuals can operate in a manner appropriate and acceptable to state or mainstream norms and/or laws. It is the non-compliance of companies paying bribes within such regulatory frameworks and the ways in which this is dealt with that is of interest in this book. In line with this, and with reference to the academic literature on regulation, a number of specific approaches have been advocated in relation to the most appropriate means of dealing with corporate *crimes*. This literature provides a broad set of concepts for comparing regulatory regimes (in, for example, the UK and Germany).

Thus, the nature and context of corporate bribery, in that it is embedded within business and industry, and often involves government aims and ideologies, creates numerous tensions. One key tension is that between the most relevant and effective form of control and response and the level of state intervention this should involve. Thinking in terms of 'regulation' provides a set of concepts for analysing how behaviour can be shaped beyond the use of traditional law enforcement and 'policing' approaches. While criminal law enforcement and prosecution remains significant, it is not only enforcement mechanisms (prosecution, penalties, cautioning, licensing and taxing and disruption and so on) but also forms of self-regulation that are key in understanding the regulation and control of transnational corporate bribery.

Shifts Towards, and Features of, New Regulatory Models

Such developments, as outlined above, have been characterised as shifts from 'Old Governance' (that is, state-centric, centralised, bureaucratic expertise, mandatory rules) to 'New Governance (that is, state orchestration, decentralised, dispersed expertise, soft law) (Abbot and Snidal 2009). This has resulted in what some analysts have termed the new 'regulatory state' (see for example Moran, 2001) or 'regulatory capitalism' (though the state retains a primary role) (see Braithwaite, 2008). This new 'regulatory state' reflects a shift away from crime control as a problem of the state and has seen a transformation of the self-regulation model, as understood in traditional British society (Moran, 2001: 22–3). As Gill (2002: 537) notes, within this 'regulatory state', the most that the authorities can do is establish a structure of enforced self-regulation.

New regulatory or new governance models such as 'responsive regulation' (Ayres and Braithwaite, 1992), 'smart regulation' (Gunningham and Grabosky, 1998), problem-solving regulation (Sparrow, 2008), 'meta-regulation' (Parker, 2002), regulation in market societies (Edwards and Gill, 2002; Gill, 2000), the 'governance triangle' (Abbott and Snidal, 2006), 'regulatory capitalism' (Braithwaite, 2008), 'really responsive risk-based regulation' (Black and Baldwin, 2010) and regulators as 'sociological citizens' (Silbey et al., 2009; Silbey, 2011) offer new ways in understanding regulatory problems and approaches. Multiple common themes can be seen throughout these models. For example, the need for a varied set of sanctions and strategies including both enforcement and self-regulatory mechanisms; the necessity of 'negotiated relationships' between the regulators and regulatees; the accomplishment of compliance; the reflexivity, responsiveness and agency of the regulators; and the involvement of non-state actors and agencies albeit within varying degrees of state intervention. As Haines notes:

> This literature places the regulator within a broad governance framework where the enforcement of rules within narrow prescriptive frameworks is eschewed in preference for policy mixes, combining instruments, third-party actors, and enforcement regimes that collectively can both 'push' and 'pull' (Gunningham and Grabosky, 1998: 259) regulatees into a reflexive appreciation of the goals the regulator wants to achieve and lead them to act in a diligent manner to bring the goals to fruition' (Haines 2011, 118–9).

However, such new regulatory models are often preoccupied with the *institutions* of regulation and their strategies – these are usually characterised by a high level of state intervention or 'steering' and are of a more formal nature (for example, an industry regulator requiring corporations to implement sufficient compliance systems). In this sense, mechanisms that emerge more independently of state influence and whose 'regulatory' impacts are secondary (for example, mechanisms that primarily aim to generate profit) are not recognised but are significant in changing market and corporate behaviour (Chapter 7).

A further problem is that such agencies are often concerned with problems that occur *within* and not *across* nation-states. Models of *transnational* regulation have been proposed (see for example Braithwaite and Drahos, 2000; Djelic and Sahlin-Andersson, 2006) such as that from Kenneth W. Abbot and Duncan Snidal (2013) who explore the key role of intergovernmental organisations in transnational regulatory standard-setting (TRSS) through regulatory strategies of 'collaboration' (engaging directly with target firms/industry groups in collaboration with international and national public interest groups to encourage self-regulation) and 'orchestration' (empowering intermediaries (for example, public interest groups, private and public-private initiatives) with similar intentions to 'enforce' self-regulation). This approach is framed within the principles of 'responsive regulation', an approach that has shaped contemporary thinking on regulation (see Mascini, 2013; Parker, 2013) though there are now attempts to move 'beyond responsive regulation' (see Grabosky 2013). Critique of the model does however exist, in particular in relation to assumptions of graduated sanctioning models and their lack of credibility when prosecutions are so rare (Chapter 6) and the relevance and robustness of the concept in relation to deregulation and neoliberalism (see Tombs and Whyte, 2013).

Contemporary Regulatory Theory and Transnational Corporate Bribery

The Innospec and Siemens cases discussed in the previous chapter indicate the sheer transnational nature of cases of corporate bribery in international commerce. It is the nature of such bribery that raises a number of significant issues for current theories of regulation, as outlined above. First, the empirical base of much of the above theory is limited to certain industry sectors, offences occurring domestically (that is, not trans-nationally), and to state agencies and regulators limited by their national jurisdiction. For example, Ayres and Braithwaite's (1992) influential 'responsive regulation' relies heavily on illustrative material from the United States, Australia and to a lesser extent Britain, and refers to specific industries (pharmaceutical, nursing homes and so on) to illustrate its arguments. Likewise, Gunningham and Grabosky's (1998) 'smart regulation' in relation to environmental policy was developed based on empirical findings largely on specific case studies on the chemical and agricultural industries in North America, Western Europe and Australia. Such models and regulatory approaches face difficulties when focusing on acts that transcend sectors, nations and jurisdictions, as in the case of transnational corporate bribery. How can a 'regulator' regulate acts that are not specific to one sector and which occur across two or more jurisdictions? This is further complicated given the differing legal frameworks that exist in different countries.

Second, and in relation to the first point, the tangibility of the nature of the object of regulation creates difficulties. It is possible to see how a regulator can focus his activities on the dumping of chemicals in rivers, or the impacts of a certain drug on individuals and populations, as such activities have tangible harms and consequences. Transnational corporate bribery, however, is less tangible in nature. There are a lack of direct victims and harms as such corruption usually involves at least two willing actors and is beneficial to both direct transacting parties. Detecting such activities raises further issues. While a river can be tested for levels of pollution, cash flows between corrupt individuals or organisations are difficult to locate, follow and attribute to responsible agents. Such cash payments may result in an official conducting his usual roles therefore further disguising the corruption. Other forms of bribery and corruption such as exchanging services are even less tangible.

Third, the regulation of industry as outlined in previous regulatory literature largely involves specific regulatory agencies tasked with controlling and managing undesirable behaviour by companies within the industry. These agencies are usually state created and are often limited in their enforcement to one specific sector. For example, in the UK the Financial Conduct Authority and the Prudential Regulation Authority (together formerly the Financial Services Authority (FSA)) are state-created, industry-funded regulators of financial institutions and cannot extend their regulatory scope beyond this sector. Such industry-specific regulation cannot be applied to transnational corporate bribery which occurs within and between many sectors (although most notably construction and manufacturing) that exist beyond specific sectors and national markets. The SFO has national jurisdiction for serious corruption but its remit incorporates a large variety of serious frauds, not just bribery (Chapter 5). This further questions the validity of regulatory models that require some form of constant negotiation between the regulator and regulatee. This is possible where an industry is regulated and may be under constant monitoring, but in cases of transnational corporate bribery such monitoring of individual companies or sectors is more complex. A company may only be monitored once a company has been prosecuted. In these cases, specific deterrence based on graduated and escalated sanctioning and enforcement strategies may prove effective. In such instances, the criminal law as argued for in deterrence models may be of more significance. As a general deterrent for all corporations operating overseas this may be less so.

Fourth, the above issues highlight the difficulty of transnational, multi-jurisdictional regulation. The legal frameworks in the US and the UK are wide-reaching allowing regulators in both jurisdictions to investigate and prosecute overseas corporations (Chapter 4). For example, a UK citizen or company working in China that is part of a joint venture with a US company or that has a listing on a US stock exchange falls into US jurisdiction under the Foreign Corrupt Practices Act. Similar jurisdiction applies to the UK Bribery Act, although guidance published at the end of March 2011 provided legal loopholes and will depend on the courts' interpretation when it comes to prosecution (Chapter 6). In other cases, peer-investigations, peer-prosecutions, and 'global settlements' often shaped through Mutual Legal Assistance are conducted but such international regulation faces numerous significant challenges such as evidence gathering from countries that have not ratified international conventions (Chapters 5 and 6). 'Ownership' of the problem or case also becomes an issue, as does potential for double jeopardy, sharing fines and confiscations (see Innospec case) and providing compensation to the relevant countries and victims. Such a clash of sovereignties reinforces the inadequacies of states and previously discussed regulatory models.

Considering the above four points, in addition to the analysis of regulation theory, a framework for understanding the 'regulatory' landscape of transnational corporate bribery is required that can account for a complex set of mechanisms, practices and relations that are organised transnationally. This chapter now sets out a framework for understanding such a landscape.

Developing an Analytical Framework

Shifting focus away from formal institutions and towards the nature of the problem enables the identification of (i) emerging 'regulatory' mechanisms that such problems imply (for example, criminal/regulatory enforcement, risk management, self-regulation), (ii) the direct and indirect actors that form part of these mechanisms (for example, state agencies, commercial enterprises, non-governmental and intergovernmental organisations) and (iii) the contexts within which such actors operate and such practices originate (for example, micro-, meso- and macro-levels; state-commercial-inter/non-governmental domains). With this in mind, it is useful to think of the regulation of *populations* of corporations within markets rather than a preoccupation with institutional responses to *individual* corporate 'offenders' and to shift attention to the emergence of a regulatory landscape that encompasses a diverse array of regulatory mechanisms in a dynamic landscape.

A useful organising framework for understanding the available 'regulatory' responses in market societies is provided by Gill (2000, 2002) and Edwards and Gill (2002). This framework foregrounds the regulation of behaviour in market societies as being *a*, but arguably *the*, principal context of modern policing in 'the West' (Gill, 2002). The framework identifies a mixture of enforcement and non-enforcement responses with regards the regulation of *populations* of actors in licit and illicit markets. Analytical focus can be shifted away from a sole concern with formal regulatory institutions (and their strategies) and from narrow conceptions of regulation towards understanding the broader processes, practices and relations that shape behaviour within corporations and markets. Using a broad and inclusive definition of regulation (as above), it is possible to understand how behaviour in market societies can be regulated by a diverse mixture of state and non-state 'regulatory' actors involved directly and indirectly in negotiating regulation. Compliance outcomes and behaviour changes are accomplished and negotiated through the interactions of such 'regulators' and 'regulatees' (that is, MNCs) over time. Viewing the regulatory landscape at the level of populations, as opposed to the level of individual corporations per se, enables analysis of the mixture of responses (for example, enforcement, self-regulatory, hybrid) that together serve to regulate the markets within which corporations operate.

Transnational corporate bribery is by its very nature a market phenomenon. For example, it involves licit corporations operating in licit markets but involves illicit activities that are dependent on 'grey' markets. 'Grey' markets are located in jurisdictions where bribery is 'common business practice' (that is, an accepted part of the local culture) and it is such markets where much transnational commerce is directed. This book utilises this framework to organise the discussion in subsequent chapters around the mixture of enforcement (for example, criminal law enforcement and civil sanctioning), self-regulatory (for example, corporate compliance, business initiatives) and hybrid (for example, mechanisms incorporating aspects of enforcement and self-regulation) that are emerging in the regulatory landscape of transnational corporate bribery and which Edwards and Gill suggest can be used to 'negotiate' compliance and regulation. Figure 3.1 demonstrates this theoretical range of regulatory practices with the horizontal spectrum relating to the range of markets from the unambiguously legal to the illegal – 'grey' markets will be found in the middle of this spectrum – and the vertical spectrum relating to the range of possible official responses ranging from full enforcement to abnegation of any regulatory effort.

As Figure 3.1 illustrates, at the top end of enforcement, sanctions are more likely to be criminal in relation to illegal markets and administrative/civil in relation to legal markets. The ellipses are therefore located correspondingly although as can be seen, the right-hand edge of 'prosecution' and the left-hand edge of 'administrative/civil penalties' indicate those cases where activities in legal markets may be prosecuted and where activities in illegal markets may be resolved through administrative/civil means. 'Disruption' of unambiguously legal markets by regulators is not necessary but disrupting criminal operations and

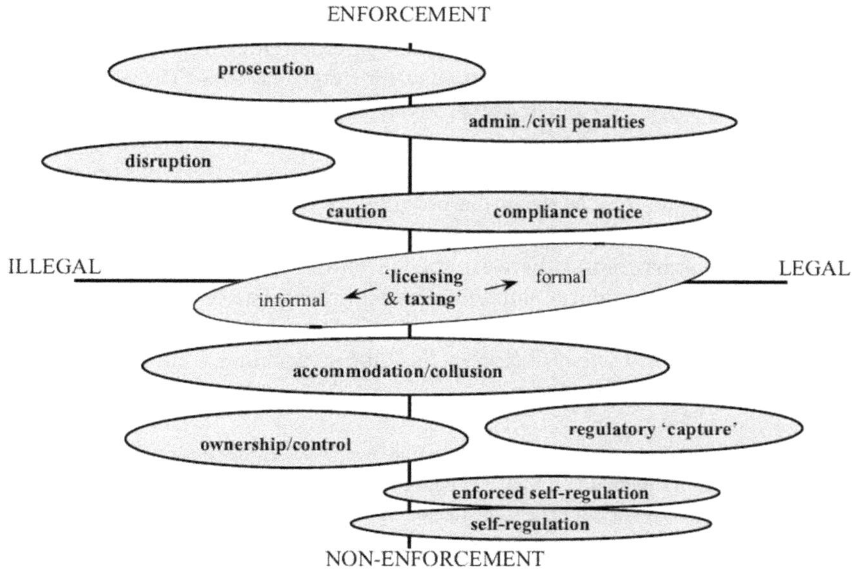

Figure 3.1 Enforcement and non-enforcement mechanisms in legal and illegal markets (Gill, 2002: 535)

markets is becoming increasingly attractive for police and custom agencies due to the higher costs of evidence gathering and the unpredictability of the outcomes of prosecution. Beneath this, the role of 'cautioning' to encourage traders to change their ways and which may be formally or informally used by police as a main alternative to prosecution, can be compared with regulators issuing 'compliance notices' in legal markets. 'Licensing and taxing', as indicated in the model, can represent varying degrees of formality where formal regulation is exercised over dangerous products that can be legally traded but require traders to have relevant licenses. Failure to comply in these cases can result in licence revocation. While illegal traders cannot be formally licensed, some circumstances occur whereby they may receive informal 'licences' from police or regulators as in the case of street traders who act as police informers. Such traders are vulnerable to sanctions and licence revocation.

In the bottom of half of the enforcement continuum, sanctions are not used at all. Within legal markets, 'self-regulation' in industry is considered the desired outcome of effective education and self-control. This suggests external, state regulation and intervention is not required or not feasible, which relates to arguments discussed above in relation to compliance. 'Accommodation and collusion' relates to the inadequate resources to pursue full enforcement that all regulatory agencies encounter. Consequently, prioritisation inevitably occurs meaning some illegal trading or regulation-avoidance takes place without a regulatory response. Thus, regulators may be aware of certain problematic activities but may be required to tolerate these where their benefits may outweigh their loss (Edwards, 2010). 'Regulatory capture' may occur due to shared ideology and/or personnel, rewards and/or threats resulting in traders 'capturing' the regulators and therefore ensuring non-enforcement. In some extreme cases, 'ownership/control' may even occur whereby the 'regulators' share in the profitability of the market. A key example of this would be the BAE Systems bribery scandal which involved a government to government arms contract between the UK and Saudi Arabia but enlisted BAE Systems as the arms producer and provider in this deal. The subsequent difficulties in investigating and prosecuting this case reflected this government-corporation relationship, amongst other factors. Thus, the conceptual framework outlined above is based on the idea that:

> … regulation is a social relationship that needs to be negotiated through a mixture of enforcement and alternatives to sanctions. A key implication of this premise is that reducing behaviour deemed problematic and harmful is unlikely to be accomplished through investment in practices of command and control alone, especially where resources for enforcement are economically, politically and/or culturally limited (Edwards, 2010: 44).

Thus, a variety of practices may be adopted by regulators towards traders and markets with the mix of enforcement styles shaped by the 'negotiated relationships' between regulators and traders. The specific nature of these relationships at any particular time and place is shaped by factors such as the available resources to regulators, the nature of their legal mandate and the political, economic and moral narration of the threat posed by traders. However, for Edwards and Gill (2002: 215), changes in the market depend not only on the actions of authorities but also on the adaptability and/or successful resistance of traders therefore such 'negotiated relationships' extend to a much broader range of interactions: this includes attempts by regulators to calculate likely outcomes of enforcement policies, costs of enforcement in relation to resources, civil rights and ethics (Beare and Naylor, 1999), as well as the study of 'evolutionary struggles' between cops and crooks that might be compared to arms races or the contest between intelligence and counterintelligence (Ekblom, 1999). It is such processes at the operational level that appear vital in any regulatory approach. Clearly, markets can vary not only in terms of their degree of illegality – although discussing markets in terms of being a 'bit illegal' or 'more illegal than legal' is itself a difficult task – but also in terms of their size, scope, geography, type of actors and products involved, law invoked and so on. The range of practices, however, can be applied to most regulatory problems. For example, by definition, *corporate* bribery is a market-based activity given its location and role within financial markets and transactions and the use of such corruption to facilitate trading and so on.

Summary

This book is concerned with the control of corporations that give bribes to foreign officials in the context of business. Significant insights can be gained from the historical differences in the way national authorities have prosecuted 'corporate crime'. These have left a contemporary legacy that further complicates *inter*-national co-operation in prosecuting *trans*-national and complexly organised corporate crimes and such historical legacies are important for understanding the limitations of criminal sanctioning by sovereign actors as an enforcement mechanism for controlling illicit corporate behaviour.

Regulation is not straightforward. The challenges discussed at the start of this chapter in relation to policing transnational crimes begin to identify the problems that responsible authorities are faced with. Furthermore, problems of knowledge and power highlight the difficulties that states face in providing effective and efficient 'policing' of problems of crime. Consequently, shifts towards regulation have taken place and traditional policing practices are now significantly similar to regulation, particularly in the area of corporate crimes.

Understandings of regulation vary amongst different actors and to the extent that different levels of enforcement and self-regulation ought to be evident in any regulatory approach. The analytical framework that shapes this research shifts analytical focus away from a preoccupation with regulatory agencies and specific regulatory mechanisms towards an understanding of the mixture of responses that are available within markets to regulate the behaviour of populations of actors. A key part of this landscape are the negotiated social relationships between regulators and regulatees that shape the extent to which regulation is accomplished. Thinking in these terms enables regulatory theory to be rethought in line with broader understandings of behaviour change through myriad mechanisms. Understanding regulation in relation to the transnational problem of corporate bribery provides insight into how such theories can be developed to deal with the exceptionality of multi-jurisdictional corporate crimes and their control.

The problem of transnational corporate bribery and a comparison of regulatory responses to this problem in the UK and Germany can empirically, theoretically and conceptually contribute to the above arguments around corporate crime regulation and control. Current theories of regulation are limited by their focus on more tangible phenomena, their focus on specific industrial sectors, their focus on regulation within specific jurisdictions and/or their focus on narrow understandings of the concept of regulation as it can be applied beyond 'regulated' sectors. Transnational corporate bribery, in contrast to these examples, is a problem of all corporations and businesses that operate internationally and is therefore not limited to any one jurisdiction, sector or regulator. Instead, a multi-agency/departmental approach to controlling corporate bribery is in existence in the UK and Germany but these traditional 'policing' authorities are adopting regulatory techniques and approaches traditionally associated with those of industry regulators (for example, enforced self-regulatory practices and persuasion) (see Chapter 6).

Chapter 4
Legal Frameworks for Enforcement: From the International to the National

> The objective of the [UK Bribery] Act is not to bring the full force of the criminal law to bear upon well run commercial organisations that experience an isolated incident of bribery on their behalf. 99% of organisations try their hardest and probably would find themselves the wrong side of this Act, simply because something had slipped through the system. What we're interested in at the SFO in administering this Act, is to go after the real offenders, and that is to say, the people who persistently – that very small minority – persistently engage in corruption to give themselves an unfair advantage over those who do behave ethically (Vivian Robinson QC, then General Counsel of the SFO, Securities Docket webcast, (13 January) 2011).[1]

Introduction

A key 'tool' in any regulatory landscape is the legal framework within which the regulator operates. The noise created by intergovernmental and non-governmental organisations such as the OECD, the UN and TI has required nation-states to evolve and adapt their legislation in order to create a more effective transnational anti-corruption and bribery legal landscape. Investigative and prosecutorial approaches have also changed in the light of these international and domestic pressures and as a result of the availability of more legal tools. The statement above reflects this. In the months following the enactment of the UK Bribery Act 2010, Vivian Robinson QC,[2] then General Counsel of the SFO (and since moved to an American-based law firm in London), implied that despite the available criminal law threat that the Act provides, the 'full force of the criminal law' would only be used in a 'very small minority' of cases that involve persistent offenders. This can only be done, however, given an appropriate legal framework. The criminal law framework is important for prosecutors given its symbolic and (potentially) deterrent effect as it enables the state (i) to negotiate regulation with corporations (that is, the underlying threat of prosecution for non-compliance – albeit this may be more rhetorical than probable (see Chapter 6)) and (ii) to be able to demonstrate to the various publics (for example, intergovernmental and non-governmental

1 Webcast available at: http://www.securitiesdocket.com/2011/01/04/january-13-webcast%E2%80%94100-days-and-counting-the-impact-of-the-uk-bribery-act-on-u-s-companies-2/ <Accessed 10/11/2013>.

2 Queens Counsel (QC).

organisations, business communities, media, activists and so on) that it is actively criminalising domestic corporations using illicit means in overseas jurisdictions.

The law, however, is alone an insufficient mechanism for changing behaviour within corporations and business but provides a normative framework within which certain activities have been condemned (usually in response to the 'moral entrepreneurship' of non-state organisations but occasionally also of political 'champions'). It is important not only to outline the legal frameworks in both jurisdictions, but also to understand and analyse how these frameworks (a) have been influenced by internal (for example, national anti-corruption activists) and external (for example, international and intergovernmental anti-corruption organisations) pressures, (b) have been transformed by national legal traditions and cultures and (c) enforced and applied at the operational level.

This chapter primarily analyses points (a) and (b) by examining the extent to which legal frameworks and legislation at the national level in the UK and Germany have been adapted and changed to come in line with international and regional conventions and guiding principles. Point (c) is explored in Chapters 5, 6 and 7. The chapter retains a focus on the relevant legislation and conventions covering 'foreign bribery', or 'international bribery', as opposed to 'domestic bribery', although where relevant, domestic bribery offences will also be outlined. At times, the content is quite technical and detailed but this is necessary for readers to understand the frameworks within which regulatory authorities must operate.

The chapter begins by considering legal frameworks created at the international and inter-regional level. Here, conventions of the OECD and the UN are analysed with the key articles and clauses being discussed. The chapter then moves on to the regional level and the provisions of the Council of Europe and the EU. The UK and German legal frameworks are then analysed with regards the extent to which the international and regional conventions are implemented within their national laws. Relevant national Acts and offences are discussed. This highlights the significant impact of the 'moral entrepreneurs' at the international, regional and national levels in evolving conceptions of the bribery and corruption 'problem'. The US Foreign Corrupt Practices Act 1977 is also discussed here, given its extraterritorial reach and therefore its relevance to UK and German corporations operating overseas. Throughout the chapter, limitations along with the strengths of the legislation and conventions will be addressed.

The key argument of the chapter is as follows: comparative analysis of the UK and German legal frameworks demonstrates a large degree of convergence but identifies fundamental and substantial differences in legal principles (for example, culpability of legal or natural persons) that identify obstacles to pursuing criminal law enforcement. Even in leading G8 economies such as the UK and Germany, not to mention those jurisdictions less developed in relation to their anti-corruption frameworks, key legal distinctions render legal frameworks ambiguous. International organisations do, however, promote a pragmatically driven preference for 'functional equivalence' which in itself demonstrates the inadequacy of criminal law alone as an anti-corruption mechanism.

The International and Interregional level

Nation-states strive to promote their own economic and corporate interests. Creating an even playing field is therefore important for those countries with corporations interested in exporting or investing overseas. In the 1970s, the US government faced internal criticism over the conduct of its corporations and subsequently enacted the Foreign Corrupt Practices Act 1977 (see below), expecting that other jurisdictions would follow suit. This did not immediately occur, however, and it took two more decades before US pressures led the OECD to create the Convention on Combating Bribery of Foreign Public Officials in International Business Transactions (OECD Anti-Bribery Convention) 1997. This Convention required key economic countries to create similar transnational bribery provisions at the national level. The second key convention is that of the UN Convention against Corruption (UNCAC) 2003. The UNCAC was more complex and organic in its creation and represented the interests of a wider number of stakeholders and jurisdictions. Both Germany and the UK ratified the OECD Anti-Bribery Convention in 1998 with national implementing legislation coming into force in February 1999 in Germany and February 2002 in the UK. At the time of writing, Germany has yet to ratify the UNCAC but signed it in December 2003. The UK ratified the UNCAC in February 2006.

The OECD Anti-bribery Convention

The OECD Convention was the first and remains the only legally binding instrument focusing on the *supply side* of bribery. The Convention deals with what is termed 'active bribery' in contrast to 'passive bribery' as differentiated in UK and German law (see below). This means the focus is on the offence committed by the person who promises or gives a bribe. That said, the Convention does not use the term 'active bribery' in order to avoid non-technical readers mistakenly viewing the briber as taking the initiative and the recipient as a passive victim (OECD 2011a: 14): it is often the case that the recipient will have induced or pressured the briber and thus be more 'active'.

The Convention seeks a 'functional equivalence' amongst the measures taken by the Parties to sanction bribery of foreign public officials. 'Functional equivalence' permits State Parties to implement any means they consider to be suitable providing they enable the requirements of Article 1 of the Convention (The Offence of Bribery of Foreign Public Officials) to be met. Thus, anti-bribery enforcement measures in each jurisdiction do not require uniformity or changes in fundamental principles of a Party's legal systems. For pragmatic and political reasons, there are therefore no requirements for harmonisation of anti-bribery measures across jurisdictions, with 'goals' (for example, reductions in bribery or increased enforcement) being prioritised above 'means' (for example, the use of corporate *criminal* liability in the UK but not Germany). This requires greater conceptual analysis of equivalence than mere technical copying would do.

The Convention is highly focused and targeted towards those countries that account for the majority of global exports and foreign investment. After opening for signature in 1997, it came into force in 1999; 60 days after five of the ten countries with the largest export shares and which represent a minimum of 60 per cent of the combined total exports of those ten countries deposited their instruments of acceptance, approval or ratification. Article 1 of the Convention outlines that Parties in relation to the offence of bribery of foreign public officials have agreed that:

> 1. Each Party shall take such measures as may be necessary to establish that it is a criminal offence under its law for any person intentionally to offer, promise or give any undue pecuniary or other advantage, whether directly or through intermediaries, to a foreign public official, for that official or for a third party, in order that the official act or refrain from acting in relation to the performance of official duties, in order to obtain or retain business or other improper advantage in the conduct of international business.
>
> 2. Each Party shall take any measures necessary to establish that complicity in, including incitement, aiding and abetting, or authorisation of an act of bribery of a foreign public official shall be a criminal offence. Attempt and conspiracy to bribe a foreign public official shall be criminal offences to the same extent as attempt and conspiracy to bribe a public official of that Party (OECD 2011a: Article 1).

The OECD Convention establishes legally binding standards to criminalise bribery (and related offences) of foreign public officials in international business transactions and provides measures to make this effective. The Convention also outlines that Parties must establish the liability of legal and natural persons for such offences and ensure effective penalties and measures are in place (though what constitutes 'effectiveness' remains undefined). Furthermore, Parties are required to establish jurisdiction when an offence is committed in or in part of their territory. As noted by TI, the obligations of the parties to the OECD Convention fall into five categories: criminalisation; money laundering; provisions regarding private sector; international cooperation; and monitoring.[3] The OECD is not able to force directly implementation of the Convention, but monitors the implementation of legislation and its effectiveness within participating countries. This is largely undertaken by the OECD Working Group on Bribery. Under the Convention, foreign bribery is a crime in all 40 States Parties (the 34 OECD members plus six non-members: Argentina, Brazil, Bulgaria, Columbia, Russia and South Africa).[4] These countries also agreed to remove tax deductions for bribe payments.

---

3 TI's overview of the OECD Convention available at: http://archive.transparency.org/global_priorities/international_conventions/projects_conventions/oecd_convention <Accessed 10/11/2013>.

4 http://www.oecd.org/daf/anti-bribery/antibriberyconventionratification.pdf <Accessed 10/11/2013>.

Key in transnational corporate bribery are the public officials and foreign countries where the bribes are directed, the definitions of which are vital. The Convention outlines that:

> a) 'foreign public official' means any person holding a legislative, administrative or judicial office of a foreign country, whether appointed or elected; any person exercising a public function for a foreign country, including for a public agency or public enterprise; and any official or agent of a public international organisation;
>
> b) 'foreign country' includes all levels and subdivisions of government, from national to local;
>
> c) 'act or refrain from acting in relation to the performance of official duties' includes any use of the public official's position, whether or not within the official's authorised competence (OECD 2011a: Article 1).

This provides a broad and inclusive definition of foreign public official. Senior politicians through managers at state-owned organisations to local police officers would all fall within this definition. Similar broad definitions are adopted in UK and German laws. Article 5 of the Convention on 'Enforcement' is also worthy of further consideration:

> Investigation and prosecution of the bribery of a foreign public official shall be subject to the applicable rules and principles of each Party. They shall not be influenced by considerations of *national economic interest*, the *potential effect upon relations with another State* or the identity of the natural or legal persons involved (OECD Convention, Article 5, 1997 [emphasis added]).

First, understanding what constitutes 'national economic interest' and how this differs from smaller economic interests is important. The Innospec case outlined in Chapter 2 clearly indicated Lord Justice Thomas' view that imposing a higher fine on Innospec would have more appropriately reflected the level of criminality but that in doing so would have resulted in immediate insolvency and would have 'affected the innocent employees of the company … [and] … caused considerable difficulties for the unfunded pension liabilities of the company …' (Judiciary of England and Wales, 2010: note 42, iii).

Second, similar concerns were raised by the OECD in relation to the BAE Systems investigation where it was argued by Tony Blair that the investigation would jeopardise relations with Saudi Arabia and subsequently the UK's national security. This scenario highlighted significant concerns on behalf of the OECD that the Convention had been breached (OECD 2007a). The independence of the judiciary from the executive is also an issue here – the legislature can impose a mandatory sentence, but can the government be criticised for 'failing' to apply the

Convention in this context? The interpretation of the courts at the national level on this matter is clearly significant, as is the interpretation of the OECD itself in deciding whether or not to criticise and even to impose formal sanctions.

The UN Convention against Corruption

The objectives of the UNCAC are:

> a) To promote and strengthen measures to prevent and combat corruption more efficiently and effectively;
>
> b) To promote, facilitate and support international cooperation and technical assistance in the prevention of and fight against corruption, including in asset recovery;
>
> c) To promote integrity, accountability and proper management of public affairs and public property (UN 2003: Article 1).

The UNCAC is the first global, legally binding instrument in the fight against corruption (UN, 2009: xvii). It requires the States Parties to implement numerous and detailed anti-corruption measures impacting upon their laws, institutions and practices. The purpose is to aid prevention, detection and sanctioning of corrupt practices and encourage the cooperation of States Parties. The Convention requires States Parties to establish a range of offences associated with corruption and attaches particular importance to prevention and the strengthening of international cooperation to combat corruption. It also includes 'innovative and far-reaching' provisions on asset recovery and technical assistance and implementation.

The UNCAC opened for signature in 2003 and came into force in 2005. It contains eight chapters and 71 Articles, in comparison to the OECD Convention that is relatively short with 17 Articles. The UNCAC, when compared to other conventions, is more detailed and extensive with its provisions and incorporates an extensive global reach: it was negotiated by representatives of more than 100 countries from all regions while civil society organisations, such as TI, also had a significant role in this process. As of May 2013, the Convention had 140 Signatories and 167 Parties, which demonstrates its wide reach.[5] As TI indicates, the obligations of the Parties fall into the following categories: preventive measures; criminalisation; international cooperation; asset recovery framework; technical cooperation and information exchange; and implementation mechanism.[6]

---

5 http://www.unodc.org/unodc/en/treaties/CAC/signatories.html <Accessed 10/11/2013>.

6 TI's overview of the UNCAC available at: http://archive.transparency.org/global_priorities/international_conventions/projects_conventions/uncac <Accessed 10/11/2013>.

The UNCAC follows an almost identical definition of the term 'foreign public official' to that of the OECD Convention, but includes also any person holding an 'executive' office of a foreign country. The UNCAC goes beyond the scope of the OECD Convention in numerous ways. For example, Articles 15 and 16 require the criminalisation of 'active' *and* 'passive' bribery of national public officials *and* foreign public officials respectively. Amongst others, Article 21 explicitly incorporates bribery in the private sector into the Convention whilst numerous other offences (for example, embezzlement, abuse of functions and so on) not included in the OECD Convention are explicitly included in the UNCAC. All these provisions are included in UK and German law (see below).

Both the UNCAC (Article 6, Section 2) and the OECD Convention (paragraph 27, commentary on Article 5) outline the importance of the independence of anti-corruption bodies. This is of particular relevance to the UK. Under the UK Bribery Act 2010, Section 10 now permits the Director of the SFO to bring proceedings without Attorney General consent. However prior to this, the Director of the SFO, despite being independent in theory, required authorisation from the politically appointed Attorney General to prosecute any overseas corruption case. The BAE Systems case brought the independence of the SFO into question following the closing down of the case by the then Director of the SFO, Robert Wardle, who was put under pressure from the then Attorney General, Lord Goldsmith, to do so.[7] The difficulty for the OECD, and for other countries, is the identification of political independence and/or its absence – although political influence can be linear, not binary, and can take various forms, for example, resource starvation or abundance without being linked to specific prosecutions. The UNCAC also prescribes the requirements of States Parties in relation to relevant processes in more detail. For example, Article 46 goes into significant depth on Mutual Legal Assistance with 30 separate points outlined as to how States Parties should afford one another assistance. In contrast, the OECD Convention outlines three points on this matter. Thus, the UNCAC covers similar requirements as the OECD Convention but goes significantly beyond in scope.

The Regional Level: Council of Europe and the European Union

The OECD and UN Conventions are global in scope, albeit the OECD Convention is specifically targeted at those countries with the largest share of international exports. There are, however, significant conventions and provisions at the regional level, although such provisions can and do incorporate countries from outside of Europe, but they retain specific focus on European matters as well as more general concerns. Of most significance are the Council of Europe and EU conventions and protocols.

7 See *The Guardian: 'Nobbling the Police'*, available at: http://www.guardian.co.uk/baefiles/page/0,2098531,00.html <Accessed 10/11/2013>.

Council of Europe (CoE)

The CoE (1999a) Criminal Law Convention 1999 came into force in 2002. As of July 2013, the total number of ratifications/accessions was 44 and the total number of signatures not followed by ratification was six. The UK signed the Convention in 1999 and ratified in 2003. Germany signed in 1999 but is yet to ratify. The Convention is also open to six non-member States of the CoE – of these, the USA and Mexico have signed and Belarus has signed and ratified.

The Convention aims for the coordinated criminalisation of numerous corrupt practices whilst also providing for complementary criminal law measures and for improved international cooperation in the prosecution of offences of corruption. Articles 2 through to 11 require signatory states to establish as offences active and passive bribery of domestic and foreign public officials, members of domestic and foreign public assemblies, officials in international organisations, members of international parliamentary assemblies and judges and officials of international courts. Active and passive bribery in the private sector must also be criminalised. The Convention further requires the corrupt activities of trading in influence, money laundering and accounting offences connected to corruption offences to be criminalised. The Convention also incorporates provisions with regards aiding and abetting, immunity, criteria for determining the jurisdiction of States, liability of legal persons, the setting up of specialised anti-corruption bodies, protection of persons collaborating with investigating or prosecuting authorities, gathering of evidence and confiscation of proceeds.

The CoE (1999b) also created a Civil Law Convention on Corruption 1999 that came into force in 2003. The UK and Germany signed this Convention in 2000 and 1999 respectively but have yet to ratify it. In the UK, ratification is dependent on finding legislative time to address the problem of the absence of appropriate limitation periods for civil actions in domestic law (GRECO 2001: paragraph 29) while the ambiguities surrounding parliamentarians in Germany present obstacles to ratification (see below). As of July 2013, the total number of ratifications/accessions was 35 and the total number of signatures not followed by ratifications was seven.

The Convention is the first attempt at defining common international rules in relation to civil law and corruption. As Article 1 states, Contracting Parties are required to provide in their domestic law 'for effective remedies for persons who have suffered damage as a result of acts of corruption, to enable them to defend their rights and interests, including the possibility of obtaining compensation for damage'. The Civil Law Convention also provides a definition of corruption, the only Convention to explicitly do so, but this is imprecise and does not distinguish between public and private corruption, legal and natural persons, or whether the advantage is for personal or organisational gain.[8]

---

8 Article 2 of the CoE Civil Law Convention 1999 states: 'For the purpose of this Convention, "*corruption*" means requesting, offering, giving or accepting, directly or indirectly, a bribe or any other undue advantage or prospect thereof, which distorts the

A number of multifaceted legal instruments have been developed and adopted by the CoE. These include:

- the Additional Protocol to the Criminal Law Convention on Corruption 2003;
- the Twenty Guiding Principles against Corruption 1997;
- the Recommendation on Codes of Conduct for Public Officials 2000, and;
- the Recommendation on Common Rules against Corruption in the Funding of Political Parties and Electoral Campaigns 2003.

These instruments address issues including the criminalisation of corruption in the public and private sectors, liability and compensation for damage caused by corruption, conduct of the public officials and the financing of political parties. The instruments provide States with the capacity to fight corruption both domestically and internationally, while compliance with the standards is monitored by the Group of States against Corruption (GRECO), which was established in 1999.

Group of States against Corruption (GRECO)

The role of GRECO, through the processes of mutual evaluation and peer pressure, is to identify inadequacies in national anti-corruption policies, subsequently advise the necessary legislative, institutional and practical reforms and provide the structures for information sharing on best practice in the prevention and detection of corruption. As of July 2013, GRECO is comprised of 49 Member States (48 European States and the USA), with membership not being limited to CoE Member States. Any State which is Party to the Criminal or Civil Law Conventions automatically accedes to GRECO and its evaluation procedures.

European Union (EU)

Within the EU, anti-corruption enforcement is shaped by two main conventions: the EU Convention on the protection of the European communities' financial interests, First and Second Protocol 1995; and the EU Convention on the fight against corruption involving officials of the European Communities or officials of Member States 1997. The Convention and Protocol 1 entered into force in 2002, while Protocol 2 entered into force in 2009. The Convention aims to tackle fraud affecting the financial interests of the European Communities and does so by requiring that fraud affecting both expenditure and revenue must be punishable by effective, proportionate and dissuasive criminal penalties in every EU country. The EU Convention on the fight against corruption involving officials of the

proper performance of any duty or behaviour required of the recipient of the bribe, the undue advantage or the prospect thereof' (Italics in original).

European Communities or officials of Member States 1997 requires each Member State to ensure that active and passive corruption by officials is a punishable criminal offence. The Convention further requires Member States to take the necessary measures to allow heads of businesses or any persons having power to take decisions or exercise control within a business to be declared criminally liable in cases of active corruption by a person under their authority acting on behalf of the business. Signature and notification from the UK and Germany have been provided for both Conventions.

In addition to these Conventions, in 1999 the EU formed the European Anti-Fraud Office (OLAF) which has inter-institutional investigative powers, with this office becoming a useful instrument in the EU's tackling of corruption. OLAF's legal status was further altered by Articles 317 and 325 of the Treaty on the Functioning of the EU which shapes OLAF's role in the coordination of Members States' cooperation against fraud. In June 2011, the European Commission (EC) established a mechanism for the periodic assessment of the EU States' efforts to address corruption. The mechanism also facilitates the exchange of best practices, identifies EU trends, gathers comparable data on the Member States of the EU and stimulates peer learning and further compliance with the EU and international commitments.

Impact of International Legal Frameworks at the National Level

The above-mentioned international and regional conventions shape legislation at the national level. They largely cover the same provisions and together provide extensive legal frameworks which are subsequently required to be implemented with legislation at the national levels following ratification. Germany has yet to ratify the UNCAC, and the CoE Criminal and Civil Law Conventions. This lack of ratification reflects the 'domestic bribery' requirements of these conventions that are not evident in the OECD Convention while the incrimination of cross-border corruption in Germany lacks consistency (GRECO 2009: paragraphs 98 and 123).

The GRECO's (2009: paragraphs 37 *et seqq.* and 106 *et seqq.*) third round evaluation report on Germany outlines these discrepancies. First, in 2006, decisions of the German Federal Court of Justice ruled out from the legal definition of 'public official' members of local self-governing bodies such as communal and city councils and county councils unless they are entrusted with administrative duties (for example, members of a supervising committee), therefore creating a gap in anti-corruption provisions at the local level.

Second, the incrimination of bribery of members of domestic assemblies under Section 108e of the German Criminal Code is limited to the buying and selling of a vote for an election or ballot. No other form of active or passive bribery is criminalised in relation to domestic public assemblies and the provisions regarding domestic public officials (see Section 331 *et seqq.* German

Criminal Code below) are not applicable to them. In addition, immaterial advantages and third-party beneficiaries are not covered. With this in mind, one could bribe a parliamentarian for an internal party vote, or bribe the wife of such a person, and face no consequences. For these reasons, Germany is unable to ratify UNCAC and the CoE conventions – a draft law incorporating amendments that would have enabled ratification to these conventions was presented in German Parliament in 2007 but not accepted.[9] The UK has yet to ratify the CoE Civil Law Convention.

The National Level: Legal Frameworks and Implementation of International Conventions

The external pressure on states to implement relevant legislation is great, but law creation also faces significant internal pressures. As a consequence of these pressures, both the UK and Germany have implemented stringent legal provisions for the regulation of *transnational* corporate bribery providing the enforcement authorities with legal frameworks to investigate and prosecute *foreign* bribery cases. Policymakers in both jurisdictions, as well as those from international and non-governmental organisations responsible for scrutinising legal frameworks, are satisfied that sufficient provisions exist for responding to the bribery of foreign officials. These frameworks are analysed in details below.

The UK

The Bribery Act 2010 came into force on 1 July 2011 and is the key piece of anti-corruption legislation in the UK. Prior to this (and analogous in some respects to the criminalisation of fraud before the Fraud Act 2006), the UK legal system presented a somewhat complex and fragmented picture of bribery, with several overlapping laws covering specific corruption offences. As Jack Straw (2009: 3) indicated in the foreword to the Bribery Bill Draft Legislation:

> Our current statutory criminal law of bribery is functional: cases are prosecuted successfully. However, it is old and anachronistic – dating back to around the turn of the twentieth century – and it has never been consolidated. Consequently, there are inconsistencies of language and concepts between the various provisions and a small number of potentially significant gaps in the law. Furthermore, the exact scope of the common law offence is unclear. The result is a bribery law which is difficult to understand for the public and difficult to apply for prosecutors and the courts.

---

9 Full draft (in German) available at: http://dipbt.bundestag.de/dip21/btd/16/065/1606558.pdf <Accessed 10/11/2013>.

Anti-bribery and corruption legislation was primarily provided under the Prevention of Corruption Acts 1889 – 1916, with amendments from the Anti-Terrorism, Crime and Security Act 2001.

The Prevention of Corruption Acts 1889–1916

The Public Bodies Corrupt Practice Act 1889 criminalised the active or passive bribery of a member, officer or servant of a public body. The Prevention of Corruption Act 1906 addressed corrupt transactions with agents. Under the Act, agents were prohibited from being involved in active and passive bribery. It also became an offence for any person knowingly to give any agent, or for any agent to knowingly use with intent to deceive his principal, any receipt, account or other document in respect of which the principal is interested, and which contains any statement which is false or erroneous or defective in any material particular, and which to his knowledge is intended to mislead the principal.

The Prevention of Corruption Act 1916 creates a presumption of corruption in certain cases prosecuted under the 1889 and 1906 Acts. If it is proved that any money, gift or other consideration has been paid or given to or received by a person in the employment of Her Majesty (or any government department or a public body) by or from a person, or agent of a person, holding or seeking to obtain a contract from Her Majesty (or any government department or public body), the money, gift or consideration shall be deemed to have been paid or given and received corruptly as such inducement or reward as is mentioned in such Act unless the contrary is proved.

Anti-Terrorism, Crime and Security Act 2001

Part 12 of the Anti-Terrorism, Crime and Security Act 2001 made amendments to the Prevention of Corruption Acts. The Act imported a ‘foreign’ element into the offences of domestic bribery under the Prevention of Corruption Act 1906 and the common law, and established nationality jurisdiction for these offences. It became immaterial if the functions of the person who receives or is offered a reward have no connection with the UK and are carried out in a country or territory outside the UK. It also gave jurisdiction for corruption offences committed overseas by UK nationals and by bodies incorporated under UK law. These amendments partially addressed the extraterritoriality requirement of the OECD Convention. Part 3 of the Act contained a provision lifting restrictions on the sharing of information by tax and customs authorities in order to facilitate criminal investigations or proceedings.

The UK Bribery Act (UKBA) 2010

The UKBA contains four distinct offences: (i) the general offences of active (offering, promising) and (ii) passive (accepting, soliciting) bribery; (iii) the bribery of foreign officials (broad definition including a variety of state officials, for example, politicians, police officers and so on and must be in the context of business commerce); and (iv) the failure of commercial organisations to prevent bribery (a form of strict liability making corporations criminally liable for the actions of their employees, subsidiaries, intermediaries (see below)). UK prosecutors are also able to use a variety of other criminal offences and legislation such as the Proceeds of Crime Act 2002 (POCA) that enables substantive bribery cases to be concluded in relation to money laundering offences, amongst others. These offences, along with key analytical issues, are now examined in further detail.

Active and Passive Bribery

The two general offences are in many respects similar to previous law. Section 1 outlines the offence of bribing another person:

> (1) A person ('P') is guilty of an offence if either of the following cases applies.
>
> (2) Case 1 is where –
> (a) P offers, promises or gives a financial or other advantage to another person, and
> (b) P intends the advantage –
> (i) to induce a person to perform improperly a relevant function or activity, or
> (ii) to reward a person for the improper performance of such a function or activity.
>
> (3) Case 2 is where –
> (a) P offers, promises or gives a financial or other advantage to another person, and
> (b) P knows or believes that the acceptance of the advantage would itself constitute the improper performance of a relevant function or activity (UKBA, 2010, Section 1).

Section 2 covers offences related to being bribed:

> (1) A person ('R') is guilty of an offence if any of the following cases applies.
>
> (2) Case 3 is where R requests, agrees to receive or accepts a financial or other advantage intending that, in consequence, a relevant function or activity should be performed improperly (whether by R or another person).
>
> (3) Case 4 is where –
> (a) R requests, agrees to receive or accepts a financial or other advantage, and

(b) the request, agreement or acceptance itself constitutes the improper performance by R of a relevant function or activity.

(4) Case 5 is where R requests, agrees to receive or accepts a financial or other advantage as a reward for the improper performance (whether by R or another person) of a relevant function or activity.

(5) Case 6 is where, in anticipation of or in consequence of R requesting, agreeing to receive or accepting a financial or other advantage, a relevant function or activity is performed improperly –

(a) by R, or

(b) by another person at R's request or with R's assent or acquiescence (UKBA, 2010, Section 2).

These offences therefore cover active and passive bribery and in doing so introduce the key concepts of 'relevant function or activity' and 'improper performance'. The former includes any function of a public nature and any activity connected with a business, performed in the course of a person's employment or performed by or on behalf of a body of persons (whether corporate or unincorporate). The person performing the function or activity must be expected to perform it in good faith or impartially or is in a position of trust by virtue of performing it. The latter will be determined by whether the function or activity is performed in breach of a relevant expectation and there is a failure to perform the function or activity which is itself a breach of a relevant expectation. The function or activity is relevant even if it has no connection with the UK and is performed in a country or territory outside the UK.

Bribing a Foreign Public Official

Section 6 is of most significance for this book. It outlines the offence of bribery of foreign public officials.

(1) A person ('P') who bribes a foreign public official ('F') is guilty of an offence if P's intention is to influence F in F's capacity as a foreign public official.

(2) P must also intend to obtain or retain –

(a) business, or

(b) an advantage in the conduct of business.

(3) P bribes F if, and only if –

(a) directly or through a third party, P offers, promises or gives any financial or other advantage –

(i) to F, or

(ii) to another person at F's request or with F's assent or acquiescence, and

> (b) F is neither permitted nor required by the written law applicable to F to be influenced in F's capacity as a foreign public official by the offer, promise or gift (UKBA, 2010, Section 6).

This offence incorporates the OECD requirement for the supply side of bribery in relation to foreign public officials as well as the active and passive bribery requirements of domestic and foreign bribery in the UN and CoE Criminal Law Conventions. The UKBA retains a similar definition of a 'foreign public official' to that of the above Conventions and again includes that bribery only occurs where the applicable national law of the foreign public official neither permits nor requires the official to be influenced.

Conceptually, there is an explicit focus placed on the intention of the bribe, which *must also* aim to obtain or retain a business or business advantage, which ties into the focus on international business transactions and the location of corporate bribery within transnational markets. In some respects, this 'business' aspect creates a narrower test than the general offences, but, conversely, the broader focus on the 'intention to influence' rather than induce 'improper performance' as in the general offences creates a wider test. That said, under the UKBA, it is only illegal to bribe a foreign official if it is in connection to business transactions, although it may be a rarity that a bribe would be given in other circumstances. Hypothetically, a corporation may bribe a foreign official to encourage changes in policy to reflect the UK's general interests, for example, with no specific business advantage linked to the bribe.

The Corporate Offence

Section 7 created substantial concern within the private sector. This Section creates a new offence of failure of commercial organisations to prevent bribery:

> (1) A relevant commercial organisation ('C') is guilty of an offence under this section if a person ('A') associated with C bribes another person intending –
> (a) to obtain or retain business for C, or
> (b) to obtain or retain an advantage in the conduct of business for C.
>
> (2) But it is a defence for C to prove that C had in place adequate procedures designed to prevent persons associated with C from undertaking such conduct.

In the UK, criminal sanctioning, as one mechanism of enforcement, is enormously limited for controlling corporate bribery because of the ease at which senior managers can sub-contract offending behaviour and distance themselves from prosecution. However, the Section 7 offence is intended to reverse current corporate liability laws by introducing the possibility of 'strict liability' for corporations failing to prevent bribery. The company may be found criminally liable even if no one within the company was aware of the bribery:

> With the new Bribery Bill you can start off like the Americans do which is proving that a bribe was paid by someone associated with the company – the association thing is quite wide – in connection with the business, obtaining/retaining that sort of thing or gaining an advantage in the course of conducting that business. The only thing then is that you test the ultimate controlling company's regime designed to stop that sort of thing going on – adequate procedures. So it's not a controlling mind, it's the opposite way round. Rather than actually having the board expressly authorise the bribery, what you have got is the board not having a good enough regime to stop it and it has got to permeate the whole of the fabric of a group's business (Former UK Investigator/Prosecutor Interview 113).

The Section 7 offence therefore enables companies to be criminally prosecuted for the actions of its 'associated persons' (for a more detailed discussion of corporate criminal liability and how this influences enforcement see Chapter 6). Section 8 defines 'associated person' as a person who performs services for or on behalf of the company. Accordingly, this person may be the company's employee, agent or subsidiary. A PricewaterhouseCoopers event[10] following the introduction of the UKBA highlighted this third-party integrity risk to companies. It was stated that the average FTSE[11] 100 company has over 50,000 external entities that it regularly interacts with and for large MNCs this can be over 100,000.

Section 7 includes a defence for companies: to activate this, they must prove that 'adequate procedures' (see UKBA guidance in Chapter 5) were in place to prevent 'associated persons' committing bribery. This places the emphasis on corporations to ensure anti-corruption procedures and compliance regimes are robust enough to prevent employees, agents, third parties or intermediaries acting for the company from committing bribery.

Facilitation Payments

The topic of facilitation payments has created much concern amongst businesses, where it has been argued that such payments are common and even suggested their criminalisation places UK business 'on an uneven playing field'.[12] Facilitation payments are otherwise known as 'small bribes paid to facilitate routine Government action' (Ministry of Justice 2010: paragraphs 44–7). For example, these could include lorry drivers required to make small payments to pass through borders, or payments given to officials to speed up the process of obtaining a trading licence or passport. Such payments could trigger the Section 6 offence

10 PricewaterhouseCoopers' seminar 'Managing 3rd Party Integrity Risk' took place 9 November 2010, London.

11 Financial Times and London Stock Exchange.

12 See *London Evening Standard: 'Bribery Act lawsuits "could ruin bosses"'*, 21/02/2011, available at: http://www.thisislondon.co.uk/standard/article-23925017-bribery-act-lawsuits-could-ruin-bosses.do <Accessed 10/11/2013>.

of bribery of foreign public officials. Where there is intention to induce improper conduct and where the acceptance of such payments is improper, the Section 1 offence of active bribery could be triggered and therefore also the Section 7 corporate offence.

Facilitation payments were unlawful under previous law and unlike the US Foreign Corrupt Practices Act 1977 the UKBA does not provide any exemption for such payments. This position ties in with the 2009 Recommendation of the OECD which acknowledges the corrosive effect of small facilitation payments, particularly on the sustainable economic development and the rule of law, and requests Member countries to encourage companies to prohibit or discourage their use (OECD 2009). The US legislation, however, predated the OECD Convention, whereas the UK's position was clearly influenced by the international pressure from the OECD, although facilitation payments were illegal under previous UK law.

The likelihood of being prosecuted for facilitation payments is low, although corporations cannot rely on this. That said, the government recognises the problems of international commerce in certain sectors in some parts of the world and that the eradication of facilitation payments is a long-term objective requiring economic and social progress and sustained commitment to the rule of law where such payments are a problem: this requires collaboration between international bodies, governments, the anti-bribery lobby, business representative bodies and sectoral organisations (Ministry of Justice 2010: para. 46). Thus, as Richard Alderman, former Director of the SFO, stated:

> … the prospects of the SFO prosecuting, shall we say, a $50 one off facilitation payment picked up by a corporate and remedied by them is remote in the extreme. That remains my view. This view though does not mean that it is open to companies to allow small facilitation payments of up to a certain amount each year. This becomes a course of conduct which is likely to lead to consideration by the SFO of a prosecution (Speech by Richard Alderman at the Association of the British Pharmaceutical Industry Legal Day, 2010).[13]

An open letter in December 2012 from the current Director David Green revised the SFO's stance on facilitation payments whereby it was reinforced that such payments are bribes and that individuals and companies using them in the course of business are at risk of criminal prosecution.[14] However, more implicitly, Green and the SFO have indicated that one-off facilitation payments are unlikely to be pursued while the SFO website states '[i]t would be wrong to say there

13 Speech available at: http://www.sfo.gov.uk/about-us/our-views/director%27s-speeches/speeches-2010/association-of-the-british-pharmaceutical-industry-legal-day.aspx <Accessed 19/04/2011>.

14 Open letter available at: http://www.sfo.gov.uk/media/225554/enforcement_of_the_uks_bribery_act_facilitation_payments_061212.pdf <Accessed 10/11/2013>.

is no flexibility' with facilitation payments.[15] Such payments in the aggregate may produce an enforcement response but this remains to be seen. In any case, identifying figures such as $50 is not a particularly useful measure against which corporations can monitor their facilitation payments given differences in exchange rates, different cultural requirements or the extortion element of much facilitation payments. The common law offence of 'duress' is very likely to be available as there are circumstances in which individuals have no choice but to make payments in order to protect against loss of life, limb or liberty (Ministry of Justice 2010: para. 48). Thus, small one-off facilitation payments are unlikely to be prosecuted by the UK authorities. This is due to the limited resources of the National Crime Agency (previously the Serious Organised Crime Agency) to deal with such payments and of the SFO to fully enforce the law. In addition, there is high level of discretion as a willingness to increase the reporting of criminal activity by corporations is likely to result in no prosecution or investigation.

However, since the UKBA came into force, individuals and corporations were required to inform SOCA or now its successor body, the National Crime Agency (NCA), of any facilitation payments made. This obligation to self-report is also in line with the OECD's 2009 Recommendation that companies 'must in all cases be accurately accounted for in such companies' books and financial records' (OECD, 2009: recommendation VI, ii). The real risk for business individuals making small facilitation payments (as well as the directors of companies who may become liable for aiding and abetting the payments) arises when the acquisition, use or possession of the criminal property (for example, financial profit from such a payment) is not disclosed to the authorities. It is then that such individuals will be committing money laundering offences under the Proceeds of Crime Act 2002 (POCA).[16] Failure to report places the individual that makes the facilitation payment at risk of criminal prosecution for the offence of money laundering, with potential for 14 years imprisonment and an unlimited fine.

Corporate Hospitality

A further area of concern is that of corporate hospitality and the potential for such hospitality, promotional or other business expenditure to amount to bribery under the UKBA,[17] although some media articles on the matter have been inaccurate and

15 http://www.sfo.gov.uk/bribery--corruption/the-bribery-act/questions-and-answers.aspx <Accessed 10/11/2013>.

16 Part 7 of the Proceeds of Crime Act 2002 criminalises various money laundering offences that may be used in corruption prosecutions.

17 See for example *The Guardian*: 'Revamped Bribery Act is giving firms the jitters', 01/04/2011, available at: http://www.guardian.co.uk/law/2011/apr/01/revamped-bribery-act-firms-jitters <Accessed 10/11/2013>.

sensationalist.[18] The UKBA guidance (see below), however, made it clear that such expenditure to improve a commercial organisation's image, or establish cordial relations, is accepted as an established and important part of doing business and such behaviour is not intended to be criminalised under the UKBA providing it is reasonable and proportionate (Ministry of Justice 2010: paras 26–32). For example, covering reasonable travel and accommodation expenses to allow foreign officials to visit a workplace, or hospitality involving fine dining and tickets to a football match at the given location would not raise the necessary inferences.

It is recognised, however, that such behaviour can be employed as bribes under Section 6. To amount to a bribe, it would be necessary to prove an intention for a bribe to influence an official in their official role and thereby secure business, or a business advantage. It will be a question for prosecutors and, later, jurors whether, on the totality of the evidence in such cases (for example, type and level of advantage offered, manner and form in which the advantage is provided, and level of influence official has on awarding contracts), the unavoidable inference is that the expenditure was intended to influence the official to grant business or a business advantage in return.

Extraterritorial Jurisdiction

Section 12 of the Act gives the UK courts jurisdiction over Sections 1, 2 or 6 offences committed in the UK but also over offences committed outside the UK where the person has a close connection to the UK. This includes British nationals, individuals ordinarily resident in the UK, bodies incorporated in the UK or Scottish partnerships. This close connection requirement does not apply to Section 7 (the corporate offence). Under Section 7, if an organisation is incorporated or formed in the UK, or the organisation carries on a business or part of a business in the UK, irrespective of where it is incorporated or formed, the UK courts will have jurisdiction.

The UK Bribery Act 2010 Government Guidance

The UKBA, in particular Section 7, was subject to much lobbying from national and international businesses before and, especially, after its passage. The issues of 'adequate procedures' and what constitutes 'carrying on business' in the UK were a particular focus of this lobbying. The government, under Section 9 of the Act, was required to publish guidance about commercial organisations preventing bribery.

---

18 See for example the *London Evening Standard* articles: *'Golf trips ruled illegal under "confusing" Bribery Act'*, 11/01/2011, available at: http://www.thisislondon.co.uk/standard/article-23912904-golf-trips-ruled-illegal-under-confusing-bribery-act.do and *'Bribery law may drive sponsors out of sport, says Formula 1 team'*, 13/01/2011, available at: http://www.thisislondon.co.uk/standard/article-23913788-bribery-law-may-drive-sponsors-out-of-sport-says-formula-1-team.do <Accessed 10/11/2013>.

This guidance was published on 30 March 2011, therefore enabling the UKBA to come into force three months later on 1 July 2011. The guidance addressed these issues but received a mixed response (as perhaps may be expected). For example, TI branded the guidance 'deplorable' and argued it would weaken the Act – Chandrashekhar Krishnan, Executive Director of TI UK at that time explained:

> The Bribery Act, as passed by the last Parliament, is one of the best anti-bribery laws in the world. But the guidance will achieve exactly the opposite of what is claimed for it. Parts of it read more like a guide on how to evade the Act, than how to develop company procedures that will uphold it (TI: website).[19]

Conversely, many private sector organisations made reference to the 'common sense' approach of the guidance.[20] The role of lobbying from business groups may have played a significant role in this, as the perspective of one leading private sector organisation indicates:

> … the final version [as compared to an earlier consultation draft] is in our view a significant improvement and we are pleased to note that many of the concerns we raised in our response to the consultation draft have to a lesser or greater extent been addressed (Personal Email Correspondence).

The guidance addressed the concept of 'adequate procedures' which raised a series of questions following the passing of the UKBA. Six guiding principles (proportionate procedures; top-level commitment; risk assessment; due diligence; communication (including training); and monitoring and review – these principles are discussed in more detail in Chapter 5) were set out along with commentary and case study examples. The guidance made clear that these are not prescriptive or a one-size-fits-all approach, acknowledging that small and medium enterprises (SMEs) will likely require different procedures to MNCs. The principles promoted a risk-based and contextual approach to managing bribery risks, with the guidance recognising that no policies or procedures are capable of detecting and preventing all bribery. It will be the final assessment of the courts that determines whether any given organisation's procedures were adequate.

Concerns were raised over so-called 'carve-outs' of the guidance. The guidance stated the following in relation to 'carrying on business' in the UK:

> The government would not expect, for example, the mere fact that a company's securities have been admitted to the UK Listing Authority's Official List and

19 See article on TI website available at http://www.transparency.org/news/pressrelease/20110330_guidance_weakens_bribery_act <Accessed 10/11/2013>.

20 See *The Independent: 'guidance notes on Bribery Act suggest common sense will rule'*, 30/03/2011, available at: http://www.independent.co.uk/news/business/news/guidance-notes-on-bribery-act-suggest-common-sense-will-rule-2256658.html <Accessed 10/11/2013>.

> therefore admitted to trading on the London Stock Exchange, in itself, to qualify that company as carrying on a business or part of a business in the UK and therefore falling within the definition of a 'relevant commercial organisation' for the purposes of section 7. Likewise, having a UK subsidiary will not, in itself, mean that a parent company is carrying on a business in the UK, since a subsidiary may act independently of its parent or other group companies (Paragraph 36, Ministry of Justice Guidance).

This statement raised two issues: first, overseas companies may be exempt from the Act; and, second, parent companies with UK subsidiaries may not satisfy the test of 'carrying on business' in the UK. Interpretations of this statement can, however, vary. For example, a UK-based investors group in conjunction with the International Corporate Governance Network wrote to the *Financial Times (FT)*[21] to express their concern that the guidance exempts certain overseas issuers in the London market from the purview of the UKBA. This 'mooted carve out', as it was termed, would be based on these companies having no other business presence in the UK apart from raising capital. They challenged the possible interpretation that this does not amount to carrying out business in the UK and argued that such a 'carve-out' could adversely impact upon the integrity of the London financial market, disadvantaging UK companies.

TI went even further, claiming that 'foreign companies could be listed on the London Stock Exchange, pay bribes and get away with it' which will disadvantage all honest companies and go back on the government's stated aim of creating a level playing field through the Act's extraterritorial reach (TI website).[22] Conversely, it had been argued that the inclusion of such overseas companies within the jurisdictional reach of the Act would negatively affect London as a capital raising market, as in the case of Kazakh companies that may be diverted away from the London Stock Exchange.[23] The then Director of the SFO, Richard Alderman, warned companies not to rely on a 'technical approach' to the Act as it will be rare that an overseas company's listing is its only connection to the UK.[24] For the SFO, if an overseas company has a presence in the UK, they fall within the scope of the Act, but it will

21 See *Financial Times: 'Investment groups seek Bribery Act assurance'*, 29/03/2011, available at: http://www.ft.com/cms/s/0/db911444–598b-11e0-baa8–00144feab49a.html#axzz1K47uE0RO <Accessed 10/11/2013>.

22 See article on TI website available at http://www.transparency.org/news/pressrelease/20110330_guidance_weakens_bribery_act <Accessed 10/11/2013>.

23 See *The Telegraph: 'Britain's new Bribery Act will encourage firms to avoid the London Stock Exchange'*, 20/09/2010, available at: http://www.telegraph.co.uk/finance/newsbysector/banksandfinance/8012137/Britains-new-Bribery-Act-will-encourage-firms-to-avoid-London-Stock-Exchange.html <Accessed 10/11/2013>.

24 See article *thebriberyact.com: 'A mirage? The Bribery Act "exemption" for overseas companies and subsidiaries'*, 18/04/2011, available at: http://thebriberyact.com/2011/04/18/a-mirage-the-bribery-act-exemption-for-overseas-companies-subsidiaries/ <Accessed 10/11/2013>.

be down to the courts to determine which circumstances satisfy the test. Thus, it is possible for a parent company with a UK subsidiary to be prosecuted for bribery by one of its other subsidiaries in a third country with the intention here being that it enables ethical UK companies not to be disadvantaged by foreign corporations using different standards and using bribery to undermine UK businesses.

Germany

The Anti-Corruption Act 1997 (*Gesetz zur Bekämpfung der Korruption*) was the last measure to improve Germany's criminal law that was solely initiated by German political actors (Wolf, 2006: 785). The Act formulated Sections 331–8 of the German Criminal Code (*Strafgesetzbuch*). Anti-bribery and corruption legislation is further supplemented by the EU Anti-Bribery Act 1998 (*EU-Bestechungsgesetz*) and the Act on Combating Bribery of Foreign Public Officials in International Business Transactions 1998 (*Gesetz zur Bekämpfung internationaler Bestechung*) – the latter Act satisfies the requirements of the OECD Convention.

The *Bundestag* has largely confined its implementation legislation to the minimum requirements of the respective international legal instruments, a policy that has led to legal inconsistencies (Wolf, 2006: 789). In 2006 the German Federal Ministry of Justice created a governmental draft of a Second Anti-Corruption Act (*Zweites Gesetz zur Bekämpfung der Korruption*) intended to bind the international conventions and provisions of the CoE Criminal Law Convention, the Additional Protocol to the Criminal Law Convention, the EU Framework Decision on Combating Corruption in the Private Sector and the UNCAC. At the time of writing, this new law has not been enacted. However, as one German prosecutor stated:

> With regards the law in Germany, I think we can be at ease. The laws are alright I think, you can apply it ok. I would say there's no need for changes (German Prosecutor Interview 212).

Thus, some are of the opinion that the law in Germany is already more than capable of addressing transnational corporate bribery.

The German Criminal Code (GCC)

All national provisions on corruption related criminal offences can be located in the German Criminal Code, in addition to the abovementioned auxiliary laws. The GCC distinguishes between *Bestechung* and *Bestechlichkeit*, and *Vorteilsannahme* and *Vorteilsgewährung*. These offences make a distinction between passive and active bribery that involve an official breaching or violating their official duties, and accepting or giving an advantage that did not result in the official breaching or violating their duties. These sections also distinguish between future and past actions, enabling the main offences of active and passive bribery, and accepting or giving an advantage to be applied in cases where the act has not yet been committed. The key clauses are outlined below.

– *Section 331: Vorteilsannahme* (acceptance of an advantage or benefit for future or past actions that did *not* involve the official breaching their duty)

> (1) A public official or a person entrusted with special public service functions who demands, allows himself to be promised or accepts a benefit for himself or for a third person for the discharge of an official duty shall be liable to imprisonment not exceeding three years or a fine (Section 331, GCC, unofficial translation).

– *Section 332: Bestechlichkeit* (passive bribery for past and future actions that induced an official to breach their duties)

> (1) A public official or person entrusted with special public service functions who demands, allows himself to be promised or accepts a benefit for himself or for a third person in return for the fact that he performed or will in the future perform an official act and thereby violated or will violate his official duties shall be liable to imprisonment from six months to five years. In less serious cases the penalty shall be imprisonment not exceeding three years or a fine. The attempt shall be punishable (Section 332, GCC, unofficial translation).

– *Section 333: Vorteilsgewährung* (giving of an advantage or benefit for future or past actions that did *not* involve the official breaching their duty)

> (1) Whosoever offers, promises or grants a benefit to a public official, a person entrusted with special public service functions or a soldier in the Armed Forces for that person or a third person for the discharge of a duty shall be liable to imprisonment not exceeding three years or a fine (Section 333, GCC, unofficial translation).

– *Section 334: Bestechung* (active bribery for future or past actions that induced an official to breach their duties)

> (1) Whosoever offers, promises or grants a benefit to a public official, a person entrusted with special public service functions or a soldier of the Armed Forces for that person or a third person in return for the fact that he performed or will in the future perform an official act and thereby violated or will violate his official duties shall be liable to imprisonment from three months to five years. In less serious cases the penalty shall be imprisonment not exceeding two years or a fine (Section 334, GCC, unofficial translation).

All the offences involve either the offering, promising, granting or demanding, allowing, accepting of a bribe or benefit to or by a public official. Section 335

('Aggravated cases'), 336 ('Omission of an official act'), 337 ('Arbitration fees') and 338 ('Confiscatory expropriation order and extended confiscation') further relate to Sections 331–4. The concept of a 'benefit' or 'advantage' within the GCC is open to broad interpretation with benefits incorporating modest gifts and hospitality. These provisions, which focus largely on the public sector and public officials (*Amtsträger*), are accompanied by Sections 299–302 of the GCC in which 'accepting and granting a bribe in business transactions' (Section 299: '*Bestechlichkeit und Bestechung im geschäftlichen Verkehr*') is covered. Section 299 states:

> (1) Whosoever as an employee or agent of a business, demands, allows himself to be promised or accepts a benefit for himself or another in a business transaction as consideration for according an unfair preference to another in the competitive purchase of goods or commercial services shall be liable to imprisonment not exceeding three years or a fine.
>
> (2) Whosoever for competitive purposes offers, promises or grants an employee or agent of a business a benefit for himself or for a third person in a business transaction as consideration for such employee's or agent's according him or another an unfair preference in the purchase of goods or commercial services shall incur the same penalty.
>
> (3) Subsections (1) and (2) above shall also apply to acts in competition abroad (Section 299, GCC, unofficial translation).

Bribery of employees (*Angestellte*) and agents (*Beauftragte*) in the private sector is accounted for. Section 298 also criminalises collusive tendering in relation to the restricting of competition through agreements in the context of public bids. Further sections of the GCC also incorporate bribery related offences. For example, Section 108e criminalises the bribing of delegates and the buying or selling of votes for an election or ballot in the European Parliament or German public assemblies, while Section 263 'Fraud' and Section 266 'Breach of Trust' may also be used in corruption cases.

Act on Combating Bribery of Foreign Public Officials in International Business Transactions 1998

The passing of this Act implemented the OECD Convention. It extends Section 334, as well as Sections 335, 336 and 338 of the GCC, by providing for active bribery of foreign officials and officials of international organisations in the course of international business transactions. It ensures equal treatment of foreign and domestic public officials in the event of acts of bribery. The main Section 1 offence states:

Equal treatment of foreign and domestic public officials in the event of acts of bribery

For the purpose of applying section 334 of the Criminal Code, also in conjunction with sections 335, 336 and 338 subsection 2 of the Code, to bribery concerning a future judicial or official act which is committed in order to obtain or retain for the offender or a third party business or an unfair advantage in international business transactions, the following shall be treated as equal:

1. to a judge:
   a) a judge of a foreign state,
   b) a judge at an international court;

2. to any other public official:
   a) a public official of a foreign state,
   b) a person entrusted to exercise a public function with or for an authority of a foreign state, for a public enterprise with headquarters abroad, or other public functions for a foreign state,
   c) a public official and other member of the staff of an international organisation and a person entrusted with carrying out its functions;

3. to a soldier in the Federal Armed Forces (Bundeswehr):
   a) a soldier of a foreign state,
   b) a soldier who is entrusted to exercise functions of an international organisation' (Section 1, Act on Combating Bribery of Foreign Public Officials in International Business Transactions 1998, unofficial translation).

Section 2 of the Act also criminalises the bribery of foreign Members of Parliament (MPs) in connection to international business transactions. Section 3 extends the scope of German criminal law to the offences of bribery of foreign public officials in connection to international business transactions and bribery of foreign MPs, as above, committed by a German abroad. Prior to this Act, it was not illegal for German nationals to bribe foreign public officials. A key similarity here with the UKBA is that large scale bribery involving foreign public officials is only illegal under German law if it occurs in the course of international business transactions thus allowing for foreign bribery not in the course of business.

EU Anti-Bribery Act 1998

This Act implements the EU Conventions. It deals with both active and passive bribery as outlined in Sections 332 and 334 GCC and essentially extends German law to deal specifically with bribery of public officials of other EU Member States and officials of the EU. These provisions include also acts of bribery committed by Germans in foreign countries, not only those committed from Germany.

Corporate Liability in Germany

Unlike the UK, corporations in Germany cannot be held *criminally* liable (for more detailed discussion see Chapter 6). 'Legal persons' can, however, be penalised under administrative law. Section 130 'Violation of obligatory supervision in firms and enterprises' of the Administrative Offences Act (*Gesetz über Ordnungswidrigkeiten*, 'OWiG') states:

> (1) Whoever, as the owner of a firm or an enterprise, wilfully or negligently fails to take the supervisory measures required to prevent contravention of duties in the firm or the enterprise which concern the owner in this capacity, and the violation of which is punishable by a penalty or a fine, shall be deemed to have committed an administrative offence if such a contravention is committed which could have been prevented or made much more difficult by proper supervision. The required supervisory measures shall also comprise appointment, careful selection and surveillance of supervisory personnel.
>
> (2) A firm or an enterprise in accordance with subsections 1 and 2 shall include a public enterprise.
>
> (3) If the administrative offence is subject to punishment, it may be punished by a fine not exceeding one million Deutsche Mark [now Euros]. If the violation of duty is punishable by a fine, the maximum amount of the fine for a violation of obligatory supervision shall be dependent on the maximum amount of the fine provided for the violation of duty. The second sentence shall also apply in the event of a breach of duty which at the same time is punishable by a penalty and a fine if the maximum amount of the fine is in excess of the maximum amount in accordance with the first sentence (Section 130, OWiG, unofficial translation).

This offence relates to violations of supervisory duties as a result of failures by senior officers of the company to supervise employees if their actions led to criminal or administrative offences. The Siemens case (see Chapter 2) demonstrated this, as in the first settlement with the Munich prosecutors a maximum fine of €1m was given. However, as was also demonstrated, an unlimited amount in the form of a disgorgement of profits can be confiscated, while there may be civil actions for compensation with aggravated penalties in some jurisdictions.

Tax Deductibility

Prior to the OECD Anti-Bribery Convention, companies were able to deduct any bribes to foreign public officials as business expenses on their tax report. In November 1998, Germany implemented the Tax Alleviation Act, subsequently preventing any deduction of taxes from bribes. This prevention of tax deduction also does not depend on the punishment of the crime. The Siemens case again demonstrates the use of tax legislation as part of anti-corruption measures as Siemens was required to pay an additional €179 million to tax authorities for deducted foreign payments as business expense. The tax authorities are also required to disclose any suspicions about expenses that may be part of criminal or administrative offences to the public prosecutors.

The US Foreign Corrupt Practices (FCPA) Act 1977

The US is keen to protect its economic interests and ensure its corporations are not disadvantaged in international business transactions. This is largely addressed by the Foreign Corrupt Practices Act (FCPA) that came into force in the US in 1977 and has extra-jurisdictional reach. The FCPA applies only to the bribery of non-US public officials (other US statutes criminalise commercial bribery for example, the Travel Act 1961)[25] and significantly impacts upon UK and German business in relation to corruption and bribery offences given the extraterritorial reach. The FCPA criminalises certain classes of persons and entities making payments to foreign government officials with the 'corrupt intention' to obtain or retain business. More specifically,

> … the anti-bribery provisions of the FCPA prohibit the willful use of the mails or any means of instrumentality of interstate commerce corruptly in furtherance of any offer, payment, promise to pay, or authorization of the payment of money or anything of value to any person, while knowing that all or a portion of such money or thing of value with be offered, given or promised, directly or indirectly, to a foreign official to influence the foreign official in his or her official capacity, induce the foreign official to do or omit to do an act in violation of his or her lawful duty, or to secure any improper advantage in order to assist in obtaining or retaining business for or with, or directing business to, any person (Department of Justice: website).[26]

While the FCPA applied to all US persons and certain foreign issuers of securities, amendments to the Act in 1998 ensured conformity with the OECD Convention while simultaneously ensuring the anti-bribery provisions also applied to foreign firms and persons acting directly or via agents to make corrupt payments in the 'territory' of the US. The term 'territory' has been broadly interpreted by the Department of Justice as their *Criminal Resource Manual* for prosecutors states:

25 The Travel Act criminalises the use of a facility of foreign or interstate commerce, for example, email, telephone, courier, personal travel and so on, with the intent to promote, manage, establish, carry on or distribute the proceeds of an unlawful activity that is a violation of state or federal bribery laws, amongst others.

26 FCPA Overview on DoJ website available at: http://www.justice.gov/criminal/fraud/fcpa/ <Accessed 10/11/2013>.

'Although this section has not yet been interpreted by any court, the Department interprets it as conferring jurisdiction whenever a foreign company or national *causes* an act to be done within the territory of the United States by any person acting as that company's or national's agent'.[27] This interpretation enables the prosecution of foreign nationals who have never been to the US, provided that they caused some act in furtherance of the offence to occur in the US, and of foreign companies who are liable for acts carried out on their behalf – a form of strict liability.

Prosecutions are often brought in relation to the accounting provisions of the FCPA that require companies with securities listed on any US stock exchange to (a) make and keep books, records and accounts that accurately and fairly reflect the transactions of the corporation and (b) devise and maintain a system of internal accounting controls (see United States Code, Title 15, Section 78m). Such provisions enabled Siemens and Innospec to be prosecuted in the US (see Chapter 2).

Conclusion: Legal Convergence

The impact of pressuring nation-states to implement international frameworks for enforcement has led to convergence and harmonisation of key legal provisions. Germany has yet to ratify the UNCAC but this relates to the requirement for the criminalisation of 'domestic bribery', which has attracted opposition from German politicians – German authorities might regard it as consistent to respond to international obligations, but to regard their domestic legislation as their own business alone. Despite non-ratification, Germany nonetheless meets all the *foreign* bribery requirements of the UNCAC due to the similar requirements of the ratified OECD Convention. German laws therefore incorporate analogous provisions to that of the UK where ratification of UNCAC has taken place. For example, active and passive bribery, bribery of foreign officials, extraterritorial reach, amongst others, are all evident. In this sense, non-ratification of the UNCAC in Germany has not made any significant difference to the policy response and enforcement context when contrasted with the UK, although the 'functional equivalence' approach of the OECD Convention does enable significant differences to remain between the UK and Germany in the legal frameworks. However, non-ratification of the UNCAC may create difficulties in mutual legal assistance should German authorities require cooperation with those jurisdictions that have not ratified the OECD Convention.

27 Manual available at: http://www.justice.gov/usao/eousa/foia_reading_room/usam/title9/crm01018.htm <Accessed 26/04/2011>.

Chapter 5
Enforcing the Law: Structure, Practice and Discretion[1]

Introduction

The available legal frameworks in the two jurisdictions, as outlined in the previous chapter, are only one part of the enforcement framework. Key to the criminal law, of course, is the extent to which it is enforced by state authorities. It is important for nation-states to ensure the legitimacy of their enforcement authorities in the face of formal monitoring and evaluation by intergovernmental and non-governmental organisations such as the OECD's Working Group on Bribery, the Group of States against Corruption (GRECO) and Transparency International (TI). But the concept of legitimacy

> … is both an output – in the sense that it is the result of multifarious influences including ideology, inequality, material interests, life experiences and social conformism – and an input, in that although it is an analytical construct rather than a human/institutional actor, legitimacy has an effect on how we behave, and what we support (Levi, 2013: 157).

Establishing consensus around what ought to be considered 'legitimate' enforcement is diverse and complex and cannot be discussed at length here (for analysis of the concept see Bottoms and Tankebe, 2012; Tankebe and Liebling, 2013; and in relation to fraud, Levi, 2013). Legitimacy here is taken to mean an expectation that responsible authorities, in line with issues of procedural justice and social fairness, investigate and prosecute all cases of bribery that come to their attention, and where not, there is a clear and transparent policy overseeing the use of discretion not to investigate or prosecute. This understanding reflects that of intergovernmental and international organisations, as well as investigatory and prosecutorial offices in the UK and Germany. Perceptions of legitimacy for different social actors are fundamental in shaping the reality of enforcement activity and with this in mind, organisations such as the OECD and TI frequently use enforcement statistics (for example, number of investigations/prosecutions)

1 An earlier version of this chapter was published as follows: Lord, N. (2014) 'Detecting and investigating transnational corporate bribery in centralised and decentralised enforcement systems: discretion and (de-)prioritisation in the UK and Germany' *Policing and Society*, DOI: 10.1080/10439463.2014.895350.

to determine such legitimacy (for example, are nation-states 'actively' enforcing bribery laws by investigating and sanctioning corporations that bribe). However, whether these provide valid indicators of enforcement responses is questionable as determining the adequate enforcement of transnational corruption is undermined by a lack of understanding of the extent and scope of the problem (see Chapter 8). Nevertheless, as discussed in Chapter 1, the position of the UK and Germany as 'active enforcers' of international bribery conventions implies enforcement responses are considered satisfactory. But the reliance on investigation and prosecution numbers is superficial and not grounded theoretically, neglecting the contextualised social relations that represent enforcement responses at the national level – analysis of the relationship between the enforcement systems, strategies and mechanisms in the UK and Germany, in addition to the legal frameworks and cultures, provides insights into the nature of the enforcement response.

With this in mind, the focus in this chapter is on how responsible anti-corruption authorities and actors located at the *national* level detect and investigate such *transnational* corporate bribery within the context of two contrasting enforcement systems, those of the UK (centralised) and Germany (decentralised). The chapter examines these social relations to develop the core analytical focus on regulation as by comparing the two jurisdictions and their enforcement frameworks, the limitations and strengths of each system can be understood. The chapter begins by contextualising the two enforcement frameworks, outlining the strengths and limitations of the centralised and decentralised structures. Understanding these contexts provides the foundation for discussion of the key practices of detection and investigation, and the evident differences and similarities (the key practice of prosecution is discussed at length in Chapter 6). Following the analysis of structure and practice, analytically, the chapter goes on to address the significant role of discretion at various stages within these practices and frameworks along with how such discretion influences the legitimacy of enforcement responses (that is, perceived levels of enforcement activities). The chapter argues that whether centralised or decentralised, and whether guided by flexible or rigid legal frameworks, formal and informal practices of discretion lead to legal and operational tensions that reduce the legitimacy of enforcement responses.

Policing Structures in the UK and Germany: Centralised and Decentralised Enforcement Systems

Two contrasting enforcement systems exist in the UK (centralised) and Germany (decentralised) which reflect geographical, historical and cultural factors but both reflect traditional 'command and control' regulatory regimes (see Baldwin and Cave, 1999). In 2005 the Serious Fraud Office (SFO) became the lead organisation in the UK for investigating and prosecuting transnational bribery and corruption. Prior to this, these responsibilities were with an extraordinary number of state agencies including the SFO, the National Criminal Intelligence Service, the 43

Figure 5.1 Key UK anti-corruption agencies

local police forces (Metropolitan Police Service in particular), the City of London Police, the Ministry of Defence Police and the Companies Investigation Branch of the Department for Trade and Industry (now the Department for Business, Innovation and Skills). The SFO now has national jurisdiction (excluding Scotland) and receives support if and when required from the Overseas Anti-Corruption Unit of the City of London Police and the various local police forces. The Financial Conduct Authority (FCA – formerly part of the Financial Services Authority) is also able to sanction regulated financial institutions for failures in anti-bribery and corruption compliance while the Ministry of Defence Police replaces the Overseas Anti-Corruption Unit of the City of London Police if the case involves allegations against Ministry of Defence employees or defence contracts to which the Ministry of Defence is a party. Similarly, the Police Service of Northern Ireland replaces the Overseas Anti-Corruption Unit of the City of London Police if the case relates to Northern Ireland. The Crown Prosecution Service prosecutes any case not falling within the remit of the SFO, and the National Crime Agency (formerly the Serious Organised Crime Agency) has special investigatory powers to support SFO investigations and may also investigate a case if not accepted by the SFO. Figure 5.1 illustrates the key authorities in the current enforcement framework.

The UK system may be considered a largely centralised system in this respect, with one lead organisation responsible for investigating and prosecuting transnational corporate bribery in England and Wales, and Northern Ireland. The SFO was established by the Criminal Justice Act (CJA) 1987 following recommendations from the Fraud Trials Committee Report (Roskill Report) 1986.

The main recommendation was for the creation of a new organisation responsible for detecting, investigating *and* prosecuting cases of serious fraud. The report stemmed from the public dissatisfaction with the UK system for investigating and prosecuting serious fraud. As Levi (1986: 394) notes, '[u]ntil the 1980s, the attitude to commercial fraud taken by all British governments could best be described as benign neglect'. It was thought to be key to have an organisation that investigated and prosecuted serious and complex frauds, an argument further reinforced by the de Grazia Review[2] of the SFO in 2008 which concluded the roles of investigation *and* prosecution must be combined when dealing with serious fraud – a model that has been evident in the US since the late 18th century. Following the creation of the Conservative-Liberal Democrat coalition in May 2010 there was suggestion that the SFO's functions of investigation and prosecution would again be separated, with its investigations becoming part of the new NCA and prosecutions being merged into the CPS. Home Secretary, Theresa May, was forced to back down on these plans with the SFO model for tackling economic crime being supported by the cabinet.[3]

The SFO's total resource budget is on a general decline (2008–09 – £53.3m; 2009–10 – £40.1m; 2010–11 – £35.5m). The budget for 2011–12 was just over £31.5m. Slight increases are planned over the next two years but a budget of £30.8m is planned for 2014–15. The SFO is able to supplement its income through monies obtained via civil settlements and awarded costs and by requesting 'blockbuster funding' from the Treasury should investigations be likely to cost more than £1.5m.[4] The SFO has two operational business areas, Fraud, and Bribery and Corruption, each led by a member of the Senior Civil Service along with case managers and case teams. These individuals are made up of permanent SFO staff including lawyers, accountants and professional investigators as well as individuals such as barristers and other external experts contracted largely as counsel to prosecute cases. The SFO, as lead central agency, represents a centralised enforcement model although cases not accepted by the SFO can be investigated and prosecuted by other decentralised police agencies and prosecutors.

The UK's centralised model can be contrasted with Germany's decentralised model where there is no lead, national agency for anti-corruption and bribery

2 Jessica de Grazia, a former senior New York City prosecutor, was commissioned to conduct a review of the SFO by the former SFO Director Robert Wardle and former Attorney General Lord Goldsmith. In the review she compared the SFO with the US Attorney's Office for the Southern District of New York (SDNY), a Federal prosecution agency, and the Manhattan District Attorney's Office (DANY), a local prosecutor's office. Review available at: http://www.sfo.gov.uk/about-us/annual-reports--accounts/annual-reports/annual-report-2006–2007/jessica-de-grazia-and-the-review-of-the-sfo.aspx <Accessed 10/11/2013>.

3 See *BBC*: '*SFO saved by cabinet revolt*' available at: http://www.bbc.co.uk/news/13585972 <Accessed 10/11/2013>.

4 See 'SFO strikes funding deal with Treasury', *Financial Times*, 18/01/2013: http://www.ft.com/cms/s/0/4cdede9e-6194–11e2–9545–00144feab49a.html#axzz2YB0JhCMU <Accessed 10/11/2013>.

enforcement. This system has geographical and historical foundations dating back to the fragmented nature of German cities and principalities as far back and beyond the fifteenth century. The unification of Germany in 1871 represented the beginnings of the federalist system, and since reunification in 1990, Germany has been made up of 16 states or *Bundesländer*. Germany has no central justice system, with the one exception of the *Bundesanwaltschaft* (Federal Public Prosecutor's Office) that deals with issues such as terrorism and has national jurisdiction. All other offences are investigated and prosecuted at the state level and this includes transnational bribery and corruption.

Within the 16 German *Bundesländer* (federal states), there are around 110 *Staatsanwaltschaften* (Public Prosecutor's Offices). Each *Bundesland* and each Prosecutor's Office can be organised very differently. For example, a Prosecutor's Office may be responsible specifically for an area such as corruption and bribery, or more broadly for a more general area such as economic crime, or they may simply be responsible for cases with defendants' surnames A–C, and so on – levels of expertise and experience therefore varies greatly regionally and nationally. Within each *Bundesland* there are a number of public prosecutor's offices, a *Landeskriminalamt* (State Criminal Investigation Office) and numerous *Polizeipräsidien* (Local Police Headquarters). The public prosecutors lead all transnational bribery and corruption cases and are supported by regional and local police during investigations. As in the UK, the German public prosecutor's office is involved in investigation and prosecution throughout the case and often conducts interrogations, analysis of documents and so on without police assistance – this dual role of investigation and prosecution is a key commonality in the policing of serious and complex crimes such as transnational bribery. The police only become involved when directed to do so by the public prosecutor, while the *Bundeskriminalamt* (Federal Criminal Police Office) can facilitate investigations at the national level.

Corruption and bribery only began to be substantially investigated following the creation of the first *Schwerpunktstaatsanwaltschaften* (public prosecutor's offices that have a special competence, in this case in the area of corruption (Specialist Public Prosecutor's Offices)). Not all *Bundesländer* have such specialist offices, but all usually have specialist departments or units that deal exclusively with corruption and bribery. For example, since 1999 in the *Bundesland* of Northrhein-Westfalia there have been four Specialist Public Prosecutor's Offices for combating corruption in existence. These are at the Public Prosecutor's Offices in Bochum, Bielefeld, Cologne and Wuppertal and together have jurisdiction throughout the *Bundesland*.[5] The Public Prosecutor's Offices, State Criminal Investigation Offices and Local Police Headquarters can directly contact and assist their equivalents in other *Bundesländer*, but the Federal

5 More information on the institutional resources of all the *Bundesländer* for fighting corruption can be found at: http://www.transparency.de/fileadmin/pdfs/Themen/Justiz/Korruptionsbekaempfung_in_Deutschland_Vergleich_Bundeslaender.pdf <Accessed 10/11/2013>.

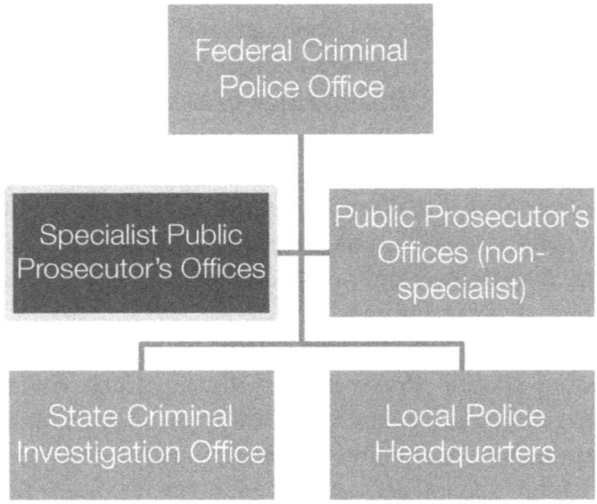

Figure 5.2 Key German anti-corruption agencies

Criminal Police Office is always informed parallel to this. The Federal Criminal Police Office operates at the national level and aids in facilitating information exchange between *Bundesländer*, collects knowledge and information of the cases and has connections to overseas authorities. The Public Prosecutor's Offices and police can also directly contact overseas authorities in the case of transnational crimes. Thus, while the State Criminal Investigation Office mainly operates at the regional level (that is, in one *Bundesland*) and the Local Police mainly operate within one district in a *Bundesland*, both are able to investigate cases throughout the whole of Germany if required, or request that a corresponding authority carries out an operation on their behalf. This must be agreed with the corresponding State Criminal Investigation Office. Figure 5.2 illustrates the structure.

Most respondents stated, however, that some *Bundesländer* are significantly more 'enthusiastic' than others in their anti-corruption investigation and prosecution efforts. The intensity varies in different *Bundesländer* due to varying political will, varying resources (financial and personnel) and varying levels of expertise. This can lead to the Public Prosecutor's Offices in some jurisdictions preferring to keep ownership over cases instead of passing them on to other authorities due to concerns that the case will not be intensively pursued. This highlights some of the difficulties of the decentralised system:

> Central organisations, for each *Bundesland* at least, would not be a bad idea. With regards personnel, if they were equipped with highly skilled staff and would accumulate expert and technical knowledge, that would be great, but it's utopian. It doesn't function practically (Country Expert Germany Interview 241).

This impracticability of central anti-corruption agencies in German *Bundesländer* relates again to the historical and geographical development of the federal states.

Each *Bundesland* has a number of small, medium and large cities and municipalities, each with decision-making powers with which the *Bundesland*, or even the nation-state, cannot always interfere. This creates a number of obstacles to reorganising the system. Respondents expressed concern over the implementation of the OECD Convention throughout Germany given that analogous implementation across the board cannot be obtained:

> The rules in Germany are valid for all *Bundesländer*. That means every *Bundesland* must actually be the same. But as so often with other themes it is the case that there are some *Bundesländer* or some Public Prosecutor's Offices that simply have more experience as they have more cases than others. Naturally, the prosecutors in the large cities have a much better sense than the smaller cities. You find that in smaller cities there are often no specialists for these issues (German Lawyer Interview 221).

In terms of resources, each *Bundesland* is responsible for funding the various investigatory and prosecutorial authorities within its borders. This can result in significant differences in available resources in each of the 16 *Bundesländer*. In a 2011 OECD report on Germany, German respondents indicated that all *Bundesländer* were sufficiently resourced for investigating and prosecuting overseas bribery (OECD 2011b: para. 118). This was confirmed by the respondents in this research, all of whom spoke of the ability to obtain resources at short notice, whether this be extra police officers for searches, extra prosecutors for large cases and whether this be in their corresponding *Bundesland* or from another *Bundesland*. Cooperation and multi-agency work functions effectively in Germany. Financial figures were not obtainable, but the respondents in this research are located in relatively affluent regions and were well resourced, equipped with multiple Specialist Public Prosecutor's Offices which indicates the political will and available resources to investigate and prosecute overseas bribery in these areas.

Comparing the Policing Structures

TI's 2012 progress report on the enforcement of the OECD Anti-Bribery convention indicates that since its entry into force in 1999 up until the end of 2011, 176 cases[6] had been brought in Germany in contrast to 23 in the UK (number includes cases in 2012) – of Germany's 176 cases, over 16 were 'major' cases, while all the UK's 23 cases were 'major'.[7] Additionally, in 2011 there were 43 investigations[8]

6 The term 'case' encompasses criminal prosecutions, civil actions and judicial investigations (that is, investigations conducted by investigating magistrates in civil law systems).

7 Cases are considered 'major' if they involve alleged bribery of senior public officials by major companies.

8 The term 'investigation' includes investigations by prosecutors and police, and excludes judicial investigations.

underway in Germany (22 in 2010) and 29 in the UK (26 in 2010). When contrasting resources, that is, personnel and funding, it can be said that Germany invests significantly more resources into anti-bribery and corruption enforcement. Most *Bundesländer* have in some form or other anti-corruption capabilities (although this can vary greatly) ensuring more cases can be investigated. Thus, available resources in part explain Germany's high case numbers, in particular the higher number of minor cases (Germany – ≤160; UK – 0(zero)). That said, the UK only brought its first corporate prosecution in 2008[9] and the subsequent statistics indicate the number of major cases, investigations and prosecutions have become more similar. But the difference in number of minor and major cases in the systems needs further analysis. Statistics alone offer no in-depth, contextualised understandings of this.

The differing enforcement systems in part explain the different levels of enforcement activity as there are strengths and limitations of both systems. The UK's centralised model enables a more consistent and coordinated regulatory approach as jurisdiction is nation-wide (see Chapter 6 for analysis of prosecution policy). However, the SFO has modest personnel and funding for an agency with national jurisdiction and therefore applies *discretionary* 'acceptance criteria' to all cases from the pre-investigation stage – this results in only large, complex cases being taken on. Thus, the centralised system creates a necessity for overt and formal practices of discretion justified through modest resources (discussed further below) due to the larger area of jurisdiction. In Germany, levels of enforcement vary across the *Bundesländer* as the extent of funding, political will and prosecutorial and investigatory expertise differs in each state. However, as responsibility lies with a multitude of actors and departments across the 16 *Bundesländer*, the central state is less able to impart one-sided and partial procedures. Centralised enforcement in Germany is impracticable and this poses concerns for representatives of intergovernmental organisations such as the OECD and GRECO who are unable to ensure harmonised enforcement throughout Germany. The decentralised system creates fragmented expertise, resources and political will with discretionary practices being less coordinated and less formal.

The structure of the enforcement systems therefore influences enforcement activity. However, within these systems, detection and investigation are also shaped by legal and cultural factors which create conditions for formal and informal practices of discretion. The article now goes on to analyse the practices involved in detecting and investigating transnational corporate bribery in some detail before moving to a discussion of how discretion in these stages materialises and how such discretion creates tensions between legal and operational frameworks and thus reduces the legitimacy of enforcement responses.

9 Mabey and Johnson paid bribes in Jamaica, Ghana and Iraq and received a total financial penalty (including a criminal fine) of £6.6m. SFO press release: http://www.sfo.gov.uk/press-room/press-release-archive/press-releases-2009/mabey--johnson-ltd-sentencing-.aspx <Accessed 10/11/2013>.

Detecting Transnational Corporate Bribery

Much overseas bribery goes undetected, or unreported, but those cases that are detected appear in numerous ways to the enforcement authorities. In the UK, referrals are the main source of cases for the SFO (although the SFO can begin an inquiry without a referral). These may come from other agencies, individuals or companies. All overseas bribery allegations related to UK companies are actively trawled through and categorised by the SFO's intelligence teams and subsequently are placed on the UK's only Anti-Corruption Register, which is held centrally by the SFO as part of a Memorandum of Understanding (MoU) with the other law enforcement agencies. The SFO's international and domestic law enforcement partners such as the FCA in the UK, the Department of Justice (DoJ) and the Securities and Exchanges Commission (SEC) in the USA, and other international organisations such as the World Bank, and so on, all refer cases to the SFO. One of the most significant sources of overseas bribery cases are leads from investigations conducted by overseas authorities where Mutual Legal Assistance (MLA) (see below) has been requested and the SFO has seen a potential UK investigation from that.

Whistleblowers, or individuals making a disclosure in the public interest (for example, coming forward to confess or allege a bribery case), are also a key source of cases. In November 2011 the SFO created 'SFO Confidential' which enables the SFO to be contacted via online reporting, email or post by individuals with knowledge of suspected corruption. Other agencies have similar reporting options; the Overseas Anti-Corruption Unit of the City of London Police has a confidential answer phone service, for example. Whistleblowers are encouraged to disclose information openly as this aids investigations and provides better protection under the Public Interest Disclosure Act 1998 (PIDA). PIDA protects whistleblowers from unfair reprisal from their employer but offers no identity protection. These individuals may come to the SFO directly, via media sources, or via non-governmental organisations and charities. Information provided by these individuals goes through the pre-investigation vetting that involves analysing the key suspects, the allegations and any corroborating information the SFO may have. This is used to determine whether there is sufficient evidence (not all evidence is required at this stage) to initiate an investigation in line with Section 1 of the CJA 1987. Cases are often discovered in internal reviews of companies, or where auditors come across cases, and in some cases competitors that have suffered due to corruption, for example, or been frozen out of bidding for certain contacts, may approach the SFO.

A significant strategy of the SFO is that of corporate self-reporting (see Chapter 6). The SFO is actively encouraging corporations to report any overseas bribery offence once the corporation has ascertained, following legal advice and internal investigations by its professional advisers, that there is a 'real issue'. Why would a corporation self-report criminal behaviour? Initially, according the SFO, 'the benefit to the corporate will be the prospect (in appropriate cases) of a civil rather than a criminal outcome as well as the opportunity to manage, with us, the issues and any publicity proactively' (2009 SFO Guidance to self-reporting).[10] Interestingly, this guidance was removed in October 2012 following a review by the SFO's new Director, David Green, but he has maintained that self-reporting is still encouraged and remains a fundamental source of cases for the SFO.

In Germany, as in the UK, determining the facts of the case, such as the form of dubious payments, or financial transactions, is of secondary difficulty to proving which advantages came from the payments: of most difficulty is uncovering the case in the first place. Capacity for anonymous whistleblowing and tip-offs is vital in Germany where all anonymous allegations are pursued. For example, one *Bundesland* has developed a 'corruption hotline' which connects directly to the State Criminal Investigation Office. Web-based systems can also be utilised to this effect. For example, Germany and the UK have seen the private sector emergence of companies such as Business Keeper AG in Germany that aim to offer 'whistleblower' services to all sizes of corporations. Of course, a number of tip-offs are false, but it is often straightforward to ascertain credible sources when the individual provides detailed facts about the organisation. Having an 'insider' who knows and understands the internal networks and systems of a corporation is highly useful. The difficulty in Germany is the lack of whistleblower protection under German law. The authorities can only protect the identity of a whistleblower when there is a threat to life or limb, or when there are substantial economic disadvantages (for example, threat of bankruptcy to a company). Employees are also able to anonymously contact ombudsmen to report corruption suspicions without the obligation to testify openly as a witness.

A second key tool of detection stems from tip-offs from other authorities: '… vital in combating international corruption is the close cooperation with the financial authorities, this is in my view, the deciding factor' (German Police investigator 2). This cooperation model, as promoted in one *Bundesland*, is the most developed in Germany: such cooperation varies significantly throughout the 16 *Bundesländer* but in this *Bundesland* attempts have been made to introduce others to such multi-agency cooperation in the area of corruption and bribery. It involves 'interdisciplinary cooperation' with the tax authorities and investigators, the accountants, auditors and the customs offices that are able to see and examine the accounts and bookkeeping of corporations. In this way, dubious payments disguised, for example, as provisions for consultancy can be detected. Without this evidence, the investigators and prosecutors do not become aware of certain cases. Key in this area is the *Steuerentlastungsgesetz* (Tax Relief Act) 1999/2000/2002. Prior to this, bribes paid by German corporations were tax-deductible but the OECD Convention required this to change. Subsequently, corporations attempting to deduct bribes from the tax are picked up by the tax authorities. There is a legal requirement for the tax authorities to notify the Public Prosecutor's Office of any

10 SFO Guidance to self-reporting available at: http://www.sfo.gov.uk/bribery--corruption/the-sfo%27s-response/self-reporting-corruption.aspx <Accessed 10/11/2013>.

suspicious tax deductions. This is a significant difference with the UK. Section 19 of the Anti-Terrorism Crime and Security Act 2001 permits but places no requirement on the UK tax authorities to disclose information subject to secrecy obligations for use in criminal investigations or proceedings.

Compliance departments in companies are also significant in detection but there is no legal obligation in Germany for the compliance departments to report any irregularities to the enforcement authorities. This reflects the *Grundgesetz* (Basic Constitutional Law) in Germany which outlines that persons cannot be required to incriminate themselves. This differs from the UK where although traditionally a 'right to silence' exists, the SFO under Section 2(2) of the CJA 1987 has special powers to require individuals to answer all questions. A criminal offence will be committed if an individual refuses to comply, though since the *Saunders* appeal to the European Court of Human Rights following the Guinness case, self-incriminating answers given under compulsion cannot be used in evidence against the person. Numerous cases are also detected following investigations into allegations from the above sources. For example, in a sort of 'domino effect', an investigation into one company often leads to suspicions of other companies and other officials and this can often develop and take cases forward.

Investigating Transnational Corporate Bribery

For the UK's SFO to open an investigation there must be 'a suspected offence which appears to the Director on reasonable grounds to involve serious or complex fraud' (CJA 1987 s. 1(3)). There is no evidentiary requirement but in practice these concepts appear unclear – a UK Memo to the OECD Working Group on Bribery in response to their Phase 2 Report stated that for there to be a 'suspected offence', there must be 'credible information to show that an offence has *probably* taken place' (OECD, 2008: para. 221). Thus, discretion is formally available at the pre-investigation stage.

Following the initiation of an investigation, a decision will be made on whether there is sufficient evidence to prosecute or proceed (for example, this could be six months into the case), and if it is unlikely that evidence will be secured, the case will be dropped – discretion is formally available following sufficient investigation. Once a case is accepted, it is taken over by a Case Manager who will be provided with the relevant resources (for example, personnel such as accountants, lawyers, professional investigators) to investigate. The investigation begins covertly until a search of premises or a company's documents or interviews with suspects are required, at which point it becomes an overt investigation. The main difficulty in corruption investigations, and what makes them distinct from other forms of economic crime, is 'proving what's the bang for the buck'. Proving the buck can be straightforward. For example, money changing hands in unusual circumstances or wrongly accounted for transactions in difficult to trace bank accounts using front companies are usually recorded somewhere. Proving the bang, or the trade-off, is more complex as it may be an inducement or a reward with no written record, making a clear understanding and *a fortiori* proof of that understanding more difficult. The solution to this often starts with the initial allegation and who has reported the case. If it has come from an insider, the foundation is usually solid. If it comes from an outsider, it is less reliable (for example, a company that missed out on a contract or a misunderstanding over a transaction). In both cases, the credibility of the individual is tested. No two cases are the same and while an insider may be a key element, charges can successfully be reached through other evidential sources (for example, strong evidence obtained from a suspect's computer).

Most cases involve the issuing of a Section 2 (CJA 1987) notice. Section 2 outlines the investigatory powers of the Director of the SFO. It enables the SFO by notice in writing to require the person under investigation to provide any relevant documents ('information recorded in any form') for the investigation. For example, this may be used on banks to provide the bank accounts of a particular individual or company in order to follow the flow of funds. It enables the SFO to obtain contracts, emails, and many other forms of document to support the investigation. If this request is not complied with, amongst other reasons, the SFO is able to issue a warrant to enter, search and take possession of any relevant documents. Thus, a warrant can only be issued once the formal written request for the documents has, for whatever reason, not been complied with. How the SFO prevents the destruction of documents in the time between is unclear, although it can request the police conduct a search under their powers. The SFO's powers were strengthened by Section 59 of the Criminal Justice and Immigration Act 2008 which enables the SFO to compel the production of documents at the earlier vetting stage of foreign bribery cases. Relevant evidence can therefore be collected earlier, swifter and more proactively in well-founded cases.

The SFO is also trying to make more use of cooperating witnesses. Section 73 of the Serious Organised Crime and Police Act 2005 (SOCPA) enables the SFO to make an agreement with defendants in exchange for a reduction in sentence, even immunity from prosecution (Section 71, SOCPA) or some form of limited prosecution. Certain cases have raised doubts as to the efficacy of this approach. For example, in connection with the DePuy International[11] case, Robert John Dougall extensively cooperated with the SFO and it was expected he would receive a lighter sentence for doing so. In April 2010, however, he received a 12-month prison sentence from the courts which jeopardised the SFO's intention to encourage whistleblowers and offer incentives in the form of 'light' sanctions. This SFO strategy was reprieved following the subsequent overturning of Dougall's sentence in May 2010. However, since this case, a number of individuals have been prosecuted, but as the SFO makes clear, it cannot unconditionally guarantee

11 DePuy made £4.5m in corrupt payments to medical professionals in the Greek state healthcare system. SFO press release available at: http://www.sfo.gov.uk/press-room/press-release-archive/press-releases-2010/british-executive-jailed-for-part-in-greek-healthcare-corruption.aspx <Accessed 10/11/2013>.

that there will be no prosecution of the corporate or its individuals even where the case was self-reported and the individuals fully cooperated (although the SFO faces significant obstacles when aiming for criminal prosecution – see Chapters 5 and 6).

In Germany, although the prosecutors are significantly involved from the first allegations or suspicions of corruption, the separation of powers in some instances can create procedural difficulties at the stage of investigation. If a Public Prosecutor's Office has no specialist corruption remit, police investigators providing initial suspicions to these non-specialists may face a barrier as such prosecutors do not possess the expertise or experience to further investigate and prosecute complex bribery cases. For this reason, the Specialist Public Prosecutor's Offices are important in order to ensure the relevant capability and will is evident.

Unlike the UK, German authorities are not required to firstly submit a notice to corporations to request documents and information. German investigators, with judicial orders, are able to go directly to the corporations and search the premises. This has the advantage that documents cannot be destroyed or removed. The public prosecutors obtain the relevant search warrants from the judge, a process which can take as little as 30 minutes or as long as four weeks. This is context dependent. For example, if a search is taking place and it becomes known that the suspect has a second residence, a warrant for this can be swiftly obtained. These searches are often not limited to one premises but involve the simultaneous searching of the private residences of all suspects in the corporation and other related organisations. These large operations can involve up 30–35 premises being simultaneously searched. These investigations involve large numbers of public prosecutors, police officers as well as tax investigators. For this reason, one prosecutor explained how corporations cannot afford not to cooperate with the Public Prosecutor's Offices in corruption cases as each search or raid creates negative exposure to their organisation. First, it is difficult and concerning for the employees of the corporations to observe and be impacted on by such searches and arrests. For example, job insecurities arise, concerns of the nature of their employer, and so on. Second, these raids are often leaked to the media and subsequent media reports can lead to reputational damage and financial difficulties (for example, share prices dropping, consumers choosing competitors and so on).

Following searches, key tools for German investigators and prosecutors are the interrogations and analyses of documents. Interrogations enable the prosecutor to ascertain key information from the accused and witnesses which can be further substantiated through an extensive examination of the confiscated documents. In Germany, one key development has enabled investigators to use telephone surveillance since 2008 but this method is not a decisive tool and only aids a small number of cases, not to mention the high costs and time that it requires. As one prosecutor explained, key in all investigations are the social interactions with the accused. This prosecutor estimated that 95 per cent of their role is based on interactions with individuals. This means being open and direct with accused individuals, determining what sort of person they are dealing with and how they can most effectively extract the desired information. Contrasting bribery suspects with suspects of 'conventional crime', this prosecutor explained that the former are often intelligent personalities, aware of their wrongdoings and therefore easier to reach and communicate openly with.

Mutual Legal Assistance (MLA)

Given the transnational and multijurisdictional nature of corporate bribery, Mutual Legal Assistance (*Rechtshilfe*, 'MLA') is of great importance to the enforcement agencies in the UK and Germany. Investigators and prosecutors, in all transnational corporate bribery cases, must cooperate with agencies in other jurisdictions in order to ascertain information and evidence. The efficacy of MLA varies significantly in different countries. For example, while the German authorities have excellent relations with neighbouring countries such as Austria and Switzerland, difficulties often emerge further afield. This can be due to simple factors such as language barriers. For example, while Germany and the UK have worked effectively together, language difficulties can emerge (while Public Prosecutors in Germany are often fluent in English, this is less frequently the case further down the enforcement regime) which requires employing interpreters and translators at high cost – one UK investigator talked of some individuals advocating automated translation as the way forward, but he (understandably) did not appear convinced about the standard of English that came out of this. As in the UK, more difficulties arise when requesting assistance from developing countries, or those countries with inadequate anti-corruption enforcement systems. Searching premises in Germany functions effectively, but determining the actual overseas recipients of bribes can prove difficult and can only work through MLA, which can take a very long time.

Some countries have been notoriously difficult to obtain information from. Lichtenstein, Switzerland and Luxembourg, for example, have traditionally had very stringent secrecy laws and provisions in relation to the banking system, making obtaining information about financial transactions and banks accounts more difficult. One UK investigator gave the example of an individual in Switzerland having 17 separate opportunities to appeal against material being transferred to the UK. Other countries may have different procedures, for example only cooperating via formal written requests rather than giving prior information via a simple telephone call, as it goes against their legal system based on *Commissions Rogatoires* between judicial authorities, not the police. In another case, the French authorities complained that a search conducted for them in the UK was of no use to them because all the UK authority had done was send them the original documents that were confiscated – as no investigator's report was attached outlining the nature of the MLA request, they were not able to use it under their system. This can make cooperation long-winded despite celerity being of paramount importance in some cases. However, one UK investigator suggested that in the view of other European countries, the UK does not have a good reputation for MLA – a view substantiated by some German prosecutors and investigators (see also Levi, 1987, showing that this is not a recent phenomenon). Even more difficult is cooperation with those countries that have no anti-corruption authorities or no political will to assist. These factors reinforce limited enforcement models at the national level. However, global settlements between the UK and the US, and between Germany and the US, have demonstrated how MLA can work effectively and attempt to address this transnational difficulty.

Discretion in the Processes of Detection and Investigation

> There's more matters for investigation than we have resources to investigate. It's always a difficult one: how many cases do you investigate? For how long do you investigate a case before you abandon it? … [O]ne measure you might have for performance indicators is how many cases do you abandon … For example, if you prosecute there's always one defendant who's found guilty as a result of a prosecution. How does that square with however many have not been taken to prosecution? On the other hand if you are not seen to be investigating a wide number, perhaps it doesn't have a market deterrent (UK Investigator/Prosecutor Interview 112).

The above detailed analysis of the processes of detection and investigation has served the key purpose of identifying that there are many opportunities for discretion to be applied by responsible authorities from the initial identification of a potential case through to decisions to prosecute or not. The key point is that enforcement authorities are only aware of those cases that come to their attention through the various practices of detection but in reality the extent and scope of the corruption problem can be presumed to be much greater as indicated by various perception studies (see Chapter 8). Such knowledge of bribery cases reflects only the extent of the resources invested into detection or the extent to which other parties are willing or able to notify the authorities:

> … when you attempt to detect corruption, you will always discover cases. When you don't attempt it, then perhaps you're in the top rung [in the 'active enforcement' section – see chapter 1] although there's potentially much more corruption in your country than you think (German Prosecutor Interview 211).

> … as corruption is a Kontrolldelikt (an offence often victimless that is only ever uncovered by the authorities), the more one invests …, the more cases come to light (German Police Investigator 231).

However, even these (relatively conservative) estimations outweigh the UK's and Germany's capacities for enforcement which can be seen in the processes of discretion throughout detection and investigation (see Chapter 5). This section explores the nature and foundation of such formal and informal discretionary practices further in the contexts of contrasting legal cultures. While discretion in the UK is overtly and publicly applied, tensions exist between law and practice for German authorities where rigid legal frameworks are often circumvented, but in both cases the legitimacy of enforcement responses is likely to be reduced as discretionary practices lead to the accommodation of many cases of corporate bribery.

Beginning with the UK, Section 3.2 of the England and Wales Code for Crown Prosecutors 2010[12] states '[t]he police and other investigators are responsible for conducting enquiries into any alleged crime and for deciding how to deploy their resources. This includes decisions to start or continue an investigation and on the scope of the investigation'. This reflects the traditional influence of the 'principle of opportunity' in the jurisdiction where a high level of discretion is significant. As Spencer (2002: 161) notes, 'it is not, and has never been, the case in England that the authorities are obliged to prosecute for all the offences that come to their attention'. For an investigation to proceed to prosecution, the Full Code Test is applied (i. is there 'sufficient evidence to provide a realistic prospect of conviction'? ii. is a prosecution required in the public interest?). Thus, due to the division of functions between the police and CPS, the discretion to prosecute is exercised in two stages: first by the police when they decide whether to institute proceedings; and, second by the CPS when they decide whether to continue the case (Spencer, 2002: 161). However, in the case of corruption, this is complicated by the independence of the SFO and its role as investigator and prosecutor which is able to use discretion immediately from the pre-investigation stage.

Given the issue of resources, the SFO makes explicit the discretionary criteria it applies to transnational bribery cases. When the SFO receives referrals or comes across potential cases of transnational bribery, this information goes through pre-investigation vetting to make sure certain criteria are met, and that the SFO has jurisdiction. By law, the SFO can investigate only those cases where there is evidence to show that serious or complex fraud and/or corruption has taken place. The SFO initially outlined the following factors that are considered before a case is accepted:

- Does the value of the alleged fraud exceed £1 million? (This could relate to the size of the contract obtained and not the size of the bribe although if it was the size of the bribe it would eliminate most cases – this reflects the formulation of these criteria at a time when the SFO did not deal with corruption, only fraud)
- Is there a significant international dimension?
- Is the case likely to be of widespread public concern?
- Does the case require highly specialised knowledge? For example, of financial markets.
- Is there a need to use the SFO's special powers, such as Section 2 of the Criminal Justice Act?

12 Code for Crown Prosecutors 2010 version available at: http://www.cps.gov.uk/publications/code_for_crown_prosecutors/introduction.html <Accessed 10/11/2013>.

The above questions have now been replaced on the SFO website with four considerations:[13] i) the scale of loss (actual or potential); ii) the impact of the case on the UK economy; iii) the effect of the case on the UK's reputation as a safe place to do business; iv) the factual or legal complexity and the wider public interest. In addition to these criteria, in determining seriousness and complexity, the SFO conducts further tests such as whether the case impacts on the integrity of the financial market, whether it involves multiple countries or evidential material being collected in multiple locations, whether it involves multiple and complex financial transactions (for example, many companies, accounts, countries and so on) and whether the investigation will need to involve a large accountancy analysis. On the issue of discretion, one UK investigator stated:

> Throughout an investigation that's fundamental, we will be considering whether this is going to go anywhere, whether criminal prosecution is the right answer, or whether there's a civil penalty that can be imposed, Serious Crime Prevention Order, you know, the variety of other outcomes that we can employ (UK Investigator/Prosecutor Interview 111).

Anti-corruption enforcement in the UK permits investigators and prosecutors much procedural discretion. If a case does not meet certain criteria, it does not require investigating by the SFO although the SFO should, where appropriate, attribute the case directly to the Overseas Anti-Corruption Unit of the City of London Police, other police forces or a prosecution authority (an OECD (2008: para. 224) report questioned whether this procedure is followed). The SFO also has no obligation to aim for criminal sanctions, given the variety of enforcement mechanisms available. As seen with the earlier statistics, there is a filtering out of smaller cases and a focus on 'major' cases. For example, cases involving 'facilitation payments' ('grease payments') are unlikely to be investigated and prosecuted by the SFO and are subsequently accommodated by enforcement agencies – focus is instead placed on corporations to eradicate such payments within and by their organisations over time. The SFO and government have also faced lobbying from small and medium enterprises that argue the costs of compliance and impact on overseas business is too onerous.[14] Thus, formal, overt discretion results in much transnational petty corruption being accommodated which in turn reduces the legitimacy of the enforcement response given the criminalisation of such bribery in the UKBA – a clear tension exists between law and operation.

In Germany, understanding discretion is more complex. The 16 *Bundesländer* are territorial units entrusted with significant wide powers and their own decision-

13 http://www.sfo.gov.uk/fraud/sfo-confidential---giving-us-information-in-confidence/serious-fraud-office-[sfo]-case-selection.aspx <Accessed 10/11/2013>.

14 See Financial Times '*Relaxation of UK bribery law on government agenda*' 28 May 2013: http://www.ft.com/cms/s/0/cab2111c-c6c8–11e2-a861–00144feab7de.html#axzz2XKZvEhvO <Accessed 10/11/2013>.

making bodies (Juy-Birmann, 2002: 292). On a simplistic level, the various sources of law (*Rechtsquellen*) are structured with the *Grundgesetz* (Basic Constitutional Law) at the top, federal law and regulations beneath this, then the constitutions, the laws and the regulations of the *Bundesländer* (Juy-Birmann, 2002: 292). Traditionally in Germany, criminal investigation and prosecution is guided by the 'principle of legality':

> The *Legalitätsprinzip* (principle of legality) is laid down in §§ 152 II, 170 I StPO (*Strafprozeßordnung* – German Code of Criminal Procedure (GCCP)) and provides that prosecution of an offence is mandatory for the public prosecutor. It demands that the public prosecutor starts investigations once a sufficient suspicion arises and that he prefer charges in cases of sufficient suspicion of an offence. To be certain that this duty is properly performed, there is an offence called *Strafvereitelung im Amt* (obstruction of criminal prosecution by an officer of the law – § 258 GCC) which can be used against an official who breaches his duty. However, in certain cases a public prosecutor may refrain from prosecuting offences for pragmatic reasons under the premises specified in §§ 153 *et seq.* GCCP (*Opportunitätsprinzip* – principle of discretionary prosecution) (Freckmann and Wegerich, 1999: 187).

The above principle is based on 'the absolute equality of all citizens before the law in criminal matters: the public prosecutor must prosecute all offences' (Juy-Birmann, 2002: 309). However, a certain level of discretion to prosecute has to an extent replaced the principle of legality in relation to pragmatism more in line with the UK system, but the requirement to investigate is seen as fundamental by actors at the operational level:

> I think it's important that we don't have discretion, that we have to investigate … we can simply say to ourselves, it's irrelevant how it is, who it comes from, whether it's the Emperor of China, or anyone else, it doesn't matter. We investigate, we have to investigate … . We very clearly have the occupational duty, in each and every case, to investigate (German Prosecutor 212).

Prosecutors are required to investigate all potential cases that come to their attention and aim to bring criminal charges where possible. Likewise, the police are required to investigate any potential criminal offence and subsequently report all evidence, in all cases, to the Public Prosecutor's Offices. This reflects the *Gleichheitsgrundsatz* (Principle of Equality), ensuring all are treated equally before the law:

> I believe the principle of legality – that we must investigate when a criminal offence has occurred – is very important, because otherwise the door of unequal treatment is opened. When decision-making is made based on what 'we just want' or 'we just don't want' to do, then the criminal law loses its justification

> ... it doesn't come across as just, and this wouldn't be accepted (German Police Investigator 231).

Thus, in Germany a more rigid legal framework exists which stipulates that prosecution of an offence is mandatory for public prosecutors and investigations *must* be commenced when sufficient suspicion arises. However, a significant difference can be observed in the treatment of natural and legal persons, or in other words, individuals and corporations. While individuals are subject to the mandatory principle of investigation/prosecution, discretion in line with the opportunity principle is evident for legal persons and corporations. Subsequently, corporations can only be sanctioned under administrative law and not criminal law (see Chapter 4).

Cases are prioritised dependent on a number of factors. For example, in Germany, the *Beschleunigungsgrundsatz* (Principle of Expediting Proceedings) ensures certain cases must be dealt with swiftly, such as those where a suspect is under arrest and there is a risk of breaching human rights. Otherwise, cases are prioritised in relation to the size of the case, with large cases subsequently given priority. The Public Prosecutor's Offices are also able to determine whether a case should be further investigated, or whether proceedings should be initiated. Thus, while the constitutional obligation to prosecute does appear very rigid, in practice, this may not be the case. One expert in Germany spoke of prosecutors who simply left cases untouched, and when probed further, stated:

> Actually they're not allowed to do that, legally they're not allowed ... [but in some cases] a file reference number will be recorded, so completely formal, but they'll carry on as if they will initiate preliminary proceedings but will conduct no investigation. It just lies there and after years it's just forgotten, it'll be discontinued due to the statute of limitations and even because apparently no evidence is produced. This occurs very frequently. It does of course depend on how well the relevant departments of the Public Prosecutor's Offices are equipped but also to what extent other authorities such as the municipal authorities are interested in it ... when no one is interested, then nobody asks 'why are you not investigating this and this despite these suspicions and despite the initiated proceedings?' This is frequently the practical problem (Country Expert Germany Interview 241).

This argument was also put forward by a number of UK respondents, one of which stated:

> What they [German prosecutors] call prosecute is actually open an investigation isn't it ... [if] nothing happens on a case in 5 years and day, it dies. I have talked to plenty of prosecutors and investigating magistrates in Europe and yes, they have got the legality principle, but they don't devote all their time and resources to cases if a case isn't going anywhere, they put it away (Former UK Investigator/Prosecutor 113).

Sections 152–7 of the *Strafprozeßordnung* (German Code of Criminal Procedure, 'StPO') do provide a number of possibilities for non-prosecution. In practice, investigators do therefore possess certain possibilities for discretion but this is not regulated on a systematic basis as in the UK with the various codes for prosecutors, and so on. For example, one investigator in Germany explained how in one case where a whistleblower called their corruption hotline but appeared uncertain about the allegations, the investigator suggested the whistleblower first submit an anonymous tip-off not disclosing the specific facts of the cases: for example, 'Mr. L has received £10m as part of an arms deal with the UK, would this be liable for prosecution?' As the investigator explained, this then does not create difficulties for both the whistleblower and the investigator. The investigator can then pass judgement on the tip-off and if there is not sufficient information can request that the whistleblower anonymously submits relevant documents to support the claim. However, if the whistleblower discloses names and sources, the investigator has no discretion in this case and must pursue. Following this, any information must be presented to the Public Prosecutor's Office who has the final decision on the case. Thus, more informal practices of discretion are evident in Germany which again creates tensions between law and practice and which can lead to rigid legal frameworks being circumvented and thus certain cases being accommodated. As in the UK case, the legitimacy of the enforcement response is undermined.

Comparing Discretionary Practices

Full enforcement of the criminal law is never possible with discretion always being evident (see Goldstein, 1960). This argument is apparent in the enforcement practices of both the UK and Germany. The constitutional obligation in Germany to prosecute so long as there is sufficient evidence provides a significantly more rigid procedural framework for prosecution than that of the UK. This, however, creates tensions between normative and practical concerns of investigators and prosecutors and the legal frameworks within which they operate. In practice, German prosecutors are able to use legal alternatives to criminal prosecution such as Section 153a StGB that enables financial penalties in certain circumstances and the creative use of the statute of limitations which for corruption cases is five years in Germany.

Despite significant distinctions between the two jurisdictions as written in law, Germany, like the UK, has numerous formal (for example, pragmatism when faced with evidential difficulties) and informal (for example, creative use of statute of limitations) possibilities for exercising discretion. Despite no strict criteria in Germany for taking on corruption cases, as the SFO uses, German prosecutors still prioritise cases based on similar factors as the UK (for example, public interest, likelihood of conviction, available resources) albeit a lack of political will may also be significant (for example, facilitation payments in UK). Thus, the key question, as one German respondent made clear, is not whether legal discretion aids or prevents effective anti-corruption, but whether or not there is political will to deal with corruption. They suggested that if anti-corruption departments within the Public Prosecutor's Offices were appropriately equipped and that a political signal was given to reaffirm an intent to investigate powerful individuals and organisations, then anti-corruption enforcement would be more effective. This respondent used the example of Siemens[15] to explain this by highlighting that if the US authorities had not investigated, the case would not have become so significant: in the end, Siemens was required to hire a law firm who uncovered the real extent of the problem internally.

Conclusion

This chapter has analysed how responsible anti-corruption agencies and actors located at the *national* level detect and investigate *transnational* corporate bribery within the context of two contrasting enforcement systems. Within these structural frameworks, responsible authorities detect and investigate transnational corporate bribery utilising a variety of different (for example, obligations of tax authorities/self-reporting and so on) but also similar (for example, use of whistleblowers/MLA and so on) mechanisms. A fundamental part of detection and investigation, however, is how discretionary practices are applied. Such discretion is recognised as a key component by intergovernmental organisations:

> … economic crime doesn't work without this kind of discretion. You have to have the freedom, for instance, to say let's concentrate on one part of the case that we can really prove and drop the rest because otherwise we will be bogged down for years and will miss prescription or something … So if you really want to be effective you have to have discretion here. The next question is, of course, should there be rules of how to apply discretion (Intergovernmental Organisation 'A' Representative Interview 411).

While discretion is key, intergovernmental organisations argue there are 'illegal forms' of discretion, for example, when considering economic and/or national interests (see above). Creating systematic frameworks for the application of discretion is therefore fundamental. While on paper the German system offers much less discretion, requiring investigation and prosecution in all cases where possible, it does not significantly differ from the overt UK system as there are a number of legal and procedural mechanisms enabling non-investigation or non-prosecution. However, with discretion being of fundamental significance in legal frameworks and in terms of practice, the key question is the extent to which this discretion is acknowledged by relevant actors (for example, prosecutors,

15 The Siemens scandal involved a system of slush funds used to pay bribes to win overseas contracts. To date, Siemens has paid a total of €2.5bn to various agencies in administrative fines while a number of managers were convicted.

enforcement authorities and so on) and the extent to which these discretionary practices are regulated on a systematic basis. In the UK, the practice of discretion appears overtly acknowledged while in Germany discretion may be more informal, but in both cases there is a tension between law and practice. Perhaps, then, there is scope for international collaboration to determine effective and systematic use of resources multi-jurisdictionally:

> When resources [are] not enough? Well, my answer to that is that you have a clear and transparent and announced policy. And I suppose you'd have to do it on a risk based approach, wouldn't you … So I think that you could let it be known that you are focusing on particular sectors, particular industries. That you're looking particularly at some country or area of the world where it seems to be particularly prevalent … so here's an idea: isn't it, that basically the OECD, that member states, ought to adopt a thematic approach and in cooperation and collaboration, that the Germans and the Brits would target the construction sector in a particular part of the world and they'd chose particular targets to have a look at. That would be one way (UK Investigator/Prosecutor Interview 112).

Risk-based approaches to resource management and discretion may provide a cooperative framework for harmonising enforcement approaches. As of yet, there is no such framework in place. (Although in a speech in October 2013 SFO Director David Green indicated that focus may soon be placed on specific sectors that are most vulnerable to economic crime, such as construction, public contracts, and oil and gas.)[16] Instead, current tensions at the stages of detection and investigation lead to the accommodation of transnational bribery cases. This in turn reduces the legitimacy of enforcement responses in line with both international and national legal frameworks as they do not have the capacity to respond to even their own conservative estimations of the problem. Additionally, the application of discretion is not always transparent.

---

16 Information on speech available here: http://thebriberyact.com/2013/10/28/construction-industry-public-enemy-no-1-for-sfo-in-sector-sweep-announcement/ <Accessed 10/11/2013>.

Chapter 6
Theories of Enforcement: Prosecution Policies

> [W]e are a prosecutor but what has to be recognised is that … effective enforcement … doesn't just mean criminal prosecutions. It means a whole gambit of any powers that you can use to enforce it including civil recovery, including Civil Companies Act offences. So we would look at it, if it goes high up in the organisation, if it is not isolated, if it's a systemic problem, then clearly nothing other than a criminal prosecution will do but then if you have, for example, they come to you and they tell you look we have done this report, we have had these systems in place, these are our procedures, this isolated case has gone outside of our procedures and has fallen through the net but we have uncovered it, we have dealt with it by getting rid of the people involved in it, we've strengthened our procedures to deal with it – then those are all factors that might sway towards a civil resolution. There's no guarantees and that's what we tell everyone that comes to us, there's no guarantees, you come to us, it's at your own choice, you come to us and we will then decide which way it goes (UK Investigator/Prosecutor Interview 114).

Introduction

The previous chapter, through analysis of the enforcement systems and practices of detection and investigation, and the application of discretion at various stages, identified structural, procedural, evidential, legal and financial obstacles inherent in the enforcement responses of responsible authorities. But it is through analysis of prosecution policy that enforcement responses are best understood. UK and German prosecutors and investigators, though socialised into the centrality of criminal law to their professional work and values, understand the difficulties of criminal law enforcement and seek to explore the available 'tools' at their disposal, as the quote above demonstrates. This chapter analyses these mechanisms within the UK and German enforcement frameworks and outlines a shift beyond traditional law enforcement practices (that is, pursuing criminal prosecution) towards the expanding use of *non-criminal* alternatives that fall within the remit of state agencies and authorities. Such enforcement mechanisms are located within what has been termed a command and control regulatory strategy (Baldwin and Cave, 1999), a strategy which is dominant in the UK and German anti-corruption approaches. The actors and organisations that use this variety of formal enforcement practices shape the formal regulation of corporations operating in legal markets.

The chapter first analyses the use of, and strengths and limitations of, criminal prosecution in the UK and Germany. Special attention is given to the most severe form of corporate sanction, debarment, or the 'corporate death penalty' as it has otherwise been termed. The increasing use of non-criminal alternatives, in particular the use of civil mechanisms aimed at ensuring changes in corporate culture, are then addressed. It is argued that investigators and prosecutors in the UK and Germany are aiming to 'negotiate' regulation through the use of a varied set of enforcement mechanisms shifting away from criminal prosecution towards non-criminal forms of enforced self-regulation, characterised by financial civil settlements and *hybrid* enforcement mechanisms including 'self-reporting', 'self-cleaning', 'monitoring' and forms of reintegrative shaming.

Criminal Prosecution and Sanctioning

Criminal prosecution of corporations (legal persons) is at the time of writing rarely used in both jurisdictions. Enforcement statistics suggest that the rate of individual (natural person) prosecutions in both jurisdictions is now similar (TI 2012) but only three substantive transnational bribery cases have involved criminal sanctioning of corporations in the UK, and Germany has seen zero criminal sanctions of corporations. In the UK, Mabey and Johnson,[1] the first corporation convicted of overseas corruption in 2009, and Innospec[2] in 2010 were both charged with 'conspiracy to corrupt' and received criminal fines (in tandem with other sanctions, for example, Civil Recovery Orders, monitoring (see below)). In 2010 BAE Systems[3] received a criminal fine for failing to keep sufficient accounting records. Thus, criminal sanctions in the UK for corporations (or 'legal persons') have predominantly involved criminal fines, confiscations under the Proceeds of Crime Act (POCA) 2002 (Part 2) and 'monitoring' as well as requirements to instil regime change and ensure effective compliance systems are in place (see 'hybrid mechanisms' below). A criminal conviction also enables powers to debar corporations under the Public Contracts Regulations 2006 (in line with Article 45 of the EU public procurement directive 2004/18/EC – see below), and to

1 Mabey and Johnson paid bribes in Jamaica, Ghana and Iraq and received a total financial penalty (including a criminal fine) of £6.6m. SFO press release: http://www.sfo.gov.uk/press-room/press-release-archive/press-releases-2009/mabey--johnson-ltd-sentencing-.aspx <Accessed 10/11/2013>.

2 Innospec paid bribes in Indonesia and were sanctioned to financial penalties and monitoring. See SFO press release: http://www.sfo.gov.uk/press-room/press-release-archive/press-releases-2010/innospec-limited-prosecuted-for-corruption-by-the-sfo.aspx <Accessed 10/11/2013>.

3 BAE Systems engaged in corruption in Tanzania and received criminal and civil financial penalties. See SFO press release: http://www.sfo.gov.uk/press-room/press-release-archive/press-releases-2010/bae-fined-in-tanzania-defence-contract-case.aspx <Accessed 10/11/2013>.

impose Serious Crime Prevention Orders and Financial Reporting Orders but these mechanisms have not yet been used. Individuals in both jurisdictions have received prison sentences (often suspended), fines and restrictions on acting as Directors.

Criminal Sanctioning in the UK

In theory, as per the Code for Crown Prosecutors and the UK Bribery Act Joint Prosecution Guidance, various mitigating and aggravating factors influence the level of criminal sanctions. In the context of bribery offences, the Code sets out a number of factors tending in favour of prosecution. For example, a conviction for bribery is likely to attract a significant sentence, offences will often be premeditated and may include an element of corruption of the person bribed, offences may be committed in order to facilitate more serious offending, and those involved in bribery offences may hold positions of authority or trust and therefore take advantage of that position. Conversely, factors tending against prosecution may include cases where the court is likely to impose only a nominal penalty, where the harm caused was minor and was the result of a single incident and where there has been a genuinely proactive approach involving self-reporting and remedial action. In law, natural persons found guilty under sections 1, 2 or 6 of the UK Bribery Act (active bribery; passive bribery; bribery of a foreign public official) on summary conviction are liable to maximum imprisonment of 12 months or to a fine not exceeding the statutory maximum (£5,000), or both. On conviction of indictment, natural persons are liable to a maximum prison sentence of 10 years, an unlimited fine, or both. Legal persons found guilty under these offences are liable to a fine not exceeding the statutory maximum (£5,000) on summary conviction, or to an unlimited fine on conviction of indictment. Any person found guilty of a Section 7 offence (failure to prevent bribery) on conviction of indictment is liable to an unlimited fine.

Bribery may also be prosecuted under money laundering offences using POCA. These powers only became available to the SFO in April 2008. Under sections 327 *et seq.* POCA (Concealing and so on; arrangements; acquisition, use and possession), persons are liable on summary conviction to maximum imprisonment of six months, a maximum fine of £5,000, or both. On conviction on indictment, there is a maximum prison sentence of 14 years, an unlimited fine, or both. Under sections 330 *et seq.* (failure to disclose; tipping off), persons are liable on summary conviction to maximum imprisonment of six months, a maximum fine of £5,000, or both. On conviction of indictment, persons are liable to maximum imprisonment of five years, an unlimited fine, or both. At the time of writing, the SFO has made use only of the confiscation and recovery powers of POCA (Parts 2 and 5) for corruption offences but mainly recovery orders. For example, in October 2008 in the first case of this sort, Balfour Beatty was required to pay £2.25m plus costs as part of a Civil Recovery Order.[4] In February 2011 MW

4 SFO press release on Balfour Beatty available at: http://www.sfo.gov.uk/press-room/press-release-archive/press-releases-2008/balfour-beatty-plc.aspx <Accessed 10/11/2013>.

Kellogg Limited was required to pay over £7m due to sums it would receive that were generated through contracts obtained by bribes made by its parent company and other third parties.[5]

Corporate Criminal Liability in the UK

On paper, as stipulated above, if bribes are large, repeated, planned or accepted as standard within a corporation, then criminal prosecution with potentially severe sanctions ought to be pursued. In practice, this has not been the case as indicated by the low number corporate criminal prosecutions and this reflects the difficulty of attributing liability to corporations in the UK. Corporate criminal liability determines whether 'legal persons' (that is, corporations) can be prosecuted under the criminal law in the same way that 'natural persons' (individual persons) can be prosecuted although there is often some relationship between the two:

> … [w]hen offences by individuals occur in a corporate context, it may be because the company's policies, culture and ethos authorize, encourage, condone or tolerate the illegal behaviour … That the individual was committing the offence on behalf of a company provides a handy rationalization for the crime (Gobert, 2011: 154).

Corporate criminal liability in the UK has traditionally required courts to locate the corporate mind for purposes of assessing *mens rea*. English judges found the 'company's mind' in the mind of persons who could be 'identified' with the company for legal purposes (Gobert and Punch, 2003: 38). This historical focus on the individual has caused the legal mind to struggle with locating *mens rea* in an aggregate entity (Punch, 2011: 111). This has remained a key difficulty in the UK:

> I mean the major problem remains that we have horrendously bad corporate liability laws. If companies are a little bit clever and export their corruption to foreign commission agents they can distance themselves sufficiently far from it so as to keep the controlling mind well out … The only reason smaller companies like Mabey and Johnson got done is the directors are actually doing the work – the controlling mind are actively involved in the work (Former UK Investigator/Prosecutor Interview 113).

The difficulty in locating the 'controlling mind', in that a company is only likely to be guilty of a bribery offence if it can be proved that the senior management and executive is involved, still remains for the general offences of active and passive bribery (s.1, 2 and 6 of the UKBA) but this is not straightforward. Companies

5 SFO press release on MW Kellogg available at: http://www.sfo.gov.uk/press-room/press-release-archive/press-releases-2011/mw-kellogg-ltd-to-pay-7-million-in-sfo-high-court-action.aspx <Accessed 10/11/2013>.

are 'conscious opponents' (Sparrow, 2008), able to export their corruption and thus distance the controlling mind sufficiently far from the bribery. The anonymity involved in international business transactions via numerous financial institutions and through difficult to access jurisdictions causes great difficulties for regulation (Elliot, 2009). Distant relationships between principals, agents and clients, and differing laws in different countries, not to mention the high level of secrecy and privacy or lack of direct victims to report, also create major problems. Thus, the nature of global business transactions creates a significant barrier to effective regulation and enforcement (Gibbs et al., 2010: 550).

However, under the corporate offence of 'failure to prevent bribery' (Section 7 UKBA) a corporation can also be held criminally liable for acts of bribery by its associated persons (employees, subsidiaries, intermediaries, sales agents, and so on) that are carried out on behalf of the corporation, in a form of strict liability. Previous to the UK Bribery Act, and as above, corporations could only be held criminally liable if it could be proved that the 'corporate mind' (that is, a board member or executive) had a direct role in the bribery. However, should the UK corporation have 'adequate' anti-bribery procedures, policies and cultures in place, this may provide a legal defence to prosecution. The inclusion of a form of strict liability into the UK Bribery Act reflects the argument that the organisation can be thought of as providing the motive, opportunity and means for such crimes in a transnational environment and across time but such factors create difficulties for legal systems based on individual liability for discrete offences at specific locations with direct causal relations (Punch, 2011: 110). However, such strict liability removes the requirement of intent and may reinforce such behaviour as 'mala prohibita' rather than 'mala in se'.

Criminal Sanctioning in Germany

In Germany, the criminal prosecution of individuals remains at a steady rate but corporations cannot be criminally prosecuted. According to an OECD (2011b) report on Germany, of the 30 bribery convictions of individuals since 2005, only 10 were for the criminal offence of bribery of foreign officials (s. 334 GCC). A further 10 were for the criminal offence of commercial bribery (s. 299 GCC) and 10 were for the criminal offence of breach of trust (s. 266 GCC). An additional four sanctions were brought for breach of supervisory duties (s. 130 OWiG) and 35 individuals agreed to civil arrangements in line with Section 153a of the German Code of Criminal Procedure (GCCP) (diversion from criminal prosecution) – 24 of these individuals were in relation to the Siemens case. These arrangements are not published, therefore the underlying offence alleged by the prosecution cannot be ascertained – further transparency is required here. In total, since the first conviction for overseas bribery in Germany in 2005 and as of May 2011, 69 individuals (35 non-prosecution agreements (NPAs)) and 7 companies (administrative fines) had been processed by the prosecutors. This presents significant evidence of the use of both criminal and non-criminal enforcement mechanisms in Germany, despite arguments surrounding the legality principle and the legal requirement to aim for criminal prosecution (see Chapter 5). Over half of individual sanctions have been concluded through non-criminal prosecution mechanisms.

In Germany, then, prosecutors are more frequently using a variety of prosecution options, in particular sections 199 and/or 266 GCC, commercial bribery and breach of trust respectively, to prosecute and sanction in foreign bribery cases rather than the Section 334 GCC that covers the specific offence of bribery of a foreign public official. The Siemens case, for example, was largely dealt with by the Munich prosecutors in relation to violations of 'breach of trust' due to the slush fund that was created – the *Bundesverfassungsgericht* (Federal Constitutional Court) confirmed that the use of slush funds can be considered a 'breach of trust'.[6] This is occurring as offences under sections 266 and 299 *et seq*. GCC can be proven without mutual legal assistance, thus enabling prosecutors to settle cases in line with the time constraints as outlined in the *Beschleunigungsgrundsatz* (Principle of Expediting Proceedings). The use of alternative offences provides prosecutors in Germany with evidential ease as the offences require less investigatory complexity and a lower burden of proof – Section 299 GCC does not require proof that the recipient of a bribe is a foreign public official, despite this likely being the case. This is therefore more cost-effective, swift and pragmatic, enabling a larger number of cases to be processed and countering the practical difficulties that emerge. This is similar to the SFO's use of anti-money laundering offences and the Section 7 UK Bribery Act offence as well as the use of civil actions for similar reasons. More notably, the use of non-prosecution agreements (NPAs) with individuals symbolises a significant shift away from criminal prosecution for reasons of practicality – where criminal prosecution is not possible, NPAs offer a 'safety net' within which individuals can be caught.

Available criminal sanctions for natural persons for the bribery of foreign officials and related offences (as outlined above) vary significantly. For the Section 334 GCC offence of active bribery of a foreign official, sentences can range from imprisonment of three months to five years or six months to 10 years in especially serious cases. Fines can be used in place of imprisonment (unless it is an especially serious case), and are mandatory should the imprisonment be less than six months. In 2010, for example, a further two former senior managers at Siemens were convicted of bribery-related offences and received suspended sentences of two and one and a half years, and corresponding fines of €160,000 and €40,000. In a case involving MAN Turbo AG, a former executive received a two-year suspended sentence and was ordered to pay €100,000 to charity. For the commercial bribery offence which is being used as an alternative, there is a possibility of imprisonment for three months to five years in especially serious cases – all foreign bribery cases have been deemed especially serious thus far.

6 Full text of the decision (in German) available at: http://www.bundesverfassungsgericht.de/en/decisions/rs20100623_2bvr255908.html <Accessed 10/11/2013>.

Alternatively, following an amendment in 2009, a maximum criminal fine of €10.8m against individuals is available. This is more than ten times the maximum fine for a corporation which can be fined up to €1m under administrative law.

For the breach of trust offence, imprisonment of one month to five years or six months to 10 years in especially serious cases is available although criminal fines for cases not especially serious can be used. In practice, the average prison sentence for the foreign bribery offence is two years and three months, the longest of which was a five-year prison sentence in conjunction with a €2.16m fine. Over half of the prison sentences were suspended. For the commercial bribery offence, no defendants were imprisoned but there is an average suspended sentence of one year and six months with fines in the majority of cases but usually not more than €20,000. For the breach of trust offence all defendants received prison sentences averaging one year and six months with fines in some cases. Thus, sanctions for the foreign bribery offence are significantly higher but as has been demonstrated, German prosecutors are adopting alternative offences to achieve swifter and more cost-effective prosecutions. Administrative sanctions for breaches of supervisory duties are also available with potential fines of up to €500,000 for negligence and €1m for intent. Such sanctions have been used where it has not been possible to prove a criminal offence. In other cases, agreed sanctions are made (under Section 153a GCCP). Settlements in these cases usually amount to twice the amount of the profit made or of the bribe given. Settlements have ranged from €600 to €50,000.

Legal persons can only be sanctioned under administrative law (see below). Sections 30 and 130 OWiG where a natural person has breached their supervisory duties enable legal persons to be fined up to €500,000 for negligence and €1m for intent. Section 17(4) OWiG ensures that the fine must be higher than the profits gained from the bribery offence. Thus, the profits of any bribery offence can be confiscated. Interestingly, the confiscatory dimension of the fines is tax deductible. Such confiscations (similar to Confiscation Orders in the UK) are significant in Germany, where the regional courts can impose financial confiscations of the profits of bribery constituting the majority of financial penalties given to corporations. As explained in Chapter 2, there is a maximum fine of €1m for corporations but an unlimited amount can be confiscated. In the Siemens case, for example, Munich prosecutors confiscated almost €600m in two separate decisions. Another example involves the MAN Group that was fined €150.6m that equated to a disgorgement of the profits made.

Sanctions for both natural and legal persons are influenced by various aggravating and mitigating factors. For example, for natural persons, the cooperation of defendants, solicitation (for example, acknowledgement by the courts that bribes are expected in certain countries), if the bribes were not for direct personal gain, or if the defendant was a first-time offender, had recompensed the company, arrived after the bribery system was in place or left the company after the offence was detected can all provide mitigation. For legal persons, the seriousness of the offence (that is, size of bribes, long-term bribery, if it was usual company practice, if senior executives involved), solicitation, the degree of cooperation (for example, voluntary disclosure) and the extent to which the company has subsequently addressed the issue are all of significance.

Corporate Criminal Liability in Germany

As alluded to above, corporations in Germany *cannot* be held *criminally* liable. The distinction between 'legal persons' and 'natural persons' has more meaning here as what a corporation does cannot be interpreted as an 'act' in German Penal Law (Hefendehl, 2001):

> The German system is based on the principle of guilt, and only someone considered a natural person can have guilt. A legal entity is an empty body and only the person able to act for the entity can realise this guilt (German Lawyer Interview 221).
>
> If there was corporate criminal liability it would be much simpler. But there isn't. We have an individual criminal law based on guilt and have to prove what the individual is ultimately accountable for and this, with such a form of criminality, is of course very difficult (German Country Expert Interview 241).

Consequently, only 'natural persons' can be held criminally liable. The responsibility of legal persons and associations of persons is regulated by the law for violations of good order, or in other words, regulatory offences (Rogall, 2011: 334). Instead, liability may be imposed on corporations by state authorities only for administrative offences (*Ordnungswidrigkeiten*) which result only in administrative fines (*Geldbußen*). Although 'legal' and 'natural' persons are separated here for the purposes of criminal liability, there is often some relationship between the two: '[w]hen offences by individuals occur in a corporate context, it may be because the company's policies, culture and ethos authorize, encourage, condone or tolerate the illegal behaviour ... That the individual was committing the offence on behalf of a company provides a handy rationalization for the crime' (Gobert, 2011: 154). The prerequisite is that as a result of the criminal offence, the company's duties have been violated or the company has been enriched or intended to be enriched. Additionally, in cases where a company's management has taken inadequate supervisory measures required to prevent bribery, the company may be held liable. For example, Section 130 'Violation of obligatory supervision in firms and enterprises' of the Administrative Offences Act (*Gesetz über Ordnungswidrigkeiten*, 'OWiG') relates to violations of supervisory duties as a result of failures by senior officers of the company to supervise employees if their actions led to criminal or administrative offences. The maximum civil fine for a corporate is €1m but this is often accompanied by the disgorgement of profits made from the corruption (as above). However, a lack of corporate criminal liability is not necessarily a problem for intergovernmental organisations:

> I don't really care whether Germany has a genuinely criminal concept or a para-criminal concept; that doesn't matter very much. I find a million Euros [maximum administrative fine for the offence] is too little and in the [name of organisation] context, it is on the lower side. I am not unhappy in the way that they apply it – on corruption they have done quite a lot in the meantime (Intergovernmental Organisation 'A' Representative Interview 411).

This reflects the 'functional equivalence' position of intergovernmental organisations that places emphasis on successful outcomes of bribery cases as opposed to harmonisation of the mechanisms adopted to investigate and prosecute, although some criticism of the penalties is evident. While such divergence at the national level may be acceptable by intergovernmental organisations, it can potentially create difficulties in Mutual Legal Assistance. In other words, some jurisdictions may be unable to assist where there is no *criminal* law element involved.

Deferred and Non-prosecution Agreements in the UK and Germany

Deferred prosecution agreements (DPAs) and non-prosecution agreements (NPAs) involve formal agreements to defer or not to prosecute a case following investigation. DPAs became increasingly prominent in the US where the Department of Justice and Securities and Exchange Commission enter into such agreements with corporations. DPAs became available to prosecutors in the UK in February 2014 following the enactment of the Crime and Courts Act 2013. They are legal mechanisms consisting of voluntary agreements between the corporation and prosecutor whereby no criminal prosecution will be pursued in exchange for the fulfilment of certain requirements. DPAs enable the symbolic aim of criminal prosecution but with deference. A criminal charge is initially made but at the end of the deferment period the charges will be dropped if the requirements are met. (NPAs are similar to DPAs but no formal charge is made). Alternatively, if these requirements are not met, the prosecutors maintain the right to prosecute at this time. At the time of writing, DPAs had not been used. However, the publication of the DPA Code of Practice in February 2014 outlined how prosecutors ought to enter into negotiations and to agree a DPA. From the DPA Code it is not clear how transparent these discretionary decisions will be while terminology is ambiguous (for example, what is 'reasonable suspicion' or 'reasonable grounds for belief'?) – analysis of DPAs is vital once they begin to be used by prosecutors. In addition, consideration must be given to the extent to which such crime polices and strategies are able to 'travel' or transfer across jurisdictions – decisive in the success and impact of such transfers are the cultural, socio-political and institutional context at the receiving end (Karstedt, 2007: 147).

As discussed above, and in Chapter 5, legal, evidential and procedural obstacles hinder the criminal prosecution of corporations. However, in this context of impracticability, enforcement authorities attempt to maintain a tough prosecutorial stance, reaffirming the role of criminal prosecution and sanctioning.

For example, the SFO Director, David Green, publicly indicated an attempt to 'toughen' the SFO's stance towards bribery and reaffirm the role of the SFO as a *prosecutor* but in reality this appears idealistic and rhetorical given the structural, legal, procedural and evidential obstacles to criminal prosecution outlined above. With this in mind, however, DPAs may provide a legitimate alternative, enabling the enforcement authorities to reinforce their prosecutorial role while continuing to shift towards 'negotiated justice' (that is, civil agreements following persuasion and dialogue between public authorities and suspected corporations) (see below for further on this shift to negotiation). That said, the likelihood of a prosecution should the terms of a DPA not be met is minimal without formal admissions of 'guilt' of bribery – the DPA Code indicates that 'there is no requirement for formal admissions of guilt': thus criminal prosecution may remain implausible.

Although DPAs are yet to be used and although there is currently no legal framework for the use of NPAs in the UK, similar mechanisms have been utilised through the civil agreements as outlined above. The only significant difference is that there is no deferral of a potential criminal charge. Individuals in both Germany and the UK have received suspended sentences which operate on a similar principle, while NPAs with individuals are now being extensively used in Germany but only as part of formal proceedings. DPAs and NPAs often require the corporation to cooperate fully, providing evidence for individual criminal prosecutions, to 'self-clean' (see below), to agree to a monitor (see below) and to make restitution payments.

Debarment: 'the Corporate Death Penalty'

The issue of debarment has been mentioned on several occasions and requires special analysis as respondents in this research repeatedly identified the heaviest form of criminal sanction as being a notable concern. Article 45 of the EU public procurement directive 2004/18/EC creates provisions for a mandatory exclusion, or debarment, of candidates or tenderers who have been convicted for certain criminal offences including corruption. The Directive allows Member States to determine implementing conditions, but only if there are overriding requirements in the general interest can the mandatory exclusion be derogated. In the UK, the Directive is enacted through the Public Contracts Regulations 2006. Part 4 (23c) stipulates that 'contracting authorities' must exclude an 'economic operator' (that is, a supplier) from public contracts if it, its directors or any other person with powers of representation, decision or control have been convicted of the 'offence of bribery'. Overseas corruption and bribery are of course not solely related to procurement, but this area creates many opportunities for corrupt behaviour.

Debarment has increased in significance internationally, with the five main multilateral development banks (MDBs), the World Bank Group, the African Development Bank Group, the Asian Development Bank, the European Bank for Reconstruction and Development and the Inter-American Development Bank

Group, signing an agreement in April 2009 ensuring that a company debarred by one of the MDBs will subsequently be debarred from all others. However, the banks 'may decide not to enforce a debarment ... where such enforcement would be inconsistent with its legal or other institutional considerations' (see paragraph 7 of the agreement). Thus, there is a discretionary element to this agreement.

Debarment has frequently been referred to as the 'corporate death penalty' given the significant financial impact it brings. For example, a corporation's business may be solely reliant on public contracts and if debarred from such contracts could potentially lose millions of pounds, face insolvency and go out of business, not to mention the reputational damage and the subsequent potential stigma attached to the corporation, its directors and employees if it continues to operate. This has wider impacts: losing such corporations as providers of employment and tax could have a detrimental impact on a country's economy at the local and national level. This raises an economic dimension for prosecutors, although the OECD Convention states that economic interests should not influence decisions to prosecute (see Chapter 4). It further creates potential for the misuse of the derogation 'get-out' by contracting authorities keen to retain certain suppliers. Debarment, however, is a complex sanctioning process. For example, corporations may face indeterminate or determinate (12 months, four years and so on) debarment, or may face suspended, conditional or voluntary debarment, and the debarment may be applicable only in certain jurisdictions, with certain organisations (for example, the MDB contracts as above) or for certain associates of a corporation (for example, Russian subsidiary of Siemens).[7] The sanction is more complex and varied than a simple exclusion or not from any given public contract.

Significantly in the UK, corporations criminally prosecuted under Section 7 UK Bribery Act for failure to prevent bribery will not face mandatory exclusion. Ken Clarke stated:

> The Government have also decided that a conviction of a commercial organisation under section 7 of the Act in respect of a failure to prevent bribery will attract discretionary rather than mandatory exclusion from public procurement under the UK's implementation of the EU Procurement Directive (Directive 2004/18). The relevant regulations will be amended to reflect this (Ken Clarke, Ministerial Statement, 30 March 2011).[8]

---

7 As an example, the World Bank Group debarred Siemens subsidiary, Siemens Russia, for up to four years for bribery, while Siemens AG and all its consolidated subsidiaries and associates agreed a voluntary two-year debarment from bidding on Bank business. See World Bank press release available at: http://web.worldbank.org/WBSITE/EXTERNAL/NEWS/0,contentMDK:22234573~pagePK:64257043~piPK:437376~theSitePK:4607,00.html <Accessed 10/11/2013>.

8 Ministerial statement on the UKBA from Ken Clarke available at: http://www.publications.parliament.uk/pa/cm201011/cmhansrd/cm110330/wmstext/110330m0001.htm#11033059000255 <Accessed 10/11/2013>.

This statement ensures debarment for conviction for the Section 7 offence is discretionary (possible but unlikely) and indirectly implies that criminal conviction for the Section 1, 2 and 6 offences will retain mandatory exclusion. This likely reflects the distinction between committing an 'offence of bribery' and failing to prevent this offence. However, how this discretion will be exercised by the SFO and other prosecutorial bodies is unclear, as is any direction as to the length of debarments, the requirements of disclosure (for example, 'rehabilitation period') in the tendering process or whether a Section 7 conviction would nonetheless lead to corporations not being considered for contracts (for example, following negative press).

The above discussion of corporate criminal liability significantly demonstrated that corporations in Germany *cannot* be criminally prosecuted. This creates a significant difference in the potential exclusion of corporations based or operating in the UK and Germany (although UK and German corporations criminally prosecuted in other EU jurisdictions are liable to debarment). This would seem to indicate an uneven playing field as the criminal prosecution of a corporation for bribery in the UK would trigger mandatory debarment under EU regulations; this is not possible in Germany. That said, German courts do have available discretion to debar companies from public procurement contracts if found liable under administrative law: but as yet, this has not occurred. As one German investigator outlined, such debarment would be desirable but other factors, as above, create obstacles for its use:

> What I would really like is that at the EU-level companies were consistently debarred for two or three years but this, I believe, is theory. This doesn't happen in practice: jobs, politics, convoluted corporations making it difficult to know where to direct attention – for example, with Siemens there may be one or two smaller subsidiaries so who do I target then? Which was the operational subsidiary? It's difficult … There are legal possibilities to debar corporations in Germany but nobody at all does this (German Police Investigator Interview 231).

Public contracts often involve large-scale projects but such projects can often only be managed by large multi-national corporations. While in previous years tenders for large-scale projects may have received a high number of bids, this is not the case currently due to take-overs that have created conglomerates, and so on, leaving only a small number of capable corporations. This creates a difficulty for debarment as if one of these multi-national corporations is debarred, the number of potential corporations is reduced. In other words, the removal of one of the few multi-national corporations able to produce large-scale projects may remove legitimate competition creating the potential for market monopolisation and unfair pricing. That said, in the majority of public contracts, given that corruption increases the scope of non-competitive awards, the debarment of corrupt corporations should increase competition by enabling access to the contracts to non-corrupt corporations (Williams, 2006: 731).

However, when economic considerations are so significant, a non-discretionary corporate debarment can appear counterintuitive. No state will ignore economic considerations, rendering somewhat utopian and idealistic requirements, as with the EU Directive and the OECD Convention, non-applicable to the 'real world'. As Williams (2006: 732–3) notes, any state aiming to adopt a strict interpretation and implementation of the mandatory exclusion will face significant costs and delays in the procurement process. Procedurally, determining the relevance of a conviction from other jurisdictions and whether a corporation has actually received a relevant conviction is difficult. Further, given the lack of clarity regarding subsidiaries and associated persons and only by incurring significant investigative costs can debarment provisions be effectively applied to persons related to convicted contractors. In any case, determining the exact procedure to be followed is not specified by the Directive.

A key prerequisite in the mandatory debarment of companies convicted of the 'offence of bribery' is the requirement of a criminal prosecution but this runs against the 'functional equivalence' concept of international anti-corruption bodies such as the OECD and GRECO (see Chapter 4). As Williams (2006: 731) remarks in her assessment of European Commission (EC) procurement directives:

> … whilst the provisions might reduce corruption in government contracts, either because they act as a sanction against corrupt suppliers, preventing them from accessing the procurement process or because they are able to deter other suppliers from engaging in corrupt practices, the tool is limited as it relies on the conviction of a corrupt supplier.

Given the criminal prosecution policies in the UK and Germany (see above) along with the difficulties in detecting and investigating bribery offences (see Chapter 5), convictions and therefore debarments are unlikely. For Williams (2006: 733–4) it appears necessary to choose between making the mandatory debarment measure effective with the attendant increased procedural and financial burdens or leaving the measures symbolic so as not to disrupt the procurement process. However, in the first case, there would be a retributivist assumption that debarment is a proportionate punishment to certain cases of corruption but the potential societal 'collateral damage' (that is, innocent individuals losing employment, stakeholders losing assets, the state losing taxes and so on) appears significantly disproportionate. Despite that, one German expert remarked,

> I'd say tough luck. Tough luck. That's just the way it is. The corporations say in response, '[debarment] costs us jobs and we might go bankrupt'. But they previously damaged their competitors through corruption who maybe went bankrupt and lost jobs because this company went against the law and was corrupt, but they never ask about that, and for this reason it's no argument for me (Country Expert Germany Interview 241).

Both arguments are empirically unsubstantiated given the dearth of debarments for corruption offences, rendering both hypotheses unfalsifiable under current circumstances. In the second case, Williams points out, there is classicist assumption that corporations (or their employees) are rational and will be deterred by strong, symbolic punishments. However, as one UK lawyer stated, ‘debarment must be a “death penalty” otherwise it has no purpose’. In other words, debarment without the destruction of a corporation is little different to a criminal fine given the corporation is essentially ‘immortal’. A key issue with debarment appears to be that of deterrence and the question of whether without debarment there is no significant deterrent for corporations. As above, a message of affordable risk may be communicated if there is no significant risk for corporations but, as discussed, the risk for individuals is much greater. Debarment, along with criminal prosecution, is therefore one significant enforcement tool that should be available to prosecutors in those cases that require it. However, the EU Directive requiring mandatory debarment creates inconsistencies at the national level, in particular in relation to guidance for prosecutors in considering the potential debarment result. One respondent from an intergovernmental organisation stated:

> I think it is a problem that the EU has this mandatory debarment that is causing trouble. It should be more flexible. It is not well thought through. It actually goes as far [to say] that under the concept of public interest one should consider whether debarment would be the consequence. It is something that we picked up in the [name of organisation] and were quite troubled about that you would not go ahead with the case because you were in fear of debarment. Now it shouldn’t be that way it should be that you go ahead with the case and the debarment issue should be made discretionary on the basis of how serious the offence is (Intergovernmental Organisation ‘A’ Representative Interview 411).

This represents a more practical approach, with debarment being reserved for those particularly serious offences of bribery, reflecting models of graduated sanctioning. Determining which offences are suitable for debarment is open to interpretation but would likely include prevalence of grand corruption and those corporations with systemic and endemic corruption throughout that do not plead guilty and that have demonstrated no intention to change the culture of the organisation.

Non-criminal Alternatives: Shifts Towards Civil Solutions to Criminal Actions

The lack of criminal prosecution in the UK and the legal inability to criminally prosecute corporations in Germany has subsequently seen an increased use of non-criminal alternatives. While a wider variety of legal offences beyond corruption and bribery offences per se are available to authorities (for example, money laundering offences, breach of trust offences and so on) for both legal (UK) and natural persons (UK and Germany), the use of non-criminal sanctioning and/or agreements in relation to these offences is prevailing. This shift aligns with Wells (2011: 13) who states 'enforcement of criminal law against corporate crime increasingly uses classic regulatory techniques of negotiation and settlement'. The non-criminal measures discussed below enable negotiation between the regulator and the regulatee and a satisfactory outcome for both parties. The influence of the US anti-corruption authorities, the Department of Justice and Securities and Exchange Commission in particular, on these anti-corruption approaches in the UK and Germany is significant. The Siemens case in Germany was largely guided by the US, and may not have been so stringently investigated and prosecuted in Germany if the US had not become involved. Likewise, the involvement of the US in the Innospec and BAE Systems cases in the UK has shaped subsequent SFO approaches. In both jurisdictions, there has been a shift towards a US style 'negotiated justice' where the use of civil agreements and non-criminal alternatives involving extensive negotiation and agreement between the authorities and the corporations has been of great importance.

Why, then, is there an apparent development towards non-criminal alternatives? UK and German investigators and prosecutors, as well as representatives of intergovernmental organisations, accept the reality of financial, evidential and procedural restraints but this shift towards civil solutions is also ideological and symbolic as these actors suggest that much corporate, economic crime requires negotiation and persuasion rather than criminal prosecution. Conducting transnational investigations and prosecutions is resource-intensive. Criminal prosecution is extremely expensive and time-consuming due to the high costs of investigation to meet the substantial evidential and legal requirements, due to the costs of recruiting external counsel and prosecutors for large complex cases and due to the ability of corporations to employ technical and expert legal teams to defend them, all of which lower the likelihood of conviction. For example, locating the 'controlling mind' of a corporation involves substantial evidential requirements which demand a high burden of proof and extensive investigatory resources as determining accountability of individuals, and therefore the corporation, in complex organisations is far from straightforward. Conversely, civil solutions are more cost-effective, with corporations often covering the costs of investigation. Civil solutions enable the prosecutorial authorities to conclude an increased number of cases as there is no requirement to prove a criminal offence and the burden of proof is lower therefore increasing the likelihood of a successful outcome. This in turn enables the authorities to extend their reach. Civil solutions to this can take several forms: financial settlements and fines; restitution via Civil Recovery Orders that include the amount of the unlawful property (for example, often profits from contracts won); and investigatory and prosecutorial costs. In relation to the demand for resources and the use of civil solutions for overseas bribery cases, one UK prosecutor stated:

> … that doesn't mean that they are any less criminal [companies that bribe compared to 'conventional criminals'], it just means that you are trying to bring

> them to justice in a way that doesn't sap all of your resource because obviously we are having our budgets cut quite drastically. So it is an extremely efficient way if they come to you and report and then correct the problem which is part of the solution, isn't it (UK Investigator/Prosecutor Investigator 114).

However, the shift towards civil responses may not only be beneficial for resources, but may also be the desirable approach for maximising impact. For example, Khanna concludes that 'if we start with the notion that corporate wrongdoing is not sufficiently deterred at present, then we would want to argue for *curtailing* corporate criminal liability and increasing the focus on corporate civil liability and managerial liability. This raises serious questions about how we regulate this area' (Khanna, 2004: 141, emphasis in original). Khanna's (2004: 95) argument is based on the premise that corporate crime legislation may be the preferred outcome for corporate interests as it: (i) satisfies public outcry; but (ii) imposes low costs on businesses; and (iii) therefore avoids legislative and judicial responses that are more harmful to their interests and sometimes deflects criminal liability away from managers and executives and onto corporations (this may be contested by convicted executives). However, Wells (2011) does not believe anyone seriously suggests private law as the only option as even Khanna emphasises the importance of public enforcement.

Nonetheless, in the current economic climate, particularly in the UK, available resources are influencing the adoption of more 'cost-effective' (or cheaper) approaches. As discussed in Chapter 5, the SFO has had its budget reduced while in Germany resources are more widely available but the decentralised system results in some prosecutors being better equipped than others. Non-criminal approaches may also be preferred due to the risk of debarment under the above-mentioned EU Directive that requires mandatory debarment of any corporation found guilty of a corruption offence. The financial consequences of debarment to a country's economy can be significant, causing tension for states between considering national economic interest and ensuring the Rule of Law. In any case, enforcement approaches to transnational corporate bribery, whether based on necessity, desire, practicability or morality, face significant challenges in the form of procedural, evidential, legal, financial and structural obstacles that hinder criminal law enforcement.

Civil Solutions

Transnational corporate bribery is a *criminal* offence but *civil* solutions are becoming more frequently used in the UK and Germany. Civil solutions can take several forms: financial settlements and fines; restitution via Civil Recovery Orders (under POCA part 5 in the UK) that include the amount of the unlawful property (for example, often profits from contracts won but also revenue); and investigatory and prosecutorial costs. Other 'hybrid mechanisms' also often form part of civil solutions (see below). Given the multi-jurisdictional nature of overseas bribery, the prosecutors may attempt to offer finality to the corporation by reaching global settlements and agreements. These settlements and agreements are often global and agreed through cooperation with other national authorities (for example, the Munich prosecutors and the US Department of Justice (DoJ) in the Siemens case, or the SFO and the DoJ in the Innospec case).

In the UK, the SFO acknowledges, however, that for such global civil settlements to be reached, the judiciary needs to be informed and involved early in the process so judges understand the reasoning behind such approaches and therefore will not present problems when it reaches the court stage. The comments of Lord Justice Thomas in the Innospec case and Mr Justice Bean in the Dougall case outline the tensions that had been created between judges and the SFO, with judges of the opinion that prior arranging of settlements could potentially erode the constitutional rights of the courts to adjudicate. One UK investigator stated:

> [The use of global civil agreements] has very recently been thrown into some question by the Innospec judgement with Lord Justice Thomas saying that you can't carve these cases up with the Americans and come to the court and expect the court to rubberstamp the outcome that you've agreed. The courts will take an independent view of what justice requires, so we're still very much in the throes of absorbing that and adapting it to the way that we do our work (UK Investigator/Prosecutor Interview 111).

Financial settlements and fines can be made up of recovery or confiscation orders, or be straightforward stand-alone fines. In the UK, nearly all civil fines have been made up of recovery orders. The SFO currently has no statutory powers to fine corporations with all civil proceedings having to go through the court. In Germany, as has been established, there is a maximum fine of €500,000 or €1m depending on the level of negligence or intent involved.

Civil Recovery Orders

In the UK, a Civil Recovery Order is an order made by the high court, not the criminal court, in order to recover property (money or assets) obtained through unlawful acts. Such orders require no criminal offence to be established. Finality can therefore be obtained without a costly criminal prosecution. For corporations, the stigma is less and debarment is avoided. The SFO obtained civil recovery powers in April 2008 following provisions in the Serious Crime Act 2007 that merged the Assets Recovery Agency into SOCA and transferred its recovery powers to other agencies. In October 2008, Balfour Beatty became the first corporation in the UK to be sanctioned with a Civil Recovery Order for bribery in Egypt. The company was ordered to pay £2.25m plus costs. A key question is whether such orders, but also criminal fines, are effective in changing behaviour within corporations. One UK prosecutor explained his view:

> I am somewhat more cynical about the way in which corporates make their money and rather suspect that they would seek to recover any fines that are imposed in relation to one lot of activity by their economic activity at a later stage. So I'm not so sure that it necessarily works in that way, nor do I necessarily think that the imposition of a fine on the company particularly changes corporate culture (UK Investigator/Prosecutor Interview 112).

Fines alone may not change corporate behaviour. For this reason civil agreements in the UK and Germany often incorporate a requirement for regime change, often in the form of 'self-cleaning' which represents a form of 'hybrid' enforcement (see below).

Hybrid Mechanisms: Shifts Toward Self-regulation

Achieving prosecutorial 'results' is important for state authorities to justify their existence and demonstrate their efficacy albeit this has proved difficult in relation to corporate bribery as above. However, engineering behaviour change within corporate cultures is equally, if not more, important when addressing corporate corruption and in reality this cannot be achieved through the criminal law alone and requires more innovative strategies. UK and German prosecutors and investigators understand this problematic but are limited by their statutory remits and the available 'tools' at their disposal. To address this, a number of key trends representing a shift away from traditional law enforcement practices towards what are termed here 'hybrid mechanisms' have emerged – such mechanisms incorporate high levels of state intervention to induce corporations to regulate their own behaviour and are more innovative and financially parsimonious.

Self-reporting

In the UK, the SFO has placed much emphasis on self-reporting and has even published guidance on how and when corporations should self-report. The SFO has held discussions with a significant number of corporations, both UK based and overseas, as well as outlining this approach at several corporate conferences which have received positive feedback and support from corporations. This private sector support stems largely from the significant incentives outlined by the SFO for corporations that voluntarily disclose details of any corrupt behaviour. The following extract from the 2009 guidance explains the incentives to corporations for self-reporting:

> … the benefit to the corporate will be the prospect (in appropriate cases) of a civil rather than a criminal outcome as well as the opportunity to manage, with us, the issues and any publicity proactively. The corporate will be seen to have acted responsibly by the wider community in taking action to remedy what has

> happened in the past and to have moved on to a new and better corporate culture. Furthermore, a negotiated settlement rather than a criminal prosecution means that the mandatory debarment provisions under Article 45 of the EU Public Sector Procurement Directive in 2004 will not apply (SFO Self-Reporting Guidance).[9]

Interestingly, this guidance was removed in October 2012 following a review by the SFO's new Director, David Green, but he has maintained that self-reporting is still encouraged[10] as can be seen in the case of Rolls-Royce who self-reported corrupt behaviour following an internal investigation.[11] But why would a corporation self-report and therefore incriminate themselves? First, criminal prosecution can be avoided with civil settlements negotiated instead. In some instances no sanction at all can be negotiated (for example, where it can be demonstrated that the corruption was down to a 'bad apple' within the organisation). As per the extract above, the SFO makes explicitly clear that it does not want to debar corporations under the EU Directive. This undermines the EU but also acknowledges the preference for a more flexible, discretionary sanctioning framework. Thus, by self-reporting, any senior executives or board members that become aware of the bribery will not be held liable, unless they are directly involved with the bribery. Second, the corporation will have greater control over any publicity, with statements potentially being jointly drafted. This negotiation between regulator and regulatee enables the corporation to manage the corporation's reputation and public image. This is a form of reintegrative shaming, although the SFO were strongly criticised by Lord Justice Thomas (Judiciary of England and Wales 2010: para. 50) for suggesting that Innospec could draft an approved press notice on their case. (This is part of an on-going struggle by the judiciary to reign in the autonomy of prosecutors in plea and sentence bargaining.) Third, the corporation can negotiate that the subsequent investigation is conducted by the corporation's professional advisers (for example, third-party legal, accountancy, investigations teams) and thus maintain a degree of control. According to the self-reporting guidance, this system of self-referral creates effective and proportionate sanctions for this type of case, aids in producing a new corporate culture and subsequently brings about behavioural change within businesses. The shift away from criminal prosecution being the traditional approach towards self-reporting strategies was summed up by one UK investigator as follows:

---

9 SFO guidance on self-reporting: http://www.sfo.gov.uk/bribery--corruption/the-sfo%27s-response/self-reporting-corruption.aspx <Accessed 10/11/2013>.

10 *Financial Times*: 'SFO toughens stance on bribery' 09/10/2012: http://www.ft.com/cms/s/0/996d051e-120d-11e2-bbfd-00144feabdc0.html#axzz2I9e4hnm9 <Accessed 10/11/2013>.

11 *Financial Times*: 'Rolls-Royce adds to SFO's in-tray' 06/12/2012: http://www.ft.com/cms/s/0/f9f76a28–3fb7–11e2-b0ce-00144feabdc0.html#axzz2I9e4hnm9 <Accessed 10/11/2013>.

> Well achieving a just outcome is the aim. Given that our cases are all at the top end of seriousness for financial crimes, the expectation has always been that prosecution will be the natural outcome. The new director … Richard Alderman [at the time of the emergence of the policy initiative], has said that we will employ a variety of the tools available to us including civil settlements and including particularly inviting companies and individuals to come forward, and often that's done with the encouragement of we will look favourably on a suggestion to deal with the case civilly rather than criminally which of course for a company is massively attractive given things like the disbarring provisions of the EU (UK Investigator/Prosecutor 111).

It is expected that corporations, on detection of a possible bribery case, will conduct internal investigations, seek advice from professional advisers and the corporation's legal teams and then make the decision to self-report or not. Should the SFO come across an overseas bribery case and ascertain that the corporation could have self-reported earlier, a criminal prosecution will become more likely (this was argued at least by SFO respondents). For example, if it should come to the knowledge of a senior officer that a bribe has been paid to gain a contract, the SFO maintains that it is vital the executive self-reports. Failure to report in such an instance has the risk of being prosecuted under a money laundering offence in line with POCA.

Following a self-report, the SFO will seek to determine if the Board is committed to resolving the issues and changing the corporate culture, if the corporation will fully cooperate, whether the corporation will agree to proposed civil sanctions, whether the corporation understands that the resolution must satisfy the public interest and be transparent (for example, a public statement) and whether the corporations would like the SFO to negotiate with other UK and overseas regulators and enforcement authorities to reach a global settlement. If these factors are satisfied, the SFO will attempt to settle the case civilly and enter into plea negotiations in line with the AG's Framework for Plea Negotiations.[12] An exception to this would be any case whereby a Board member had engaged in a corrupt activity and perhaps benefited personally from the bribery. Such cases will likely lead to a criminal investigation and prosecution.

There are no data available on the effectiveness of this self-reporting approach. An article from the *Financial Times*[13] suggested that since the inception of the approach in 2009 up until August 2011, only 10 companies had self-reported. According to the former SFO Director, Richard Alderman, this lack of self-reporting was attributable to the uncertainty over how judges respond to

---

12 Full text of AG's guidelines on plea discussions available at: http://www.sfo.gov.uk/media/111905/ag_s_guidelines_on_plea_discussions_in_cases_of_serious_or_complex_fraud.pdf <Accessed 10/11/2013>.

13 *Financial Times: ' "Plea bargaining uncertainty" hits SFO drive'* 07/08/2011: http://www.ft.com/cms/s/0/c55f88e6-bf6f-11e0–898c-00144feabdc0.html#axzz1WWTWzWSA <Accessed 10/11/2013>.

such deals. (The introduction of DPAs may increase certainty.) Furthermore, the lack of incentives for individuals to self-report needs addressing, given that an individual who cooperated and gave evidence may only receive a few months less in jail than someone who did not cooperate but then pleaded guilty in court at the first available opportunity. Such incentives to cooperate provide alternatives to traditional enforcement approaches involving formal sanctioning:

> … the penal mindset of most people that are attracted to investigation and prosecution is that we tend to believe in sanctions as a way of behaviour change rather than incentives, so I do think some kind of incentives would help (UK Investigator/Prosecutor 112).

But for such incentives to be credible and certain, Alderman believes guidance from judges in sentencing bribery is required. One former investigator/ prosecutor was more critical, however, suggesting that the companies are not concerned with reporting to the SFO given the risk of prosecution by the SFO is in any case small (that is, the SFO lacks a sufficient 'big gun' (see Ayres and Braithwaite, 1992)):

> People are not scared of the SFO and in the area of international corruption they are not scared of the SFO in comparison to the Department of Justice and the Securities and Exchange Commission because it is a lot easier for these to actually levy penalties than it is for the British jurisdiction. The feedback I am getting is that people aren't going to self-report unless they have to in those circumstances. Too much at risk, poor corporate liability. If they get clobbered by the Americans then they will report to the UK as well but not otherwise (Former UK Investigator/Prosecutor Interview 113).

Nevertheless, in March 2012 Alderman outlined that since the coming into force of the UKBA, this number of self-reporting corporations had doubled to over 20 indicating further progress.[14] This promotion of self-reporting is continuing under the new SFO Director, David Green, who has indicated that civil recoveries will remain prominent in appropriate cases. This was demonstrated with Oxford University Press who agreed a Civil Recovery Order for overseas bribery in July 2012.[15] Such an explicit self-reporting approach does not exist and is not actively promoted in Germany though this may change. As one German police investigator suggested:

14 SFO press release: http://www.sfo.gov.uk/about-us/our-views/director%27s-speeches/speeches-2012/enforcing-the-law-on-fraud-and-corruption-does-self-reporting-pay.aspx <Accessed 9 August 2012>.

15 SFO press release on OUP: http://www.sfo.gov.uk/press-room/latest-press-releases/press-releases-2012/oxford-publishing-ltd-to-pay-almost-19-million-as-settlement-after-admitting-unlawful-conduct-in-its-east-african-operations.aspx <Accessed 10/11/2013>.

> Since the Siemens case, industry companies have approached the authorities and said "we've found these dubious payments", this never happened before then … They do this because they basically want to stop these corruption schemes in their firms but until now, this is only happening for corruption at the national level, not for overseas corruption. It hasn't gone so far as yet (German Police Investigator Interview 251).

Corporations notifying the German authorities of bribery are likely to receive more lenient responses, often in the form of self-cleaning requirements.

Self-cleaning

The principle of self-cleaning has only become a well-established legal concept in some EU Member States, such as Germany and Austria (Arrowsmith et al., 2009). In Germany, the concept of 'self-cleaning' as a 'sanction' was used most notably in the Siemens case. Self-cleaning mitigates the likelihood that corporations will be debarred form public contracts. As Arrowsmith et al. (2009: 257–8) note, 'the general idea would be that an economic operator can regain the possibility of participating in public contracts by demonstrating that it has taken effective measures to ensure that wrongful acts will not recur in the future'. Of course, preventing future criminality cannot be guaranteed, but the likelihood of future acts of bribery can be reduced.

Based on their analysis of jurisdictions that recognise the concept of self-cleaning but mainly Germany, Arrowsmith et al. (2009: 259–61) suggest that four key measures will usually take place: clarification of the relevant facts and circumstances; repair of the damage caused; personnel measures; and structural and organisational measures. Corporations are first required to actively assist with the criminal proceedings in order to clarify the facts and the responsibility of all individuals involved. This must be comprehensive and swift to ensure subsequent self-cleaning measures appropriately reflect the facts of the case, otherwise the process may not be credible. In particular, there is often a preference for special audits by outside certified public accountants or other independent persons. Second, any financial damage caused must be repaired. Third, the corporation must immediately and comprehensively dismiss the shareholders, executives and employees involved in the criminality. All such individuals must be prevented from having any further influence on the management of the corporation (for example, shareholders may have trust agreements enabling them to recall their share in the corporation at any time), or in cases where the individual had minor involvement, dismissal with notice, a termination agreement or a reprimand may also be appropriate. These personnel measures are a key component of the self-cleaning process. Fourth, future misconduct must be prevented. This can include in-house training for staff and creating binding company guidelines, standards and codes. Other measures may include the appointment of intra-corporate or external compliance officers to assist whistleblowers and the establishment of compliance departments, amongst others. Such organisational and structural measures are key in preventing future wrongdoing.

Self-cleaning, while already established in the German anti-corruption system, is becoming more significant in the UK (although less formal) in line with the increased use of civil agreements and the 'adequate procedures' defence to Section 7 of the UK Bribery Act (see above). Corporations agreeing to civil settlements are frequently required to implement the four key measures outlined above, while adequate compliance procedures are required for corporations aiming to prevent and detect bribery within their organisation. But effectiveness of such requirements for culture change is unclear and difficult to measure. As things stand, apart from cases that involve the use of monitoring (see below), the anti-corruption authorities do not revisit and reassess the extent of the culture change. However, should a corporation be found to have reoffended and not have sufficiently enacted such changes, according to UK prosecutors this would increase the likelihood of criminal prosecution (although this may be more rhetorical than probable given the difficulties and obstacles faced in prosecution).

Monitoring

As part of self-cleaning and other civil fines, corporations in both the UK and Germany may be required to have a monitor in place for a set period of time. The monitor may be nominated by the corporation, but must be accepted by the authorities. It is the duty of the monitor to ensure compliance regimes and self-cleaning are effectively carried out and to ensure satisfactory culture change within the organisation. It is in relation to monitoring that contemporary theories of regulation that encourage regulators to be responsive may have the most relevance in relation to regulating transnational bribery. For example, a monitor would be able to recommend an increase or decrease in the severity of enforcement sanctions to the prosecutors therefore reflecting models of escalated or graduated sanctioning (see for example Ayres and Braithwaite (1992)). However, the actual obstacles to such escalation (for example, difficulties obtaining overseas evidence for criminal prosecution) may render such models impracticable.

Third-party Influence and Coordinated Responses

Cases of transnational corporate bribery inevitably involve many jurisdictions, and this is increasingly the case given the extraterritorial reach of the UK Bribery Act 2010, US FCPA and to some extent the German anti-bribery laws (Chapter 4). In the current landscape corporations are liable in multiple jurisdictions given their involvement in international business and this has impacts for enforcement responses at the national level. The above discussion identifies the mixture of criminal, civil and hybrid policy responses to cases of transnational corporate bribery in the UK and Germany but there is an assumption that such mechanisms are alone products of the efforts of national enforcement authorities (for example, SFO, public prosecutors) in the two jurisdictions following detection and investigation. In practice, however, the influence of third-party jurisdictions and their enforcement agencies, in particular the Department of Justice and Securities and Exchange Commission in the US, in some cases shape whether a case will be investigated and prosecuted in the UK and Germany:

> If the American law enforcement and tax authorities hadn't investigated Siemens, then the proceedings would have never become so big because ultimately Siemens were obligated to pay a law firm to uncover the extent of the internal problems. This is not possible in Germany. We have no corporate criminal liability. The public prosecutor's office must firstly want to investigate and if they do want to investigate then of course they have huge problems in detecting the main suspects and finding corresponding documents within a large, well-known corporation (German Country Expert Interview 241).

A similar scenario shaped the investigation of Innospec by the SFO. In this case the US authorities were highly influential in instigating an SFO response and subsequent sanctioning (Chapter 2). Had the US authorities, within the framework of their extra-jurisdictional reach under the FCPA, not investigated these cases, it is unclear whether Innospec and Siemens would have been pursued in the UK and Germany respectively. Of course, it is impossible to infer for sure whether or not this is the case but it can be said that in these instances the role of the US was highly influential in shaping the enforcement agenda in the UK and Germany. This raises the question of how inter-jurisdictional influence and coordinated responses are organised and carried out. In general, both UK and German investigators and prosecutors view their relationships with the US positively and speak of the benefits of information and evidence exchange and the ability to coordinate their investigations and prosecutions. As indicated by one public prosecutor in Germany, the US authorities are frequently praised:

> We have excellent cooperation with the Americans, it really functions well. You can really praise them in the Siemens case. They were unbelievably fair and very, very competent, the Securities and Exchange Commission as well as the Department of Justice. Unbelievable, really great. It worked really trustingly – not once was anything passed to the press, you can really rely on them 100% and they were also fair in the process … They behaved very fairly. So, excellent with the Americans, though of course we have other countries that are more difficult, that's for sure (German Public Prosecutor Interview 211).

However, an element of caution is required given nation-states often seek to protect their own economic and political interests. The overarching influence of the US on both the UK and Germany needs transparency and due consideration.

One German police investigator felt US involvement often reflected their interests at the time:

> With the US, I believe there is always the national aspect. I think sometimes they give the impression that they have double standards in terms of whether it relates to one of their own corporations or to a German or international corporation … I have experienced that they proceed against US firms … When it relates to things which happen in third-party countries, so in the Third World or so, then you get very little support from America, even if local firms are involved. So it's difficult. You notice that from case to case it depends on what America has interests in (German Police Investigator Interview 231).

One former UK investigator/prosecutor was more critical, in particular in relation to how the fines or financial confiscations were often weighted towards the US authorities, even in cases where the criminality was predominantly in the UK and Germany:

> You have got pressure being put on all the time from say the Americans … Siemens had nothing to do with the Americans but the Americans got the lion's share of the money out of it. Most of BAE had nothing to do with America but they got the lion's share of the money. Innospec – the holding company was quoted in America and that's enough for them to get the lion's share out of it (Former UK Investigator/Prosecutor Interview 113).

There is no formal framework in place to determine the allocation of cases or which jurisdictions ought to retain ownership over a case. To allocate appropriate jurisdiction, some respondents indicated that this is best done on an ad hoc basis as decisions to investigate are often made before evidence is available to make an informed decision. One example involved a UK case that the SFO investigated for seven years. The long time span was due to difficulties in tracing the flow of money through various different jurisdictions and the time taken to obtain mutual legal assistance. Once the end of the money trail was ascertained, the principal beneficiary and therefore the principal criminal act was actually in the US. At the start of this process, allocation of jurisdiction would have been the UK and nowhere else but the most natural place to prosecute was actually the US. In such scenarios, early definitive rulings can be restrictive thus a more flexible and developing approach is required. As one UK investigator/prosecutor stated:

> I think there are one or two mechanisms in place. For example, what if you've got a case that could be prosecuted equally well in the US or the UK, how do you manage that? Well it's only a problem if both have started investigating. If only one's got it there's not a problem. So in those kinds of situations you do need some kind of arbitration mechanism or mediation mechanism to determine where it is and there is a protocol between the Attorneys General of the UK and

> the US to try and coordinate that. Equally they're working towards some kind of allocation of jurisdiction rules for criminal matters in Eurojust. As soon as you make the rules cast iron then you're gonna find there are some gaps, so it needs to be flexible. And that's it isn't it, the difficulty arises where both want to do it rather than [neither] … . and there's no mechanism in place if neither wants to do it and that's probably because you don't need a mechanism for that because if there's more cases to investigate and prosecute than you've got resources to be deployed, it's just not an issue is it (UK Investigator/Prosecutor Interview 112).

This is a relatively new area as only since the early 2000s have nation-states began to engage in the enforcement of transnational corporate bribery. Issues of ownership and allocation in particular in light of third-party influence and involvement require systematic analysis and the development of bilateral or multilateral frameworks within which such concerns can be addressed.

Joint Investigations

The consequence of this third-party involvement is the need for coordinating investigations with other jurisdictions. As an example, a typical international bribery case might involve a company from Italy, a company form France, a company from Germany and a company from the UK with the UK company being the subsidiary of a US holding company. Determining who should investigate and prosecute in such scenarios is complex. Often we see the creation of joint investigation teams:

> So the Americans have this kind of joint task force type concept where you put together ad hoc a group of people to deal with the matter. The difficulty is long term funding of those arrangements and whilst the political will might be there to begin with, later on it dissolves … So joint investigation teams, something to speed up the process of exchanging data and exchanging evidence across the team is something that needs to be worked on. So, the issue that we need to work on as the investigations become more multinational is actually working the multinational investigations and working through the practicalities of doing that (UK Investigator/Prosecutor Interview 112).

Such investigations will involve coordination (for example, determining which authority should pursue which aspect of a case) and cooperation (for example, sharing evidence and providing assistance). Should a case merit prosecution, it may be the case that one jurisdiction will subsequently solely pursue the case to prosecution or that different offences in different jurisdictions will be pursued by different authorities in order to maximise impact and prevent double jeopardy. Establishing which authority has 'ownership' over cases will vary, dependent on factors such as the most appropriate jurisdiction (for example, where did the bribery take place), likelihood of successful prosecution (for example, more favourable corporate criminal liability laws in the US), public interest (for example, is it in the interests of one jurisdiction more than another to take the lead), amongst others. Such joint investigations are commended by investigators and prosecutors as they enable the building of relationships between active enforcement authorities but also accept the need for temporary measures in these scenarios. However, as above, national interests are reflected in decisions to engage and cooperate with specific cases and as one German police investigator suggested:

> The level of assistance often depends on how interested the other jurisdiction is in the case (German Police Investigator Interview 252).

Should such measures become permanent, issues of sovereignty and nationality are invoked. Furthermore, it is not clear how more permanent teams would be funded and where ultimate decision-making responsibility and accountability would lie. It was also common for all respondents to suggest the likelihood of the formal development of regional anti-corruption authorities (for example, an EU Anti-Corruption Office) beyond the sovereign state was small and would be beset with practical difficulties (for example, as is the case with regional and international policing authorities such as Europol and Interpol).

Prevention and Reduction as Part of State Responses

In the UK, law enforcement is traditionally reactive in its approach to sourcing cases and responding to offences. However, as seen in Chapter 5, the SFO utilises a mix of reactive and proactive detection mechanisms. While referrals from other agencies may be reactive, the SFO through self-reporting (see below) and encouraging whistleblowers has developed more proactive strategies, and this proactive approach is further reflected in the preventative mechanisms being adopted. UK investigators and prosecutors within the SFO are very clear that the statutory remit of the organisation is to focus on investigation and prosecution. This trend is very evident in the responses of UK respondents to the question of prevention and reduction, which is of secondary importance. However, the organisation has adopted elements of a more resourceful approach which recognises the wider picture of changing corrupt corporate cultures and preventing overseas bribery. Reduced resources may influence this, as may an acknowledgment that gaining leverage against corporate bribery can be supplemented by alternative strategies.

Consequentialist theories of punishment are very much evident in the form of specific and general deterrence, and rehabilitation. As part of civil settlements (discussed below), as in the Innospec case, corporations are required to introduce anti-bribery and corruption compliance regimes and remove those corrupt or complicit board members, executives and employees as part of an initiative to change corporate culture and subsequently prevent further bribery. This may be viewed as a form of specific deterrence with an element of rehabilitation. Corporations that have not been charged or investigated are also being encouraged to approach the SFO with the intention of obtaining advice as to how to improve the compliance systems and comply with the law. (In the event of an investigation into such a company, these meetings would not provide any mitigation during prosecution.) The published Guidance on the UK Bribery Act, for example, outlines six key principles of compliance systems: proportionate procedures; top-level commitment; risk assessment; due diligence; communication (including training); and monitoring and review. While these are not compulsory, they aid corporations aiming to introduce or improve their compliance systems. This represents a wider preventative approach, aimed at ensuring the compliance of corporate cultures, although it is not known whether this actually reaches corrupt organisations or only those organisations that are otherwise ethical. These principles represent a form of enforced self-regulation. Albeit the principles are not prescriptive and corporations are not regulated to ensure they have effective compliance systems, if investigated for bribery by their associated persons (for example, third parties, subsidiaries, agents) as per Section 7 of the UK Bribery Act, they can provide a defence to the offence. This in turn pressurises corporations into introducing the principles into their systems, albeit the government accepts that commercial organisations vary in terms of size, resources and capability, and so on, and thus intends the principles to be flexible and outcome-focused. The six principles are briefly explained below:

> *Principle 1* Proportionate procedures – bribery prevention procedures should be proportionate to the risks the commercial organisation faces and to the nature, scale and complexity of the organisation's business activities. They should also be clear, practical, accessible, effectively implemented and enforced.
> *Principle 2* Top-level commitment – top-level management (for example, board of directors, owners or other equivalents) should be committed to preventing bribery by persons associated with their commercial organisation. A zero-tolerance culture towards bribery should be fostered.
> *Principle 3* Risk assessment – the commercial organisation should assess the nature and extent of its exposure to potential external and internal risks of bribery on its behalf by associated persons. The assessment should be periodic, informed and documented.
> *Principle 4* Due diligence – the commercial organisation should take a proportionate and risk-based approach to applying due diligence procedures in respect of persons who perform or will perform services for or on behalf of the organisation in order to mitigate identified bribery risks.
> *Principle 5* Communication (including training) – proportionate to the risks it faces, the commercial organisation should seek to ensure that its bribery prevention policies and procedures are embedded and understood

throughout the organisation through internal and external communication, including training. This should include a secure, confidential and accessible 'speak up' procedure.
Principle 6 Monitoring and review – the commercial organisation should monitor and review procedures designed to prevent bribery by associated persons and make improvements where necessary. Monitoring and review should be regular and also be conducted in response to other stimuli such as governmental changes in countries where they operate.

These procedures, although not prescriptive, provide a prevention framework for corporations to regulate their own behaviour – this extends beyond traditional enforcement practices towards the manufacturing of an indirectly enforced self-regulatory landscape (see Chapter 7). UK investigators, however, still view more traditional forms of general deterrence as effective mechanisms for behaviour change. For example, it is taken for granted that in certain cases, criminally prosecuting a corporation can serve as a deterrent to other corporations:

> … when every boy in the class sees Johnny getting taken to task, it's a deterrent to their activity. Enforcement has a deterrent effect and that is therefore a preventative effect but that is different from taking all the classmates of little Johnny aside and saying you do realise that it's naughty to do what little Johnny has done (UK Investigator/Prosecutor Interview 112).

Thus, elements of more traditional understandings of prevention along with more innovative strategies of prevention are evident within the SFO. However, as another respondent explained, such prevention is not measureable, making it more difficult to assess the impact of the SFO.

As in the UK, the German authorities have a statutory remit aimed at repression. Mechanisms of prevention, however, are frequently adopted in Germany in combating corruption and bribery, but there is no legal requirement to do so, and this voluntariness was reflected in the attitudes of some respondents. The potential benefits of preventative action are, however, largely understood amongst investigators and prosecutors in Germany, although as in the UK, German investigators also acknowledge that the effectiveness of prevention cannot be measured:

> Well, we're the police and an investigatory authority and it's our main duty to prosecute. But like in many other areas of criminality, you quickly realise that certain areas can't only be combated by the police, or only through prosecution. That's why I consider it also important … that in the cases we investigate, we also identify ways to prevent [corruption] in future (German Police Investigator Interview 251).

This respondent is explicitly acknowledging the limitations of criminal prosecution and 'policing' in changing behaviour. This respondent argued that criminal prosecution serves a number of key purposes: it expresses what the state wants, or does not want; it speaks to the public and has therefore a symbolic influence; and it creates a feeling of justice. However, they also suggested that prosecution alone cannot deal with corruption: in the long run, prevention is most important, but strong repression goes hand in hand with prevention. Education in this process is vital, as is the need to encourage and ensure that corporations change, and want to change, their own behaviour: a need to trigger self-regulatory practices. This respondent also acknowledged the key role that institutions such as TI play in shaping this self-regulatory landscape 'since the state alone can't do it'. While repression is the responsibility of the authorities, prevention is the responsibility of a number of institutional settings.

In the State Criminal Investigation Office in one *Bundesland*, this education process involves giving frequent talks internally and externally to explain how corruption can be prevented. It also involves frequently publishing documents and brochures available to corporations on a variety of corruption-related issues. For example, events aimed at addressing representatives of corporations and SMEs are held in conjunction with anti-corruption organisations such as TI. In addition, non-state agencies provide much material and guidance on effective compliance in Germany, as in the UK (see Chapter 7).

As outlined above, the UK has published specific guidance with regards adequate procedures in relation to the law. No such formal, all-encompassing document exists in Germany, but investigators and prosecutors do nevertheless convey similar principles to commercial organisations. For example, the significance of 'the tone from the top' was frequently referred to when attempting to implement culture change within corporations, as was the need to review compliance systems. Thus, while no extensive document exists, similar messages are being conveyed. Relating to the focus placed on interdisciplinary cooperation in Germany, an interdisciplinary working group was created and has provided numerous publications on differentiating customer care and corruption and triggering prevention.

One investigator was strongly of the opinion that there is not prevention without repression, a view reinforced by one prosecutor who did not consider preventative measures as part of their remit. On the subject of changing the behaviour of corporations, this prosecutor stated:

> … the main incentive from our side is the fear of criminal prosecution. Actually, that's the only stimulus that we can actually apply. We can't go giving out prizes in the sense that you say, 'ok, the corporation is great'. We can't do that so our incentive is primarily, that those who are clean or will in any case see that they're better off than those who don't care. We are a pure criminal prosecution authority, we don't do anything other than prosecute criminal offences … We don't do anything with prevention. It's not our field (German Prosecutor Interview 212).

This prosecutor did acknowledge that awareness was increasing about the newly found significance of compliance and the role of corporations in monitoring their own behaviour, but remained of the view that prosecution is the main task of the Public Prosecutor's Offices. Thus, a mixed response in Germany with regards to prevention exists.

Conclusion

The key argument of this chapter is that whether the enforcement system is centralised or decentralised and whether there is corporate *criminal* liability (UK) or not (Germany), prosecutorial convergence in the two jurisdictions is evident not only in relation to criminal prosecution but also in relation to the use of non-criminal measures although variances are evident. Key in this shift is the significance of negotiation between the regulator and the regulatee. In both jurisdictions there is a trend to use non-criminal approaches for both individuals and corporations (NPAs and civil sanctions), as well as a wider variety of criminal offences to deal with overseas bribery (for example, money laundering, breach of trust and so on). Whether criminal or civil/administrative approaches are used, every case has involved financial penalties for the corporation in both jurisdictions. This regulatory mix of enforcement mechanisms indicates how responsive regulators can be within their legal frameworks but also demonstrate the strengths and limitations of criminal prosecution for such complex transnational crimes (for example, legal, evidential, procedural, financial obstacles). With this in mind, a variety of non-criminal alternatives are enabled and encouraged given discretion in the context of:

i. structural (for example, decentralised or centralised systems), financial (for example, costs of criminal prosecution), evidential (for example, transnational investigations and burden of proof), legal (for example, difficulties surrounding corporate criminal liability) and procedural (for example, prosecution policies) obstacles;
ii. ideological and symbolic arguments (for example, efficacy of prosecution or persuasion to deal with 'corporate' offenders); and.
iii. wider economic (for example, risks of debarment/losing corporates as tax and employment providers) and security (for example, counter-terrorism when dealing with states where corruption is evident but security cooperation is required).

Balancing national interests in the light of scrutiny from organisations such as the OECD, GRECO and Transparency International is challenging but civil responses appear to appease both sides. However, while civil outcomes reduce the stigma for corporations, they may also fail to satisfy public demand for social fairness and retribution, creating an image of such offences as wrong because they are prohibited rather than inherently or morally wrong. However, traditional policing approaches that favour criminal prosecution cannot in themselves achieve behaviour change in relation to transnational corporate bribery. Instead, this chapter has demonstrated the ways in which UK and German investigators and prosecutors are 'negotiating regulation' through a variety of enforcement sanctions including criminal prosecutions, civil sanctions and a variety of innovative, enforced self-regulatory approaches such as self-reporting and self-cleaning. Through these mechanisms, the SFO and German prosecutors are creating a regulatory role in which they police, supervise and monitor all corporations and in extreme cases criminally sanction those not complying with the law. This approach demonstrates the shift in policing practices towards activities traditionally associated with industry regulators; the similarities between policing and regulation are more analytically significant than their differences (Gill, 2002).

The criminal law, however, provides a normative framework within which certain activities have been condemned and remains significant for prosecutors for its symbolic and (potentially) deterrent effect in order for the state (i) to negotiate regulation with corporations and (ii) to demonstrate to the various publics at the national, regional and international levels that it is actively enforcing the law against corporations that bribe overseas. However, given international frameworks of 'functional equivalence' (where outcomes are placed above means), we need to rethink how the criminal law ought to be used to deal with *corporate* offenders given i) the unlikelihood of prosecution due to the above obstacles, ii) the inevitable considerations given to national interests and iii) ideologies of 'negotiated justice'. The leverage that is offered by supplementary models of control and influence needs to be fully explored. Hybrid mechanisms provide innovative responses but the following the chapter considers a range of self-regulatory mechanisms that are emerging in the regulatory landscape.

Chapter 7

Theories of Self-regulation: Manufactured and Organic Self-regulatory Practices

> What I envisage is a kind of complex form of hybrid regulation … I think that we are moving the way of hybrid [regulation], meaning the outlines are given like here (points to the organisation's 'good practice guidance' addressed to companies). [For example], it doesn't say what you have to do about facilitation payments but you have to find a way to regulate them. You can have various options and for me this is the place where self-regulation comes in. The same thing with gifts, to define what is an adequate gift and what is an illegal gift. Anything between a little present and a Rolex so that is something you had better leave to self-regulation. So the framework has to be created by states or by international bodies and then leave it to the private sector to find its own insight (Intergovernmental Organisation 'A' Representative Interview 411).

> I believe the task of the authorities, or the task of the state, is to provide a system through which it's ensured that when the rules of the game are not adhered to consequences are threatened and implemented. This, I believe, is important (German Lawyer Interview 221).

Introduction

Theories of enforcement characterised by the prosecution policies of formal state agencies are alone an insufficient means of regulating transnational corporate bribery and changing corporate behaviour. Enforcement mechanisms from debarment and criminal prosecution to civil agreements and hybrid mechanisms that are available to state anti-corruption authorities gain *some* level of regulation but substantial difficulties are encountered which reduce the legitimacy of these responses (Chapters 5 and 6). Academic debates over state capacities to respond to corporate crimes, and crimes more generally, have led many to argue that even in advanced developed countries the sovereign state is no longer solely able to provide security, law and order and crime control within its territorial boundaries (Garland, 2001) and this has been accompanied by subsequent shifts towards a focus on the 'responsibilisation' of non-state agencies and actors (Garland, 2001; O'Malley, 1992). Although some commentators propose that state capacities for enforcement do exist (see Slapper and Tombs, 1999, 186; see also Almond, 2013;

Pearce and Tombs, 1998; Tombs and Whyte, 2007; Tombs, 2011), even where political will and resources may be evident, the 'real' obstacles posed by such transnational problems to state authorities hinder enforcement.

In the area of transnational corporate bribery, informational asymmetries (for example, the enforcement authorities are unable to obtain sufficient knowledge, evidence to prosecute) mean that criminal and regulatory enforcement alone are unlikely to sufficiently impact upon the problem and therefore need to be supplemented by self-regulatory mechanisms. Starting from the position of the state, such developments have been characterised as shifts from 'Old Governance' (that is, state-centric, centralised, bureaucratic expertise, mandatory rules) to 'New Governance (that is, state orchestration, decentralised, dispersed expertise, soft law) (Abbot and Snidal, 2009) where concepts of 'governance' are characterised by the steering of public and private groups (Kooiman, 1993: 255) and the 'triggering' of self-regulatory practices (Teubner, 1998). However, such new regulatory models are often preoccupied with the institutions of regulation and their strategies – these are usually characterised by a high level of state intervention or 'steering' and are of a more formal nature (for example, an industry regulator requiring corporations to implement sufficient compliance systems). In this sense, mechanisms that emerge more independently of state influence and whose 'regulatory' impacts are secondary (for example, mechanisms that primarily aim to generate profit) are not recognised but are nonetheless significant in changing market and corporate behaviour.

The chapter begins by conceptualising the nature of these self-regulatory practices that may be of a more manufactured (that is, high state intervention) or more organic (that is, minimal or no state intervention) nature. Analytically, these mechanisms emanate from the micro- (for example, individual corporations), meso- (for example, individual markets) and macro- (for example, multi-sector/transnational initiatives) levels, and originate within three main 'domains' (state, commercial and intergovernmental/non-governmental). The mechanisms involve both state and non-state 'regulatory' actors, reflect varying levels of formality (for example, mandatory-voluntary), can be specific or general and may be direct and/or indirect in their influence. The chapter argues that while mechanisms of a manufactured nature reflect contemporary regulation theory (where there is a preoccupation with regulatory agencies and formal mechanisms), understanding organic mechanisms offers new ways of thinking about 'regulation'. Thus, the argument is not that regulatory strategies ought to be directed away from the manufactured responses of 'regulatory' agencies (for example, state regulators; orchestrating intergovernmental organisations) as such governmental authorities create important formal frameworks and ought to retain a primary role. However, shifting focus to the broader regulatory landscape to understand informal and organic mechanisms informs analytical and theoretical understandings of behaviour change within corporations at risk of being involved in transnational bribery.

Conceptualising the Self-regulatory Landscape

Determining appropriate levels of state intervention is challenging as nation-states must simultaneously manage expectation, scrutiny and pressure from anti-corruption intergovernmental and non-governmental organisations whilst ensuring they promote and support the business interests of their corporations:

> If the state remains involved [in regulating and sanctioning corporations] we are confronted with risks that the system is biased for the sake of strategic positions abroad if it comes to international bribery cases. Would that mean that having a much more liberal model leaving it entirely to the private sector? Would that be better? I am not sure. I think also in the private sector there is a tendency sometimes to put the 'dust under the carpet'. No I think that for the time being the state should remain involved (Intergovernmental Organisation 'B' Representative Interview 311).

Too much state intervention may increase the risk and/or perception of 'strategic positioning' abroad as nation-states promote their interests. For example, the BAE Systems case demonstrated the importance of large commercial enterprises to national economic and security interests (see Chapter 1). But nation-states and their enforcement agencies and regulators are able to implement mechanisms with varying levels of intervention where at one extreme enforcement mechanisms such as public prosecution leading to corporate debarment are available (see Chapter 6), while at the other extreme, minimal or no state intervention within a liberal model that encourages market and corporate self-regulation is possible. But the implementation of self-regulation is problematic (press regulation in England and Wales and the Leveson Inquiry[1] into the culture, practices and ethics of the press following malpractice and corruption scandals demonstrated this). Thus, it has been argued that 'while private regulation has resulted in some substantive improvements in corporate behaviour, it cannot be regarded as a substitute for the more effective exercise of state authority at both the national and international levels' (Vogel, 2010: 68). It is important then to retain a regulatory landscape that involves varying levels of state intervention.

Traditionally, self-regulation covers a wide range of institutional arrangements and can differ according to the degree of monopolistic power (for example, whether all suppliers in a given market are regulated), the degree of formality (for example, is legitimacy derived from a legislative framework?), their legal status (for example, are the rules binding?) and the degree to which outsiders participate in rule formulation and enforcement, or in other ways supervise the system (Ogus, 1994: 108–9). In other words, self-regulation may refer to non-legally binding standards established for a particular firm or industry, or to rules formulated by a self-regulatory agency but approved by the state, as in enforced

1 http://www.levesoninquiry.org.uk/ <Accessed 10/11/2013>.

self-regulation (see Ayres and Braithwaite, 1992). Gill (2002: 536) suggests that in legal markets, it is self-regulation within an industry that will be viewed as the desired outcome of effective education and self-control. He goes on to suggest that due to the limitations of the sovereign state, and the power and knowledge problems that arise, the autonomy of some areas of social life has become so extensive that the notion of effective outside regulation is abandoned. As Clarke (1990: 225) states, 'the private context of business offences, their complexity and frequently their ambiguity make the formality and precision characteristic of law difficult and require the extensive commitment of resources, which, as in all legal enforcement systems, are limited'. Consequently, governors are forced to abandon ideas of effective outside regulation and aim for the mere triggering of self-regulatory processes (Teubner, 1998: 406–9).

Taken in its broadest sense, then, self-regulation may refer not just to rigid and formal models of industry regulation, but also to more expansive conceptions of a variety of self-regulatory mechanisms with little or no state intervention and formality. The self-regulatory mechanisms in this book reflect both aspects. Accompanied by a high level of state intervention, self-regulatory mechanisms take a more manufactured form. In other words, these mechanisms are organised by the state with the specific intention of developing self-regulatory mechanisms within international commerce. Self-regulatory mechanisms may also emerge organically – these mechanisms emerge independently of the state or with minimal state intervention and are products of the initiatives and/or policies of individual corporations, industries, business in general or other non-state sources. It may not be the primary intention of such organic mechanisms to regulate the behaviour of corporations but they may do so as a secondary impact (for example, commercial enterprises seeking profit through selling compliance may also change behaviours in corporations).

The level of formality of both manufactured and organic self-regulatory mechanisms can also be analysed. For example, both state and non-state manufactured and organic self-regulatory mechanisms may have mandatory or voluntary elements and may exist within formal (for example, prescribed) or informal (for example, general guidelines) frameworks. For example, the manufactured imposition of a 'monitor' by the state as part of a civil agreement will be mandatory but may be informal insofar as the corporation retains responsibility for how changes may be implemented within the organisation. In contrast, organic transnational business initiatives do not compel corporations to join but are voluntary. However, once associated with such initiatives, corporations agree to more formal frameworks and guidelines with which they should operate. Figure 7.1 outlines the self-regulatory framework within which various mechanisms have emerged.

The vertical spectrum implies a separation of state intervention with no state influence in the bottom half; but in reality, the state can still influence self-regulatory mechanisms in this area in the same way that non-state organisations can influence the mechanisms of the state. The primary actors, however, in the

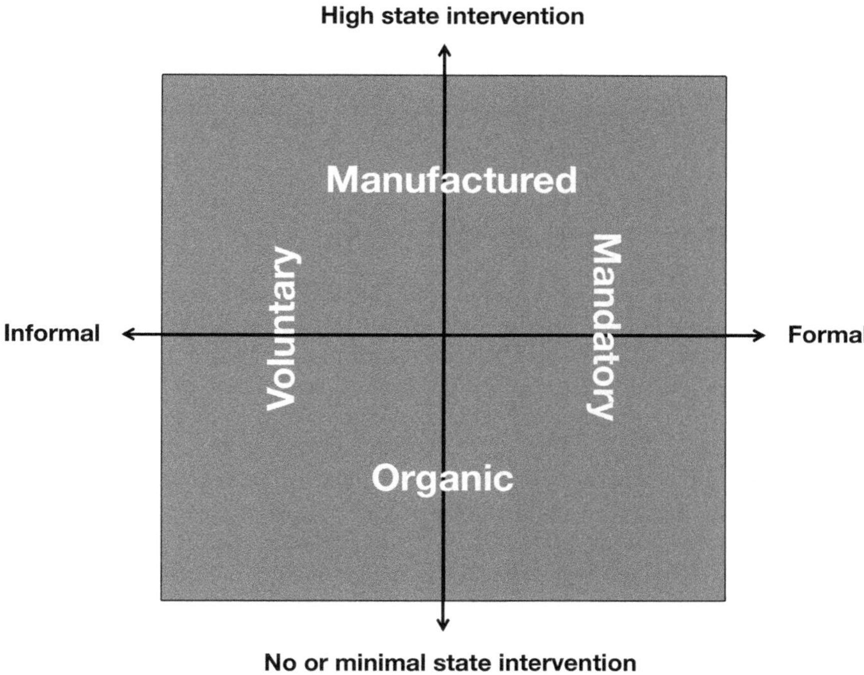

Figure 7.1 Conceptualising self-regulatory mechanisms

top half of the spectrum are state actors and agencies, with non-state actors and organisations being of primary importance in the bottom half. In the same manner, the informal/formal spectrum relates to the voluntary or mandatory requirement of the self-regulatory mechanism although it is acknowledged that some voluntary agreements may subsequently lead to mandatory elements and vice versa. Thus, in some cases, self-regulatory mechanisms may involve a significant degree of cross-over in relation to the level of formality and level of state intervention but the majority of self-regulatory mechanisms in relation to the problematic of transnational corporate bribery fall into specific areas.

A useful organising framework for understanding these mechanisms and their primary actors is in relation to the levels at which they emanate and the domains within which they originate. For example, self-regulatory mechanisms have emerged at the micro-level (i.e. at the level of individual corporations); at the meso-level (i.e. at the level of individual markets/industries); and at the macro-level (i.e. at the level of multi-sector and transnational initiatives). Furthermore, such mechanisms emerge within three main domains: state, commercial; and intergovernmental/non-governmental. These categories are not comprehensive, as other organisations not discussed here may also be important in changing corporate behaviours (e.g. media pressure). These mechanisms may also be specific or general. Specific mechanisms are focused on individual corporations while general mechanisms aim at the regulation of 'populations' of corporations. The following section analyses these mechanisms in relation to these dimensions (see also Table 7.1, p. 8).

Self-regulatory Mechanisms at the Micro-level

Manufactured and organic mechanisms emerging at the micro-level originate from the state and commercial domains and reflect practices and relations principally directed at *individual* corporations. These mechanisms include informal dialogue, lateral litigation, monitoring, self-cleaning, self-investigation and self-reporting (see Table 7.1 for explanation). All these mechanisms (bar lateral litigation) are manufactured by the state but involve varying levels of formality and intervention, for example, informally, state regulators may enter into discreet dialogue at the request of corporations; formally, state regulators may impose strict requirements on corporations as in the case of self-cleaning following sanctioning. In addition, some mechanisms may shift from voluntary to mandatory (for example, self-reporting leading to imposed self-cleaning). Self-investigation and self-reporting, although manufactured by the state, may also be triggered by corporations themselves. For example, internal corporate compliance systems may uncover suspicious behaviour which is investigated (either internally or using external professionals) and presented to the enforcement authorities with the intention of negotiating favourable sanctions. (For more in-depth analysis of these responses, see the section on 'hybrid mechanisms' in Chapter 6 in line with shifts towards self-regulation as part of enforcement responses.)

A key analytical aspect of the origin of each of these mechanisms is the nature of the regulator-regulatee 'negotiation' which provides the framework and relations for such mechanisms to function and thus for compliance to be accomplished:

> One [way] is engaging with those companies who are ethical companies and want to do the right thing. We are already doing that. I'm already having lots of good conversations with good companies who want to make sure their systems are OK and we give them our views, there are no non-prosecution guarantees but it is just our views on what we think are adequate from our experience of seeing others. So we engage with those good companies and we very much welcome them coming to talk to us and we are happy to have that dialogue and that is part of the preventative side of this. We are looking to get out there and get the message out there and help people to get to the right place if they are not there already (UK Investigator/Prosecutor Interview 114).

In the UK and Germany, law enforcement authorities actively engage with the private sector at corporate conferences and seminars whereby prosecutors and investigators are present on panels and discussion groups. Corporate representatives can approach regulators during scheduled sessions but also informally. Through such meetings, regulators and corporations are able to develop relationships which can subsequently lead to the negotiation of self-regulation and compliance. Corporations have also been advised to contact overseas British officials working in jurisdictions where the corporation operates or intends to initiate business. Corporations can obtain informal advice on appropriate operating procedures from local British officials who are knowledgeable of the cultural and legal frameworks in the 'high-risk' foreign jurisdictions within which business might take place. Corporations are then able ensure proportionate systems and risk assessments are in place. These practices represent a key relationship between the regulator and the regulatee, a relationship which appears as prominent in the majority of literature in regulation theory.

Such relationships reflect the needs of nation-states to be seen as being active in responding to transnational corruption in light of international pressure and scrutiny from organisations such as the UN, OECD and Council of Europe. As Chapter 6 indicated, UK and German investigators and prosecutors (in addition to representatives of intergovernmental organisations) accept the reality of enforcement obstacles and are shifting towards negotiation and persuasion rather than criminal prosecution. Such persuasion is viewed as a means of changing behaviour within individual corporations by requiring the corporation to self-regulate its own behaviour under varying levels of state pressure and oversight and thus being a suitable outcome for both regulators and regulatees:

> If you look at the kind of whole ethos of the [UK] Bribery Act, it is built around people policing themselves, organizations policing themselves, especially Section 7 [corporate offence for failure to prevent bribery by employees, subsidiaries, intermediaries etc.]. It's a self-perpetuating thing that we want companies to then have adequate procedures in place to stop this happening. Ultimately if we don't prosecute anyone because everyone's got perfect systems well that's a great place to be, probably utopian in its vision, but it's very important for us to look at this change in behaviour (UK Investigator/Prosecutor Interview 114).

Thus, the state's intention with such mechanisms is to encourage corporate self-regulation but whether such self-regulation is more effective when enforced by the state with a stronger mandatory dimension or not has been frequently debated. For example, self-regulation, when enforced, may reflect negotiations between the state and individual corporations that result in flexible, particularistic standards and enforcement and which views self-regulation as a form of subcontracting regulatory functions to private actors (Ayres and Braithwaite 1992: 102–3). Enforced self-regulation 'envisions that in particular contexts it will be more efficacious for the regulated firms to take on some or all of the legislative, executive, and judicial regulatory functions. As self-regulating executives, firms

Table 7.1 Self-regulatory mechanisms at the micro-, meso- and macro-levels

Level	Self-Regulatory Mechanism	Primarily Manufactured or Organic i.e. high or low state intervention?	Origin i.e. state, commercial, inter/non-governmental organisation?	Formality i.e. prescribed framework/ rigid structure?	Specific or General i.e. individual or populations?
MICRO (e.g. individual corporations)	Informal dialogue	Manufactured	State	Informal – voluntary	Both
	Lateral litigation	Organic	Commercial	Formal – voluntary	Specific
	Monitoring	Manufactured	State	Formal – mandatory	Specific
	Self-cleaning	Manufactured	State	Formal – mandatory	Specific
	Self-investigation	Manufactured	Commercial/state	Formal – mandatory and/ or voluntary	Specific
	Self-reporting	Manufactured	Commercial/state	Formal – voluntary	Both
MESO (e.g. individual markets)	Co-regulation	Manufactured	State	Formal – mandatory	General

Key Actors	Description
i. Regulator ii. Corporates	– Building relations between regulator-regulatee to advise on behaviour change/anti-bribery policies. – Specific: Discreet meetings/dialogue. – General: Regulator representatives at corporate conferences.
i. Corporates ii. Plaintiff/litigant	– Competitors, shareholders, customers litigate for losses derived from corporate bribery. This has most notably been considered by corporations that have missed out on contracts due to bribery. Such litigation is legally and theoretically possible but remains an unknown possibility due to various obstacles e.g. difficulties in proving losses, risk of being 'outlawed' within the market, financial costs of litigation.
i. Regulator ii. Corporates iii. Monitor	– Independent monitors for fixed periods e.g. prosecutor/corporate-identified specialist firm, required as part of criminal or civil sanction.
i. Regulator ii. Corporates	– As part of civil and non-prosecution agreements, corporates required to 'self-clean' i.e. involves the corporation clarifying the relevant facts and circumstances of the corruption, repairing the damage caused, removing involved personnel and taking further structural and organizational measures.
i. Corporates ii. Regulator	– Corporations employ external, independent legal/investigatory firms to investigate suspected bribery, the findings of which are passed to the regulator to form part of case: can be instigated by the regulator following formal suspicion or by the corporate itself following detection. – Specific: requirement of formal sanctions. – General: encouraged within the market.
i. Regulator ii. Corporates	– In the UK, explicit Serious Fraud Office (SFO) policy offered probable lenient sanctioning (i.e. civil settlement) to corporations reporting corrupt behaviour within their organization. Remains a key mechanism but new SFO director removed self-report guidance and shifted powers to determine sanctions away from corporate to the Director. – Specific: individual corporations encouraged following informal dialogues. – General: all at risk corporations targeted within markets.
i. Regulator ii. Corporates	– Co-regulation theory refers to industry-associated self-regulation that involves a certain degree of state oversight and/or ratification (Grabosky & Braithwaite, 1986: 83) e.g. Financial Services Authority (FSA) (now the Financial Conduct Authority (FCA) and the Prudential Regulatory Authority (PRA)) in the UK and the Federal Financial Supervisory Authority in Germany monitor corporations to ensure sufficient compliance systems to prevent bribery and corruption (plus more) are in place.

Table 7.1 ***Concluded***

Level	Self-Regulatory Mechanism	Primarily Manufactured or Organic i.e. high or low state intervention?	Origin i.e. state, commercial, inter/non-governmental organisation?	Formality i.e. prescribed framework/ rigid structure?	Specific or General i.e. individual or populations?
MESO (e.g. individual markets)	Industry/ sector specific initiatives	Organic	Commercial	Formal – voluntary	Both
	Market-based incentives	Organic	Commercial	Informal – voluntary	Specific
	Private-private compliance	Organic	Commercial	Informal – voluntary	Specific
MACRO (e.g. multi-sector/ trans-national initiatives)	Non-state compliance guidance and tools	Organic	intergovernmental/ non-governmental organisation	Formal – voluntary	Both
	State compliance guidance	Manufactured	State	Informal – voluntary	General
	Transnational business initiatives	Organic	intergovernmental/ non-governmental organisation/ commercial	Formal – voluntary	Both

Key Actors	Description
i. Industry associations ii. Corporates iii. Regulator	– Industry specific anti-bribery and corruption initiatives usually form part of a broader intention to promote industry specific goals e.g. in the UK the Association of the British Pharmaceutical Industry (ABPI) is a trade association founded and funded by the industry and representing the views of research-based pharmaceutical companies in the UK – the ABPI's 'Code of Practice' in relation to bribery and corruption was published following 'informal dialogue' with the SFO – it indicates that while the SFO reserves the right to take action against member corporations, it will not routinely intervene with actions covered by the Code.
i. Corporates	– Corporations may promote their compliance programs (most likely after these have been 'certified' by legal experts and consultants) as a means of attracting business and therefore creating financial benefit. Corporations 'sell' their compliance concept to potential investors, partners, contracting agencies, etc., as a means of generating business, but also to reassure shareholders and regulators.
i. Corporates	– Private consultants, accountancy firms, and legal firms etc. are targeting at-risk corporations and subsequently hired to advise them on how to respond to bribery that may come to their attention, how to introduce adequate compliance procedures and systems and how to comply with the law. By employing such external firms, in many cases companies are able to receive third-party 'certification' to verify the quality of their compliance systems.
i. Non-governmental organisations ii. Intergovernmental organisations iii. Corporates	– Intergovernmental organisations such as the Organization for Economic Cooperation and Development (OECD), United Nations (UN) and Group of States against Corruption (GRECO) provide guidance and mechanisms which corporations can implement and adapt to respond potential and actual bribery and corruption. – Non-governmental organizations such as Transparency International also provide guidance and models of best practice. – General: Publications, handbooks etc. made available online for all corporations. – Specific: Intergovernmental and non-governmental organisations may also speak directly to corporations.
i. Regulator ii. Corporates	– State guidance from prosecutorial and investigatory agencies as state departments in relation to bribery legislation as well as how to implement anti-bribery and corruption compliance systems e.g. state guidance on the interpretation of the Bribery Act 2011.
i. Transnational organizations ii. Corporates	– Global, multi-industry initiatives that assist corporations in creating anti-bribery and corruption frameworks and providing tools with which to respond to internal and external bribery and extortion problems e.g. notable roles of organizations such as the International Chamber of Commerce (ICC) and the World Economic Forum Partnering Against Corruption Initiative (PACI) that provide initiatives that corporations can join and mutually support each other and promote best practice ideas.

would monitor themselves for noncompliance; and as self-regulating judges, firms would punish and correct episodes of noncompliance' (Ayres and Braithwaite 1992: 103). For Ayres and Braithwaite, it is important for such 'enforced self-regulation' to be embedded in schemes of escalating interventions where public enforcement (detection, punishment, prosecution) is retained but as discussed previously, the obstacles to enforcement practices inhibit escalation to more punitive sanctioning. That said, such processes are prominent here, in particular reflecting mechanisms of monitoring and self-cleaning at the micro-level but also co-regulation at the meso level (see below). However, determining which 'contexts' are appropriate for self-regulation in this model is also problematic. One option would be to develop a risk-based approach:

> I think that as far as self-regulation is concerned you might be able to do that if you've got an acceptable method of measuring whether a corporate culture is high risk or low risk and you might move into the self-regulation area a corporate that has effectively a low tolerance of corruption and bribery as a culture. But that presupposes that you have already done the basic work to work out what is a low risk environment … I suspect that it'll be another 10 years or so before we start seeing or being able to judge whether the measures that are put in place to try and affect corporate culture change have been effective (UK Investigator/Prosecutor Interview 112).

Currently no systematic analysis of risk-based self-regulation has been conducted by anti-corruption agencies in the UK and Germany, but the self-regulatory mechanisms manufactured by the state have been implemented based on a variety of mitigating factors. For example, the level of cooperation by a corporation, whether the corporation admits guilt, the extent of the corruption problem, whether the corporate self-reported the corruption and so on, all influence the ability of the state and corporation to negotiate appropriate responses. However, the long-term impact of such mechanisms on changing corporate cultures requires further substantiation as currently state authorities do no revisit concluded cases while sufficient time has not passed to determine their efficacy. Interestingly, such a shift toward culture changes within corporations was considered part of the 'remit' by UK investigators and prosecutors while German respondents maintained their remit remains focused on criminal prosecution and sanctioning and that culture change ought to be the responsibility of industry and corporations themselves.

Beyond state manufacture at the micro-level, an interesting but unknown potential area emerging more organically from the commercial domain is that of lateral litigation: 'the fear of what is called "third-party litigation", as it's known in the trade, can be huge' (UK Lawyer Interview 121). This refers to the risk of a corporation being sued by its competitors. For example, if in a hypothetical bidding process for a public contract, company A, which put in an equally good, if not lower, tender, in comparison to company B, subsequently lost out on the contract because company B was mysteriously allowed to re-tender and lower its tender because there was a change in specification to accommodate them, then it is likely due to corruption. If company B is then later investigated and sanctioned for bribery in this contract there is potential for company A to litigate against company B. While there has been suggestion that this may occur in the near future, at the time of writing, no such litigation has taken place. While such lateral litigation is legally and theoretically possible in both the UK and Germany, its emergence remains unclear:

> … [t]he problem is you would never be able to prove the causality. It is true that even if it is proved somebody has bribed, you still can't prove that you have lost because of that unless in a very rare case somebody testifies to that but there might be other competitors so you will never prove the causality. General Electric has been asking itself whether they should go against Siemens saying we have lost out in the 10 cases but I don't think it works. You have to prove too many other things (Intergovernmental Organisation 'A' Representative Interview 411).

Further difficulties include the unlikelihood of a company, despite their innocence, to report and/or make public the corruption as they may be viewed as an 'informer' and subsequently be ostracised within the industry sector, losing contracts as a result. This risk is too high for companies, added to by the financial costs of litigation which must be covered by the companies themselves. Similarly, class actions are legally possible in both the UK and Germany:

> You might have class actions in those countries which permit class actions because shareholders will say that now you have been named and shamed the stock price has gone down therefore the value of their investments has gone down and they can sue. One of them suing would be an irritation but twenty thousand of them suing can [be a problem] and that happens from time to time (UK Lawyer Interview 121).

Again, the likelihood of this occurring is at the time of writing unknown but such actions may begin to take place. Similar difficulties such as the cost of litigation, proving causality, and so on, exist.

Thus, predominantly manufactured but also organic mechanisms directed towards individual corporations to facilitate self-regulation are evident at the micro-level. The manufactured mechanisms analysed here reflect contemporary theories of regulation (see above) where the state retains a formal, 'steering' role in persuading or enforcing self-regulation as common characteristics are evident. However, the potential for organic mechanisms of self-regulation also becomes evident at this level where the state has no role in enforcing or persuading corporations to shift to self-regulation, but where individual corporations operating within the market identify practices to serve their own interests (for example, remuneration) but which indirectly regulate targeted corporations. This message may be communicated to other corporations at risk of offending behaviour.

Self-regulatory Mechanisms at the Meso-level

Manufactured and organic mechanisms emerging at the meso-level originate primarily, and more organically, from the commercial domain and reflect practices directed towards 'regulating' corporations at the level of *individual* markets, industries and sectors. These mechanisms include co-regulation, industry-/sector-specific initiatives, market-based incentives and private-private compliance (see Table 7.1 for explanation). Again, these mechanisms are characterised by both formal and informal frameworks (for example, handbooks provided by industry regulators or options for corporations to employ external compliance specialists) and can be both voluntary (for example, company decisions to 'sell' or market their compliance systems) and mandatory (for example, requirement of corporations to abide by industry standards). They may be targeted at specific corporations (as in the case of companies offering certification schemes to corporations perceived to be operating in at-risk jurisdictions) or at sectors or industries generally (as with industry regulators).

In relation to those mechanisms emerging from the commercial domain, a key analytical aspect in the origin of these mechanisms is how self-regulation relates to the importance that private sector organisations place on economic and business interests (for example, maintaining market position, profit creation) as this can lead to the emergence of direct and indirect mechanisms of regulation. With this in mind, the emergence of private sector 'regulatory' mechanisms has become something of an industry in itself in a similar manner to that identified by Nils Christie (2000) in relation to increasing prison populations in the US at that time when the potential for and occurrence of privatisation of many aspects of the prison system led in part to crime control becoming an industry. He states '[t]he crime control industry … . provides profit and work while at the same time producing control of those who otherwise might have disturbed the social process' (Christie 2000: 13).

The current private sector role in anti-corruption regulation can be considered an extension and contemporary example of these processes. For instance, in one sense public-private boundaries have become blurred even to the extent that companies suspected of transnational corporate bribery may be required to hire and pay external auditors, legal/accountancy firms, professional financial investigatory firms and so on, to investigate them and pass on all findings to the state agency responsible for investigating and prosecuting corporate bribery as part of 'self-reporting' and 'self-investigation' (as above). However, in addition, international pressure to conform to anti-corruption standards has presented numerous opportunities for private sector companies and organisations both in the UK and Germany and their actions provide a form of self-regulation that has emerged organically at the market level but which is largely voluntary. With this in mind,

> compliance is … a new business market for legal firms. So, once some legal firms take a look at this compliance market, they grow like fungi on it. Much has

> happened here [in preventing corporate bribery] but it's not just the task of the public prosecutor but also, however, the task of corporations, of consultants, and of lawyers (German Prosecutor Interview 211).

Thus, within this context, mechanisms emerging from the commercial domain create an environment whereby the market, through basic profit-making principles, is able to generate self-regulatory processes within those corporations and markets at most risk of transnational bribery in international commerce. In this sense, such organic mechanisms are not primarily concerned with developing self-regulation but with furthering the corporate interests of the creators – the self-regulatory impacts, however, are secondary as corporations buy into these services (for example, whistleblowing companies selling their services to corporations (i) generates profit for the corporation but (ii) improves anti-bribery compliance). These mechanisms have emerged organically, that is, independent of state influence, within the market but remain informal with no mandatory requirement on behalf of corporations to do so. Corporations are, however, making use of these services for a number of reasons: first, to mitigate the risk of prosecution and provide a legal defence if investigated; second, to support an awareness that ethical business practices and effective compliance can in turn generate income in fair markets and that corruption itself distorts the market and increases the costs of business; and, third, to symbolically communicate to shareholders, clients, partners, charities, pressure groups, and so on, that the organisation is socially responsible.

The shift towards such organic mechanisms has been influenced by the significant pressure that has materialised within the private sector where cultures of fear are being created, as key reports and key players sensationally frame and narrate the risk of bribery. For example, two notable publications include a PricewaterhouseCoopers (2010) report entitled, 'Will you act now or pay later?, and a KPMG (2010) report entitled, 'Blessing in disguise: How the UK Bribery Act creates opportunities for better corporate culture and control'. This latter report begins with the following paragraph:

> Some business people see the new Bribery Act as a piece of politically correct window dressing. Not so: this law has teeth, and the prosecutors are deploying accordingly. Moreover it threatens to ensnare those we would normally think of as innocent; those whose only crime is not to have taken active steps to prevent corruption (KPMG, 2010: 1).

Whatever the motivation of the companies that create such discourse ('consciousness raising', consultancy fees), there is no doubt that such publications and other sources emanating from the private sector provide a useful source of information on anti-corruption and anti-bribery compliance and raise business awareness. Such methods play a role in promoting (in)formal social control and self-regulation of corporate behaviour and cultures. Large corporations, as well as medium sized enterprises (less so small enterprises given proportionality arguments), are keen to ensure they have rigorous compliance models able to regulate the behaviour of their employees, subsidiaries, intermediaries and other third parties and therefore comply with external pressure in the form of legal standards and lobbying from intergovernmental/non-governmental organisations. The extent to which all businesses, small, medium or large, are able to implement such self-regulatory compliance systems is questionable given issues of resources and likelihood of being involved in bribery despite operating in at risk jurisdictions:

> [o]ne can say that the large corporations, so those with turnovers of several billion, that many of those corporations have in any case already established very good functioning compliance systems and take care of corruption prevention in these systems (German Lawyer Interview 221).

This may (or may not) be the case for the majority of large corporations, but cases such as Siemens have demonstrated that even such corporations may not take their compliance systems seriously. In any case there has been a significant expansion within the private sector towards private-to-private compliance and other market-based self-regulatory mechanisms but for such systems to function effectively, a positive corporate culture needs to be created and appropriately supported and accepted:

> Corporations must themselves do something … There must be clear rules: what is allowed and what isn't allowed, and this needs to be communicated … It must be discussed with each other, teams must be educated. An atmosphere must be created in which one is able to immediately address [corruption] cases. So one is jointly armed against it. So one says 'no, we're not accepting that, we're not getting involved' … If someone is left alone, the danger is great and they may become weak. But if everyone is in a team in which they feel comfortable and where the others won't want to betray or deceive them, and want to have secrets, then it's hard to become corrupt (German Police Investigator Interview 231).

Private consultancies, accountancy firms, legal firms and so on are being hired to advise multi-national corporations on how to deal with any acts of corruption that may come to their attention, how to introduce 'adequate procedures' and sufficient compliance systems and therefore how to comply with the law and manage the bribery problem. A number of firms have also emerged in the private sector that aim to offer 'whistleblower' services to all sizes of corporations. Business Keeper AG[2] in Germany is one example of this where for a monthly or yearly fee (the size of which depends on the size and revenue of the company) corporations can subscribe to the use of the Business Keeper Monitoring System that provides a certified, internet-based communication platform through which the subscribing

2 Website available at: http://www.business-keeper.com/whistleblowing-compliance.html <Accessed 10/11/2013>.

company's employees can report irregularities, abuses and risks. Whistleblowers can choose to remain anonymous or not and it is claimed that the whistleblower's identity is completely protected and that leads cannot be decrypted or interpreted by third parties including Business Keeper AG. An examiner (*sic*) (for example a compliance officer in the subscribing company, an anti-corruption investigator, an ombudsman and so on) can enter into direct dialogue with the whistleblower who continues to provide information. Such organisations provide corporations operating transnationally that may be at risk of bribing with a self-regulatory mechanism aimed at giving employees the opportunity to 'speak up' and inform the company or the regulator of potential criminal activity.

Online companies have also been created which seek to offer e-learning solutions to assist corporations in need of introducing anti-bribery and corruption training as part of their compliance systems.[3] These training courses are often customisable and can be sector specific, offering information on various aspects of bribery such as its consequences, the company's policy on bribery-related risks (for example, corporate hospitality), due diligence and associated persons and so on. Online tools are also provided to assist employees in their decision-making when faced with uncertain situations and potentially corrupt actions. Such e-learning solutions are also available from other non-profit sources. The UN Global Compact and the UN Office on Drugs and Crime jointly provide an e-learning tool that uses six interactive learning modules to further the audience's understanding of the Global Compact's principles against corruption as well as the UNCAC as it applies to the private sector. Online, video modules cover issues including receiving and giving gifts and hospitality, facilitation payments and corruption, the use of intermediaries and lobbyists, corruption and social investments and insider information. Both organisations encourage corporations to integrate this e-learning tool into their own anti-bribery and corruption learning frameworks requiring no fees or subscriptions to do so, unlike the private sector equivalents.

By employing such external firms, in many cases companies are able to receive third-party 'certification' to verify the quality of their compliance systems:

> Yes, the industry's being used and there is a lot of third party certification. One motivation is to have a document in your filing cupboard that you pick up when something goes wrong and you say we are well organized here we are – they certified it. The alternative is that you proactively go out with it and say this is our business model – we are the best – you don't risk being cheated with us (Intergovernmental Organisation 'A' Representative Interview 411).

Rigorous compliance regimes can mitigate the decision to prosecute. The Section 7 offence of the UK Bribery Act 2010 in relation to 'adequate procedures' has not

3 For an example see: http://www.inmarkets.com/anti-bribery-training.html <Accessed 10/11/2013>.

yet been tested with the meaning of 'adequate' therefore remaining unclear. But corporations may promote their compliance programs (most likely after these have been 'certified' by legal experts and consultants, as above) as a means of attracting business and therefore creating financial benefit. This marketing of a company's compliance program may be based on the premise that it will generate more income (minus the costs of implementation and monitoring) through obtaining more contracts as contracting agencies are more likely to award contracts to overtly ethical companies. As one intergovernmental organisation representative indicated:

> I think the award is the market. It has to pay on the market otherwise they won't do it because business is motivated by self-interest. So if it pays to be compliant, well, you evade risk but also it is a selling argument, then OK, it works. If you ruin your career as a manager by not complying or the other way round, if your company has a better image and this reflects on the books at the end and that is the motivation' (Intergovernmental Organisation 'A' Representative Interview 411).

Additionally, as a PwC report in Germany demonstrated, corporations with a positive culture are more frequently and more convincingly able to communicate their strict anti-corruption policies externally with the result that their employees appear 'incorruptible' and subsequently find themselves less frequently in situations where bribes are expected (PwC (Germany) 2010: 4) or indeed demanded. Siemens is one example of this promotion of a corporation's compliance system. Following the bribery scandals, as discussed in Chapter 2, Siemens implemented significant regime change including a substantial overhaul to the anti-bribery and corruption compliance system. A presentation from a Siemens compliance officer argued 'Siemens has fundamentally changed and is now seen as an industry benchmark in compliance and sustainability'.[4] Siemens has actively promoted and marketed their compliance approach, 'selling' the concept to potential investors, partners, contracting agencies, and so on., as a means of generating business, but also to reassure shareholders and regulators (Siemens had a monitor appointed by the DoJ/SEC to watch their compliance progress). In June 2011 Siemens reported a potential bribery scheme to the US and German authorities with it being suggested Siemens was keen 'to showcase its revamped compliance program' – Siemens pointed out that the subsequent Munich investigation, rather than being a mark against the company, was actually a positive as it demonstrated that sufficient measures are in place to prevent a corrupt deal taking place.[5] Such is the influence

4 Presentation available at: http://www.siemens.com/sustainability/pool/collectiveaction/ourlearnings/pdf/Siemens_ComplianceProgram_EN.pdf <Accessed 10/11/2013>.

5 See *Wall Street Journal* blog *Corruption Currents*: *'Siemens Compliance Program Made The Catch, Company Says'*, 10/06/2011 available at: http://blogs.wsj.com/corruption-currents/2011/06/10/siemens-compliance-program-made-the-catch-company-says/ <Accessed 10/11/2013>.

of Siemens' compliance programme, the six guiding principles outlined in the UK government's 'adequate procedures' guidance for Section 7 UKBA can all be found in the Siemens programme (albeit the UK guidance is not as extensive or detailed). This marketing of a company's compliance programme may be based on the premise that it will generate more income (minus the costs of implementation and monitoring) through obtaining more contracts as contracting agencies are more likely to award contracts to overtly ethical companies. Alternatively, it may be a means of satisfying the demands of regulators and intergovernmental/non-governmental organisations. In either case, the secondary benefit is that risk may be evaded, with the primary benefit for the corporation being that such promotion of a company's compliance program can provide financial benefits. This is an example of secondary, organic self-regulation.

Sector-specific and/or industry-specific anti-bribery and corruption initiatives initiated by the state have also emerged. Such state-triggered mechanisms reflect current regulation theory where preoccupation remains with the 'regulatory' agency. These initiatives usually form part of a broader intention to promote industry-specific goals and have become more prominent since the increased focus on transnational bribery at the international and national levels. For example, co-regulation represents a form of self-regulation manufactured by the state which imposes mandatory requirements on regulated corporations to ensure anti-bribery compliance under oversight from the state. The Financial Services Authority (FSA) is an example of such co-regulation. The FSA was set up by government and was accountable to Treasury Ministers and therefore Parliament. The government was responsible for the overall scope of the FSA's regulatory activities and powers. However, the FSA operated independently of government but had statutory powers in line with the Financial Services and Markets Act 2000. The organisation had rule-making, investigatory and enforcement powers to meet these statutory objectives. The FSA was a company limited by guarantee and was funded by the financial services industry, that is to say, the organisations that it regulated. The FSA regulated most financial services markets, exchanges and firms (over 29,000) and influentially set the standards that they were required to meet. If these standards were not met, the FSA could take action against these firms. As part of its remit, the FSA ensured that corporations had sufficient compliance systems to prevent bribery and corruption with particular cases reinforcing its ability to regulate and enforce the law to encourage its standards to be met. For example, the FSA fined insurance broker Willis Limited £6.895m for failings in its anti-bribery and corruption systems and controls.[6] According to the FSA, these failings created an unacceptable risk that payments made by Willis Limited to overseas third parties could be used for corrupt purposes. In 2013, the FSA was split into the Financial Conduct Authority (FCA) and Prudential Regulation Authority (PRA) with the above responsibilities allocated to each organisation. In Germany, the equivalent organisation is the *Bundesanstalt für Finanzdienstleistungsaufsicht* (Federal Financial Supervisory

6 http://www.bbc.co.uk/news/business-14233610 <Accessed 10/11/2013>.

Authority, 'BaFin') which has a similar function and remit, working independently but subject to oversight by the *Bundesministeriums der Finanzen* (Federal Ministry of Finance). However, as one UK prosecutor indicated:

> Where are we in relation to regulation? The FSA for example – its approach is a risk based approach and what a risk based approach means is that you focus for greater scrutiny those organisations which on some kind of scale you consider to be more likely to be at risk. Now that in one way is a way of trying to use thin resources more rationally and more effectively but the very fact that you are having a risk based approach suggests that you don't have enough resources to regulate to the same standard and scrutiny every part of the market (UK Investigator/Prosecutor Interview 112).

Thus, such co-regulatory agencies represent a more traditional form of industry-wide self-regulation as understood within more narrow conceptions of self-regulation, but this approach implicitly points to the lack of resources and/or inability of the state to regulate whole markets to the same degree of scrutiny.

But sector/industry-specific mechanisms can also be more organic. An example of this in the UK is the Association of the British Pharmaceutical Industry (ABPI) which is a trade association founded and funded by the industry and representing the views of research-based pharmaceutical companies in the UK. In June 2011 the ABPI published guidance in the form of a MoU for its members (who make up 90 per cent of the UK industry) on the overlap between the UKBA and the APBI's Code of Practice that is administered by the Prescription Medicines Code of Practice Authority. This was published following liaison ('informal dialogue') with the SFO and outlines the SFO's support for the self-regulation policy of the industry, indicating that while the SFO reserves the right to take action against member corporations, it will not routinely intervene with actions covered by the ABPI's Code of Practice. Similar provisions and initiatives of trade associations can be found in Germany. Remaining with the pharmaceutical industry, for example, in 2004 the Association of the Research Based Pharmaceutical Companies (*Die Mitgliedsunternehmen des Verbands Forschender Arzneimittelhersteller*) founded the *Freiwillige Selbstkontrolle für die Arzneimittelindustrie e. V* (Voluntary Self-Control for the Pharmaceutical Industry) which outlines a code of practice incorporating anti-corruption elements.

Thus, at the meso-level, where self-regulatory mechanisms emerge at the level of markets and industries, there is more often an organic component and commercial involvement as opposed to direct state intervention. Understanding these organic mechanisms enables a broader notion of regulation to be analysed. Such mechanisms may have primary or secondary impacts as they reflect agendas and interests beyond state concerns with ensuring adequate compliance. For example, the market creates opportunities for profit creation through the establishment of companies utilising the culture of fear and concern over bribery as narrated and constructed by state, commercial and international organisations.

With this in mind, organic mechanisms, in particular those of a secondary nature, offer new ways of thinking about regulation beyond a focus on specific regulatory agencies and in response to the nature of the problem.

Self-regulatory Mechanisms at the Macro-level

At the macro-level, a mixture of informal organic and manufactured, and state, commercial and intergovernmental/non-governmental organisations' self-regulatory mechanisms are evident. It is at the macro-level that international self-regulatory standards and rules are created for implementation by governments and corporations. (There are clear commonalities here with Abbot and Snidal's (2013) 'transnational regulatory standard-setting'.) In this sense, the origin of self-regulatory mechanisms at the macro-level is often through the moral entrepreneurship of organisations and actors where agendas based on informed moral and ethical principles in relation to corruption are pursued – it is such entrepreneurship that has framed the (self-)regulatory responses at the micro- and meso-levels:

> Rules are the products of someone's initiative and we can think of the people who exhibit such enterprise as *moral entrepreneurs* (Becker 1973: 147, emphasis in original).

If, as Howard Becker noted, 'crusading reformers', unsatisfied by the current rules and profoundly disturbed by some given evil, exist in society, then in relation to transnational corporate bribery, these moral entrepreneurs are largely to be found within intergovernmental organisations and other campaigning organisations: '[o]ne of the most significant changes in recent years is that the "who" in "who governs?" must now be expanded to include the participation of nongovernmental and noncorporate actors' (Haufler, 2006: 92). International organisations such as the UN, the OECD and GRECO, as well as non-governmental organisations such as TI, Global Witness and Global Financial Integrity, amongst others, shape and narrate the anti-corruption landscape and subsequently develop anti-corruption 'rules' with the intention of influencing corporate behaviour: '[the] fact is … [c]ompliance does not appear free willingly but results from increasing pressure from outside' (PwC (Germany) 2010: 3).

These organisations have influenced self-regulatory mechanisms within corporations in two main ways. First, they have narrated and constructed the bribery problem by producing discourse on the extent and nature of corruption, on state enforcement and so on, and in doing so aim to influence legal frameworks which subsequently increase pressure within the private sector to conform to anti-corruption laws. Second, they have directly produced policy documents specifically for corporations to assist them in creating effective compliance regimes and thus assist them in regulating their own behaviour. Such mechanisms have emerged organically but provide formal, voluntary standards for corporations. For example, the OECD (2010) published a document entitled 'Good Practice Guidance on Internal Controls, Ethics, and Compliance' which is based on findings of the OECD's Working Group on Bribery as well as consultations with the private sector and civil society. This document provides a framework and guidelines for corporations at a high level of generality which can be implemented as corporations wish. This reflects the 'functional equivalence' position of the OECD that promotes 'goals' ahead of 'means'. Providing such frameworks accounts for the diverse nature of corporate cultures, enabling corporations to adapt mechanisms suitable for their organisation:

> Corporate cultures can be so multifaceted … I have a lot to do with various corporations and it's unbelievable. It's almost like with natural persons. You can feel just how different the cultures are when you go into a corporation, you can just tell what type of culture it is and because they can be so varied, I don't believe you can say that the authorities must bear responsibility [for each corporation] (German Lawyer Interview 221).

TI (2010) has published guidance on good practice procedures for corporate anti-bribery programs in relation to the UK Bribery Act. This document is much more wide-ranging, extensive and detailed than the official guidance by the UK government or the framework provided by the OECD above. It provides analysis of the UK Bribery Act in addition to practicable and operational guidance on creating a sufficient control environment, risk assessment, policies and procedures, implementation, applying due diligence and monitoring and review. Other key initiatives include the United Nations Global Compact which is a strategic policy initiative for businesses reinforcing that the private sector shares responsibility for addressing corruption and bribery. Although a voluntary initiative, there is a mandatory requirement for participating businesses to annually disclose certain performance changes. Additionally, non-profit organisations such as TRACE provide several core services and products such as due diligence reports on commercial intermediaries, model compliance policies, online resources centres, in-person and online anti-bribery training and research on corporate best practices. These initiatives are directed towards populations of corporates operating in specific sectors. Through their critical reports, policy frameworks, practical guidance, increasing public awareness and support and/or via political lobbying, such organisations play a significant role in shaping legislation and advising companies on good practice and behaviour, to 'strengthen development, reduce poverty and bolster confidence in markets'.[7] As TI[8] states:

---

7 OECD website: http://www.oecd.org/department/0,3355,en_2649_34855_1_1_1_1_1,00.html <Accessed 10/11/2013>.

8 TI website: http://archive.transparency.org/news_room/faq/corruption_faq#faqcorr3 <Accessed 10/11/2013>.

> We are committed nonetheless to the core values and principles that have guided our work from the inception of our movement in 1993. The basic principles of TI's anti-corruption struggle have been defined from the start: coalition building, proceeding incrementally, and remaining non-confrontational. What does this mean? TI believes that keeping corruption in check is only feasible if representatives from government, business and civil society work together to agree on a set of standards and procedures they all support. TI also believes that corruption cannot be rooted out in one big sweep. Rather, fighting it is a step-by-step, project-by-project process. TI condemns bribery and corruption vigorously and courageously wherever it has been reliably identified, although TI does not seek to expose individual cases of corruption. Finally, TI's non-confrontational approach is necessary to get all relevant parties around the table.

The evocative, rhetorical and symbolic language used by TI indicates the enterprise of such organisations whereby the long-term goal is to implement rule and enforcement change through moral persuasion. Board members of TI national chapters, and other such organisations, are largely constituted of individuals with extensive experience with anti-corruption who emanate from legal, business and political backgrounds and these individuals, due to their knowledge and expertise, can hold significant influence over legislature. TI highlights its key accomplishments as putting corruption on the global agenda by breaking the taboo against speaking out on corruption, as playing a vital role in anti-corruption conventions (TI was involved in drafting UNCAC and was closely involved in the OECD Anti-Bribery Convention) and as raising standards in public life by helping to define certain behaviours as corrupt, such as the improper acceptance of gifts. Whether such rule changes, as Becker suggests, will be good for those companies, is largely dependent on perspective (some in business view bribery as common practice and a cultural necessity in order to facilitate legitimate commerce and would not consider themselves as 'outsiders'). However, it has to be agreed that in relation to the class structures that Becker referred to, those in less favourable positions stand to benefit from the rule changes.

Also at the transnational level, a number of global, multi-industry organic initiatives have emerged to assist companies in creating anti-bribery and corruption frameworks. These initiatives provide formal, voluntary frameworks, albeit once joined, corporations face mandatory requirements (for example, appropriate compliance systems). This industry and market-based mechanism demonstrates a significant level of cooperation and mutual support and provides a means of triggering changes in corporate behaviour through the promotion of good practice by significant international 'players'. Most notable are the roles of the International Chamber of Commerce (ICC), and the World Economic Forum Partnering Against Corruption Initiative (PACI). The ICC considers itself the 'voice of world business', speaking with authority on behalf of corporations throughout the world in different sectors. The Anti-Corruption Commission of the ICC encourages self-regulation by enterprises in confronting issues of extortion and bribery and provides business input into international initiatives to fight corruption. In 2005 the ICC published a revised version of its 'Rules and Recommendations to Combat Extortion and Bribery' that provides substantive rules and implementation procedures for voluntary application by enterprises. The ICC has also published a number of versions (most recent 2008) of a handbook on international corporate integrity and fighting corruption. The World Economic Forum's PACI is a transnational, multi-industry initiative that provides a platform for companies to commit to developing, implementing and monitoring anti-bribery and corruption programmes and systems through peer network meetings and the use of private sector-driven support tools. The PACI's rationales for addressing corruption are fourfold, there being significant financial, legal, ethical and socio-economic incentives to do so. For example, PACI states that corruption increases the costs of doing business globally by 10 per cent on average, while doing business with integrity attracts and retains principled, motivated employees and ethically oriented investors (although not if you have a product that is inferior to others and costs insufficiently less to get the business other than by corruption).

Below such international organisations, nation-states also produce anti-bribery compliance frameworks directed towards the private sector as a whole, encouraging corporations to voluntarily implement recommendations. For example, the UK Bribery Act 2010 compliance guidance explains the policy behind the law and aims to support commercial organisations of all sizes and sectors in understanding what sorts of procedures can be put in place to prevent bribery. Such guidance is not prescriptive, taking a more informal, voluntary approach, but is targeted at all corporations who might commit transnational bribery. The decentralised nature of Germany's anti-corruption system (see Chapter 5) whereby each *Bundesland* is responsible for anti-corruption enforcement, but without specific anti-corruption agencies, means that publications are more likely to be produced at this level, emanating from specific public prosecutors and/or State Criminal Investigation Offices. For example, although no such formal 'guidance' on the law exists, as it does in the UK, enforcement agencies are still able to advise corporations on appropriate anti-bribery mechanisms. One initiative from one *Bundesland* reflects the interdisciplinary approach of the *Bundesland* whereby a 'working group' (made up of representatives from enforcement, academia, lawyers, private sector corporations, courts and so on) has over the last few years published guidance on hospitality and corruption. This publication presents corporations with a traffic light system that can be used to determine what constitutes bribery or accepted business practice. For example, individuals are advised as to what is allowed ('green'), what is prohibited ('red') and what requires authorisation ('yellow/amber'). According to the document, 'the objective of the traffic-light concept is to describe an operational framework that is to be satisfied and clearly defined by corporations in the framework of their compliance strategies in addition to the agreement of standards whose communication and training are permanently monitored for compliance'.[9]

9 Taken from publication provided during data collection.

A key theme throughout these mechanisms in both the UK and Germany is the how change in the corporate culture can be engineered and how this needs to be shaped around an anti-bribery ethic within the corporation itself. Reflecting the six guiding principles to the UK Bribery Act (see Chapter 4), one German lawyer stated:

> In order to change corporate cultures, I believe, there is one point that is absolutely the most important point. The most important point that is more important than any instruction is 'the tone from the top'. The management must make a clear decision whether they take it serious or whether don't take it serious. When the management takes the middle ground, then it can't be that great of a compliance system … . This was the case at Siemens as well as other corporations where they introduced a system but the 'tone from the top' was just not congruous and then the best system is of no use because the people don't have the spirit to say 'we simply stand for doing things correctly'. This spirit must be borne out of the corporate culture (German Lawyer Interview 221).

This outlines the practical difficulties when triggering compliance systems that are able to reduce the occurrence of bribery. For example, while state compliance guidance may provide frameworks within which corporations can locate their self-regulatory models, there is the risk that such models will not be fully supported, a concern also raised by both UK and German prosecutors and investigators:

> … I am not sure that the current mechanisms that are being tried for changing corporate culture will necessarily be that effective. You know, the kind of corporate ethos policy and so on, because if you have a look, the US has had those running for many years and it doesn't seem to have necessarily reduced the number of either serious frauds perpetrated by senior managers or indeed corruption matters (UK Investigator/Prosecutor 112).

The impact of such initiatives on changing corporate cultures requires further substantiation. However, both manufactured and organic mechanisms at the macro-level, emanating from the state and commercial domains but primarily from intergovernmental/non-governmental organisations, noticeably shape the anti-corruption landscapes at the micro- and meso-levels. Their origin reflects processes of moral entrepreneurship, as opposed to commercial interests or being the result of pressure or scrutiny placed on nation-states.

Key Reference Groups

A number of key reference groups can be found within this conceptual and self-regulatory framework, each with influential roles in creating the regulatory landscape in relation to the self-regulatory practices that are emerging. These groups are not conclusive or all-encompassing and may overlap or significantly interact, but the following represent key groups that emerged during the research.

– *The corporates*: not a restrictive category, this refers to any company, their overseas subsidiary, partnership, and so on, that on the whole as a legal entity operating overseas requires sufficient anti-bribery and corruption compliance mechanisms in order to regulate its own behaviour and provide a defence against extensive bribery legislation. Corporations may develop their own self-regulatory practices from within, employ the 'profiteers', take advice from or learn from literature provided by the 'moral entrepreneurs' and/or the 'negotiators', or be part of inter-corporate initiatives and academies providing information on 'best practice'.
– *The profiteers (other private sector organisations)*: this includes legal firms, accountancy firms, and so on, with expertise in anti-bribery and corruption along with companies founded specifically for the purpose of selling (and profiting from) their anti-bribery and corruption compliance systems, whistleblower systems and so on. All such companies may be employed by corporations as a means of strengthening their anti-bribery and corruption measures.
– *The moral entrepreneurs (non-private sector organisations)*: non-governmental organisations, intergovernmental organisations, charities and so on. These individuals and organisations play a significant role in lobbying government and business, subsequently influencing changes in legislation and placing bribery and corruption on the agenda. These organisations also 'negotiate' with the corporates, giving advice and providing literature on how rigorous compliance can be implemented and so on.
– *The negotiators (state regulators)*: regulatory agencies, government departments, political corruption 'champions' and so on. State actors play a significant role in negotiating, formally and informally, effective compliance regimes within corporations, leading to the emergence of self-regulatory practices. Hybrid mechanisms are also adopted to trigger self-regulation within the business sector.
– *The victims (individuals and corporations)*: those facing the negative consequences of bribery and corruption may also influence forms of self-regulation within the market. Corporations that lose out on contracts due to bribery, disgruntled shareholders of corporations that have bribed or of corporations that have lost out on contracts, employees made scapegoats and unfairly dismissed, and so on, may aim to litigate or bring class actions against corporate enabling a form of market self-regulation.
– *The others*: representatives of transnational business initiatives; also the media have significantly pressured enforcement responses and also pressured corporations.

The negotiation of self-regulation therefore incorporates a varied set of practices each with varying levels of state intervention and formality, and involves a wide range of non-state actors and agencies. The incorporation of non-state actors echoes earlier regulatory models such as Gunningham and Grabosky's (1998: 398) expanded pyramid model of smart regulation that argues for the importance of first parties (government as regulator), second parties (business as self-regulator) and third parties (both commercial and non-commercial) in broader understandings of regulation. A key theoretical difficulty, however, is their promotion of escalation of enforcement responses by any set of parties, as in hierarchical pyramids originally proposed by Ayres and Braithwaite (1992) – but when standards are not met in relation to transnational corporate bribery, criminal prosecution can rarely be reached due to the obstacles outlined earlier. However, as with these regulatory models, such self-regulatory practices as discussed here distort the boundaries between the 'public' and the 'private', and reflect the distribution of responsibility away from the state as sole provider of security, law and order and crime control.

Conclusion

Informational asymmetries mean that criminal and regulatory enforcement alone are unlikely to adequately reduce transnational bribery, and need to be supplemented by self-regulatory mechanisms. While some leverage is gained through enforcement practices, a regulatory landscape is emerging that also incorporates a variety of manufactured *and* organic self-regulatory mechanisms. These mechanisms emanate from the micro- (for example, individual corporations), meso- (for example, individual markets) and macro- (for example, multi-sector/transnational initiatives) levels and originate within three main 'domains' (state, commercial and intergovernmental/non-governmental). Within these three domains self-regulatory mechanisms have emerged that involve both state and non-state 'regulatory' actors, reflect varying levels of formality, can be specific or general and may be direct and/or indirect in their influence.

Some of these mechanisms, in particular those 'manufactured' within the state domain, reflect contemporary regulation theory (that is, state 'steering', negotiation, reflexive/responsive). Mechanisms that emerge more organically, however, offer new ways of thinking about 'regulation' in particular where the primary objective/intention may not be one of 'regulation'. In this sense, self-regulation is an artefact of the domains from which the mechanisms emanate as different agendas and interests shape their origin (for example, nation-states appeasing international scrutiny; commercial organisations furthering economic interests; moral entrepreneurship). However, the effectiveness of these emerging self-regulatory mechanisms remains unclear. Thus, the argument is not that regulatory strategies ought to be directed away from the manufactured responses of 'regulatory' agencies (for example, state regulators; orchestrating intergovernmental organisations) as such governmental authorities create important formal frameworks and ought to retain a primary role. However, shifting focus to the broader regulatory landscape to understand informal and organic mechanisms informs analytical and theoretical understandings of behaviour change within corporations at risk of being involved in transnational bribery.

Chapter 8
Understanding 'Regulatory' Performance and Determining 'Adequate' Enforcement

Introduction

A recurrent theme throughout this book is the pressure placed on nation-states by domestic and international actors to respond to transnational corporate bribery. At the international level pressures come from supra-national organisations such as the European Union (EU); intergovernmental organisations such as the United Nations (UN) and Organisation for Economic Cooperation and Development (OECD); and international, non-governmental organisations and campaign groups such as Transparency International (TI), Global Witness and Global Financial Integrity. These act through the development of international standards and conventions with which nation-states are morally and politically compelled to sign up to and implement and undertake peer review, monitoring and evaluation of states to ensure sufficient progress is being made. At the domestic level, local campaign organisations and pressure groups such as non-governmental organisations, voluntary and third-sector organisations, and those representing the interests of private-sector enterprise (who may at times be perpetrators and at other times victims) also encourage the state to engage in the effective enforcement, regulation and reduction of transnational corporate bribery.

As discussed in Chapter 1, these concerned parties often focus on law enforcement and other control mechanisms as appropriate policy responses which reflect the symbolic and moral nature of criminal justice. However, this creates tensions with national governments where there has traditionally been a preference for regulation (preferably 'self-regulation'), persuasion, negotiation and non-criminal responses to white-collar and corporate offenders (see Chapter 6; see also Slapper and Tombs, 1999; Wells, 2011; Nelken, 2012). Both self-regulation and the aversion to criminal prosecution combine ideology with pragmatism: the state considers its economic interests (that is, the prosecution of large corporations may adversely harm the generation of employment and tax) and/or the difficulties of prosecuting white-collar offenders (that is, the prosecution of well-resourced 'conscious opponents' (Sparrow, 2008) where difficulties of individual/corporate attribution of these crimes creates obstacles). Whatever the motivation, criminal prosecutions face significant procedural, evidential, legal, financial and structural challenges that reduce their plausibility and legitimacy as agents of crime control, crime reduction and justice. While shifts to self-regulation, as discussed in this book, can supplement enforcement responses, the real impact of these manufactured and organic mechanisms is unknown in the light of a dearth of data and the relatively recent emergence of such practices. Such obstacles to regulating the problem of transnational corporate bribery imply the question of how we then determine what level of 'regulation' is enough.

It remains a key issue, therefore, to understand the performance of regulatory responses and to understand when enforcement and self-regulatory responses are considered to be adequate. But how do we gain an understanding of when particular sorts of enforcement responses are sufficient and adequate, both in the instant case and taking all enforcement responses together? We can only properly assess levels and impact of state and non-state activity against transnational corporate bribery and their adequacy when we understand the levels (for example, extent and scope) and organisation of such crimes. In light of this, relative to what variables are levels of enforcement and (self-)regulation understood? How can we develop an appropriate 'threshold', against which levels of enforcement and (self-)regulation can be compared? If this is a serious problem at the national level, it is a far more difficult problem transnationally, where consistent data on both the harms and enforcement practices are unobtainable.

This chapter explores these questions and discusses their implications for methodological approaches to researching transnational corporate bribery and the subsequent implications for policing strategies. The chapter begins by considering what is and ought to be understood by 'regulatory' performance, followed by a brief analysis of the need to understand extent and scope for performance measures to have value. The chapter then goes on to explore available data to inform extent and consider current performance measures, arguing that as we can only ever understand *some* level of the problem, current performance measures cannot provide valid indicators of levels of enforcement. Instead, research and policing strategies that aim to understand the organisation and processes of transnational corporate bribery and the corresponding impact of intervention, disruption and prevention strategies provides a more useful indicator of 'regulatory performance'. The chapter concludes by outlining potential data sources and models for understanding 'regulatory performance'.

Understanding 'Regulatory' Performance

To determine 'adequate enforcement', we need to understand the available mixture of control responses. Competing (if often merely implicit) ideologies are significant given in the area of white-collar and corporate crimes there have been conflicting approaches to the most appropriate model of criminal justice and law enforcement (see Chapter 3 for detailed analysis of contemporary regulatory models). Generally, policy responses to white-collar and corporate crimes in most European jurisdictions can be located within a spectrum of 'regulatory' mechanisms. At one end of the spectrum, these are characterised by a variety of enforcement practices such as criminal prosecution, debarment, civil sanctioning, disruption/reduction/intervention strategies and licensing mechanisms where the state frequently retains a primary role in both the strategic and operational response. But at the other end policy responses also incorporate various levels of self-regulation within business and industry such as compliance mechanisms and industry/sector regulation that cover a wide-range of institutional arrangements and can differ according to the degree of monopolistic power, the degree of formality, their legal status, and the extent to which outsiders participate in rule formulation and enforcement (see for example Ogus, 1994: 108–9). The level of state intervention in such practices is often reduced, although such practices may be manufactured/stimulated by the state (for example, as part of criminal/civil sanctioning or enforced self-regulation) or may be more organic in their creation (for example, business initiatives, market responses embodying mutual self-interest). Such responses may be targeted at specific offenders or at the markets within which such offenders operate. Also, a variety of 'regulatory actors' is evident that includes both state (for example, law enforcement, industry regulators) and non-state (for example, commercial enterprises, voluntary organisations, business communities) organisations and actors.

But if we take 'enforcement' to include both traditional policing responses as well as mechanisms of (enforced) self-regulation and the corresponding multiplicity of 'regulators', we need to understand the extent and impacts of all such practices, not to mention states or conditions of 'non-enforcement' that may take the form of accommodation, collusion and/or regulatory capture where the state has no desire or is unable to provide a formal response (for analysis of these concepts see Edwards and Gill, 2002; Gill, 2002). But even if an understanding of both enforcement and non-enforcement is obtained, understanding regulatory performance, as above, is part ideological. In the absence of clear evidence for most white-collar offences about 'what works' under what circumstances, it is difficult to adjudicate between preferences for enforcement and regulation, just as there remain tensions between 'equal punishment for all' and a purer effectiveness with minimal punishment necessary perspective.

With this in mind, there is a clear problem with current attempts to understand adequate 'regulatory performance' as crude indicators of levels of enforcement (in its narrow sense) such as prosecution numbers (see below) are often used to determine how active any given jurisdiction may be in dealing with these problems and thus neglect the performance of broader 'regulatory' practices of negotiation, compliance and self-regulation. If we accept we need to understand performance in relation to this broader notion of regulation, a second problem arises in the realisation that determining how 'adequate' and 'effective' such enforcement and self-regulation practices are requires an understanding of the extent and scope of the problem. How then can we understand extent and scope?

Understanding the Extent and Scope of Transnational Corporate Bribery

> Reports that say that something hasn't happened are always interesting to me, because as we know, there are 'known knowns'; there are things we know we

> know. We also know there are 'known unknowns'; that is to say we know there are some things we do not know. But there are also 'unknown unknowns' – the ones we don't know we don't know (Donald Rumsfeld, former US Defence Secretary, 2002).[1]

When Donald Rumsfeld spoke of 'known knowns', 'known unknowns' and 'unknown unknowns' in relation to weapons of mass destruction in 2002, he took a phrase from business vocabulary to distinguish between things we know that we know, things we know we do not know, but can anticipate their existence, and things we do not know that we do not know, and therefore cannot anticipate their existence. While these phrases may have several indirect and direct meanings and therefore can be used for rhetorical purposes (for example, to refute accountability), they do point to a significant criminological limitation – the 'dark figure' of crime – that is of significant relevance in relation to transnational corporate bribery. The extent and scope of transnational corporate bribery remain difficult to estimate for the following reasons: (1) the complexities of ascertaining who if anyone is *legally* responsible for the conduct; (2) the relative 'invisibility' of such crimes, the range of actors, their relations and transactions (that is, insufficient knowledge, statistics, theory, research, control, politics and panic (see Davies et al., 1999: 5–23, for more extensive analysis of the characteristics of 'invisible crimes'); (3) the lack of identifiable consequences (for example, direct victims or harms often obscured); and (4) the knowledge and power problems faced by the state in attempts to understand corporate subsystems (see Mayntz, 1993).

In relation to white-collar and corporate crimes more generally, attempts have been made to infer extent and scope from diverse data sources such as official statistics (limited to 'enforcement' responses), perception studies, victim surveys (individuals and organisational), self-report studies and, where accessible, private-sector data (Levi, 2011). More specifically in relation to corruption and bribery, in the TI *Global Corruption Report 2007*, Kaufmann et al. (2007) identified six myths in relation to corruption measurement. Myth 1, 'corruption cannot be measured', is from the authors' perspective not the reality. They suggest corruption can be measured (i) by gathering informed views of relevant stakeholders (for example, firms, public officials, non-governmental organisations, experts and so on), (ii) by tracking countries' institutional features (for example, to determine opportunities of incentives for corruption and therefore provide useful indications of the possibility of corruption) and (iii) by careful audits of specific projects (for example, financial audits and comparisons of spending with the physical output of projects in order to provide project specific corruption). Myths 2 and 3 relate to the vague, generic and unreliable subjective data that is obtained from perception studies. The authors argue that perceptions of corruption are sometimes the best and only information available, suggesting that perceptions matter directly in that they

1 Quote used in article *BBC*: '*Rum remark wins Rumsfeld an reward*', 02/12/2003, available at: http://news.bbc.co.uk/1/hi/3254852.stm <Accessed 10/11/2013>.

influence individuals' behaviour towards institutions and so on. This may be the case but it does not inform an understanding of measurement or extent. Kaufmann et al. also suggest specific survey questions that enable more specific and focused findings (although it could be said such questions remain distanced from the social context); and that any kind of data measurement involves an irreducible element of uncertainty. Myths 4 and 5 suggest that though the nature of corruption makes it virtually impossible to satisfy policymakers' desires for objective measures, specific, focused surveys can aid in identifying priority areas for action. Myth 6, the notion that countries perceived to have high levels of corruption also have fast economic growth, is also challenged by the authors who argue that in the medium to long term adverse effects can be seen. In short, available empirical data is weak, and no strategy will yield a perfect measure of corruption.

Where collected by the state, data may also be inaccessible, although recording practices vary by jurisdiction. In the UK, for example, the Serious Fraud Office (SFO) maintains an Anti-Corruption Register of all suspicions, allegations and cases of corporate corruption but these figures are private, although other enforcement agencies are granted access. SFO data are available only in their Annual Reports and prosecutions are included in Ministry of Justice statistics, but not in recorded crime data. Likewise, neither general victimisation and self-report studies (for example, Crime Survey for England and Wales) nor business victimisation surveys (Home Office, 2012) have ever included crimes by corporations against consumers, workers or taxpayers in the UK or elsewhere. Similar difficulties exist elsewhere, such as in Germany, where enforcement statistics are centrally collected and inaccessible within the individual *Bundesländer*.

Beyond official statistics, attempts to measure corruption have been made in numerous ways – some focus on the number of corrupt transactions that take place in a country, others analyse the amount of money that changes hands as part of corrupt transactions (Bardhan, 2006: 342). Theoretical models have measured corruption as a percentage of government officials that are willing to accept a bribe (Çule and Fulton, 2005) and by the size of the bribe (Cadot, 1987; Choi and Thum, 2005). Other methodologies include the use of public expenditure tracking surveys, service provider surveys and enterprise surveys to collect quantitative micro-level data (Reinikka and Svensson, 2006). In addition, there have been approaches involving axiomatic measurements that entail formal definition of potentially important properties of a measure and then classification of measures according to such properties (Foster et al., 2009) and approaches involving corruption-victimisation measures based on survey research (Seligson, 2006). International organisations, such as the World Bank and the World Economic Forum, have conducted large-scale surveys, but the main source of data more broadly comes from studies of perception, such as TI's Corruption Perceptions Index and Bribe Payers Index, but such studies are methodologically limited by their focus on perceptions only. The key question is whether the trend data produced provides valid indicators of corruption, even if numbers might not be accurate. In this sense, some measures may be more convincing than others, for example, self-report surveys and victimisation studies may offer more reliable data than perception studies, while the collation of empirical datasets may increase understanding of levels of transnational corruption. However, retaining the analytical focus on measurement of the problem can inform us only of *some* level extent and scope.

In sum, the limitations in measuring and understanding the extent and scope of corruption – especially transnational corruption – raise the question as to how an appropriate 'threshold', against which enforcement and self-regulatory efforts can be compared, can ever be determined. Given this flaw, against which variables should 'adequate enforcement' be measured and, more specifically, can 'adequate enforcement' ever be determined?

How Do We Determine the Adequate Enforcement of Transnational Corporate Bribery?

Current Approaches to Determining Adequacy

According to TI's 2013 progress report on the enforcement of the OECD Anti-Bribery Convention 1997, only three European countries (Germany, the UK, Switzerland) are considered to be 'active enforcers' of foreign bribery. The remaining European countries included in the report are located within the categories of 'moderate', 'limited' or 'little or no' enforcement. Levels of enforcement are assessed using arbitrary thresholds that aim to consider a combination of the share of world exports of a country along with the number of investigations, cases and sanctions for foreign bribery in the most recent four year period. For example, thresholds for enforcement are based on a country's actual percentage of world exports together with a points system that weights different enforcement actions: 1 point for commencing investigations (pre-trial phase), 2 points for commencing cases (trial phase of a legal procedure), 4 points each for commencing major cases or concluding cases with sanctions, and 10 points for concluding major cases with substantial sanctions. (It is unclear why these points thresholds have been allocated.)

Substantial is defined by TI as sanctions that include 'deterring prison sentences, large fines, appointment of a compliance monitor, and/or disqualification from future business'. In previous reports TI failed to define what was meant by substantial and in this instance defines it ambiguously. For example, there is no clarification of what length or form of prison sentence begins to act as a deterrent (should suspended sentences be included?), or whether 'large fines' are considered in relation to an individual's or company's overall turnover and profits, or whether a monitor ought to be appointed by the enforcement authorities rather than the corporate – these are key issues. The blanket application to multiple jurisdictions of this methodology also fails to consider local contexts, for example, understanding in which jurisdictions corporations conduct their overseas business and in which sectors are they involved is necessary for meaningful comparison. In the report, the UK and Germany required scores of 152 and 344 to be categorised as 'active' and scored 251 and 464 respectively in addition to meeting the requirement of commencing or concluding at least one major case in the four year period. The general trend appears to be the larger the share of world exports, the more 'active' a country is at enforcing the OECD Convention – this superficial methodology reinforces the need to understand enforcement responses in the context of the proportion of all bribery cases, otherwise such analyses are meaningless beyond raising awareness of corruption and bribery.

In previous reports, the methodology employed by TI used cumulative raw numbers (for example, number of prosecutions, investigations and cases since the OECD Convention came into force) combined with a country's share of world exports. The use of raw numbers rather than the proportion of estimated cases dealt with again presented problems for understanding levels of enforcement as well as for comparative understandings between jurisdictions. In TI's 2012 report, 'active enforcers' referred to those countries with a share of world exports over 2 per cent and with at least 10 major cases on a cumulative basis, at least three of which were initiated in the last three years and resulted in 'substantial sanctions' (see above). The category 'active enforcer' could also be given to those countries with less than 2 per cent world export shares but these countries had to have brought at least three major cases, at least one of which resulted in substantial sanctions and at least one case pending that was initiated in the last three years. Again, these thresholds were arbitrary and were not premised on any logical foundation (for example, it is unclear why the threshold was 10 major cases – it is possible that this was set as a number that allows a 'reasonable number' of countries to meet the target). The UK and Germany were identified as 'active' enforcers – from the dates when the OECD Convention came into force in the respective countries up until the end of 2011, Germany has concluded 176 cases (of which more than 16 were 'major') and the UK had concluded 23 cases (all 'major' – and until August 2012).

In both approaches, enforcement is considered more active and acceptable once a certain number of investigations and prosecutions are being regularly concluded or when prosecution numbers satisfy the informed perspectives of those 'moral entrepreneurs' that played such a significant role in the generation of rules. But how such measures reflect a reduction in prosecution numbers due to effective prevention strategies through, for example, corporate compliance and/or situational measures that remove the opportunities for corruption is uncertain. Prosecution numbers without an understanding of proportion are an insufficient measure of 'enforcement/regulatory performance'.

Although the TI statistics incorporate economic variables such as share of world exports as comparison points, meaningful comparisons cannot be made, given the lack of recognition they give to other key variables, not to mention the social context of regulation and bribery. For example, against what denominator are these enforcement statistics being measured for them to represent active enforcement? While world export shares may be used as markers for the categorisation of these jurisdictions within 'active enforcement', this gives a false picture of active enforcement in terms of the broader regulatory landscape e.g. prevention, disruption and reduction strategies, and therefore may fail to explain how local regulatory regimes and cultures might better explain these (apparent) differences.

For example, hypothetically it may be the case that Germany has high levels of undetected corruption but retains the 'active enforcer' category for prosecuting a small percentage of this corruption; while other jurisdictions such as Finland or Sweden have lower perceived levels of corruption than Germany[2] but may be prosecuting a higher proportion of these – the percentage of all corruption offences being prosecuted is currently unknowable in any country. Likewise, the Netherlands are considered to have 'little or no enforcement' but according to TI's Bribe Payers Index 2011, corporations from the Netherlands are least likely to bribe abroad which may reflect a more effective set of self-regulatory mechanisms but which receive no recognition in enforcement numbers. Neither do the statistics distinguish between different cases as can be seen with the Siemens case which accounts for over 20 of the prosecutions in Germany, which distorts the picture. International studies such as TI's Bribe Payers Index and Corruption Perceptions Index inform understandings of the extent of transnational bribery, perhaps more so than estimations of the problem by enforcement authorities (whose estimations are based on those cases that come to their attention). In addition, other variables such as the number of companies registered; the size of the corporation and its importance in the economy; the type of products traded; the Gross Domestic Product; and the available enforcement resources along with many significant legal, procedural, evidential and financial processes are not acknowledged. These variables would provide different measures against which prosecution numbers could be considered. Thus, 'active enforcement' in current terms does not necessarily reflect effective anti-corruption systems or measures and does not inform any understanding of the extent of the corruption problem.

An understanding of extent requires the collation and analysis of multiple data sources. Such data sources do exist to some extent and emanate from the private, public and third sectors and are located at the local, national and supranational level (see Table 8.3). In this sense, such sources provide proxies for the missing data outlined above and provide data on both traditional enforcement mechanisms of state investigation and prosecution but also mechanisms of a self-regulatory nature.

2 They are both ranked as less corrupt in TI's Corruption Perceptions Index 2012 although perception-based surveys have obvious limitations. The sample of respondents for TI's CPI is calculated using data from 13 sources. 2012 results available here: http://cpi.transparency.org/cpi2012/results/<Accessed 10/11/2013>.

Table 8.1 Potential data sources at the micro-, meso- and macro-levels

Level	Key organisations	Data
Micro	Individual corporations and business enterprises operating transnationally.	– Data on contextual factors such as how often bribes are requested from corporations and in which areas (geographical and business) etc. (see points 1–6 below).
	Media outlets	– Accounts of investigative journalism as developed through sustained and focused investigations. – Exposés on multi-national corporations e.g. *The Guardian* and BAE Systems.
	Activist groups	– Case construction and analysis to support lobbying and moral entrepreneurship. – Exposés
Meso	Industry and trade associations of transnational sectors and markets.	– Industry/trade data generated through member surveys and monitoring of financial transactions and market performance.
	Whistleblowing organisations external to corporations.	– Data on reported cases from multiple sectors/industries, internal/external reporting and responses and outcomes.
Macro	National/regional level enforcement and regulatory agencies.	– Data collated on number of cases detected (via myriad sources), on number of cases investigated (or not) and of number of cases concluded (whether (non-)prosecution or closure).
	International organisations e.g. non-governmental organisations such as TI.	– Large-scale survey data based on self-report studies, victimisation surveys and studies of perceptions etc.
	Intergovernmental organisations e.g. OECD, UN.	– Country monitoring to establish enforcement activity whereby investigation and prosecution numbers are collated for jurisdictions.
	Transnational business initiatives e.g. World Economic Forum.	– Market/sector data generated through disclosure of financial transactions by member corporations and data collected through member surveys.

To determine 'adequate' or 'active' enforcement, consideration needs to be given to the variety of enforcement *and* self-regulatory mechanisms, along with aspects of repression *and* prevention/reduction. Determining an appropriate 'threshold' against which enforcement and self-regulatory mechanisms should be compared is problematic for a number of the reasons outlined above. However, a useful place to start would be within the social contexts where such bribery and corruption occur and where the necessary and contingent relations of corporate bribery can be fully explored and understood. For example, in addition to the methodologies outlined above (such as victim surveys and self-report studies and so on) data collected by and on corporations' anti-bribery and corruption compliance departments with regard to the following processes would aid understandings of the impacts of self-regulatory mechanisms:

1. The number of corporations implementing 'certified' anti-bribery and corruption compliance systems and the extent to which these are regularly monitored and adapted, for example, as compelled by formal or informal self-regulatory mechanisms.
2. The frequency (for example, how often are bribe requests made to the company), intensity (for example, how insistent are bribe requests), intention (for example, facilitation of otherwise legitimate service, to win or maintain business contracts, to be accepted in the tendering process and so on) and type (for example, cash bribes, services, hospitality and so on) of bribery and the extent to which these factors change over time and correlate to different localities.
3. The risk assessments of foreign jurisdictions that are conducted by corporations or third-party experts (for example, how is the risk of corruption determined?), and the extent to which these risk assessments change over time and why. For example, have corporate compliance mechanisms reduced bribe frequency in country A and in what ways?
4. The identification and recruitment of potential bribers within the corporation by external solicitors/demanders of bribes for example at which organisational level are employees approached (for example, executives, middle-managers, low-level employees), do these represent particularly 'at risk' positions (for example, high contact with foreign officials, independent positions and so on), are certain corporate departments consistently approached (for example, telecommunications, construction and so on)?
5. Public disclosure and increased transparency of payments made to foreign public officials and governments for public contracts (in line with the Publish What You Pay (PWYP) initiative in the extractive industries: http://www.publishwhatyoupay.org/).
6. Public disclosure of country-by-country reporting of financial performance broken down into production, profits, sales and costs to enable transparency of contracts and transactions and discrepancies to be identified.

These processes represent only some of those involved in bribery but an understanding of these would inform an understanding of transnational corporate bribery and more specifically, an understanding of 'effective' prevention and control. The impact of corporations' compliance mechanisms on the regulation of transnational corporate bribery could therefore be measured over time. For example, to what extent are companies operating in high-risk country A receiving fewer bribe demands/requests over time, and how has this been influenced by company policies? Of course, such an approach assumes both that the majority of corporations are good, ethical organisations willing to collect such data accurately and honestly. (There may be many legitimate reasons why they would not wish to such as too much transparency on their legitimate business transactions that may influence competition and the market.) It also focuses only on the 'demand-side' of bribery, or passive bribery. Those corporations actively committing bribery would unlikely be reached without some form of mandatory, regulatory intervention (albeit compulsory self-reporting is arguably a violation of the privilege against self-incrimination). If corporations can be encouraged or compelled to collect such data, an understanding of the impacts of self-regulatory mechanisms on bribery reduction could be explored (although gaining access to this data without formal regulatory coercion would prove difficult). Thus, the problem of transnational corporate bribery could be made more tangible through methodological innovations in researching the organisation of serious crimes such as corporate victim surveys; but also by altering the research question to ask how known incidents of bribery were organised and what such 'known knowns' do for criminological understanding. The latter would assist corporations' own efforts as well as criminological thinking.

As things stand, however, how 'adequate' or 'active' enforcement may be cannot be determined without some inference about the volume of crime from victim surveys and self-report studies along with official records and other sources of data (for example, corporations). Given the difficulties of detection and accessing corporate subsystems, while the above proposal may begin to bridge this gap, this knowledge is currently not available, nor is it plausible that it would be in the near future. This in addition to the less tangible nature of transnational corruption reinforces the location of transnational corporate bribery amongst the 'known unknowns'.

Moving Beyond Estimations of Extent and Scope Towards Understanding 'Organisation'

Two problems are evident. First, determining adequate levels of enforcement only makes sense in relation to accurate judgements about extent and scope but this latter endeavour is methodologically idealistic. Second, the only attempt to address adequate enforcement across Europe comes in the form of the above comparison of prosecution numbers by TI. However these adopt a narrow view of enforcement that is limited to the investigation, prosecution and sanctioning of transnational corruption – this gives us no insight into those enforcement practices characterised by prevention and self-regulation and which incorporate the widely accepted role of non-state actors and organisations. Furthermore, as argued throughout this book, the complex organisation of corporate bribery presents obstacles to prosecution and conviction, rendering criminal law enforcement implausible in the current control landscape – the difficulties when criminally prosecuting corporations, the shift towards civil settlements and negotiation, the need to use resources effectively, the evidential burdens of transnational investigations and so on inhibit the policy response of the UK and Germany to address transnational bribery. Although some regulation is possible, the enforcement capacities of responsible agencies and actors cannot meet even the most conservative estimate of the 'need' or 'demand' for prosecutions, even more so in times of austerity.

Understanding these limitations may assist policymakers, legislators and agents of control in improving current practices. Granted that there may be a demand for punishing bribery as just deserts and social fairness, irrespective of the deterrent impact, other approaches are possible either as substitutes or as supplements. With this in mind, in addition to developing estimations of the incidence, prevalence and concentration of transnational bribery and corruption, the analytical focus could be shifted onto the *modus operandi* of *how* those incidents of bribery (that do come to the attention of the authorities and are successfully dealt with) have been organised (see Edwards and Levi, 2008) and onto the particular technical and social characteristics and relations of transnational bribery would supplement more reactive policies. For example, white-collar crime reduction has been analysed through an 'opportunity perspective' approach, the tools of which are predominantly situational crime prevention, routine activities theory and crime pattern theory (see Benson et al., 2009; Benson and Simpson, 2009). Based on the 'crime triangle' (that is, motivated offender, opportunity and capable guardians), the propensity to commit offences is assumed and analytical focus is placed on 'opportunity structures'. By identifying the features of the immediate 'situations' within which white-collar crimes take place and the processes involved, it is possible to intervene and reduce (or perhaps displace) such crimes. Understanding the 'technical' dimensions of corporate bribery is clearly important for enforcement authorities. However, such approaches must be supplemented with an understanding of the 'social' dimensions (that is, the necessary and contingent relations (see Edwards and Hughes, 2005) of corporate bribery and the nature of these relations in different geo-historical contexts). Intervention strategies incorporating both dimensions guided by risk-based assessments of potentially corruptible markets, sectors, corporations and individuals can strategically shape the enforcement response.

In other words, it is important to understand the processes, relations and routine activities of white-collar and corporate crimes in the context of political, cultural and economic structures. For example, analysis of the necessary involvement of particular actors (for example, executives, corporations) in particular economic sectors (for example, construction, finance, defence and so on) and in contingent legal or cultural contexts (for example, UK, Germany) informs an understanding of why such crimes are organised in specific societies. Understanding the organisation of transnational corruption over time and in different places informs enforcement practices of intervention – to render social problems such as transnational corruption sufficiently 'tangible', there must be some 'known knowns' from which the impact of self-regulatory and non-repressive mechanisms can be understood. Additionally, analysing context informs an understanding of the impact of mechanisms designed to respond to or reduce corrupt activities. For example, in an enforcement culture of non-prosecution and negotiated civil sanctioning, the ripple effect of one or two notable criminal prosecutions is likely to have a greater impact within business and the market in terms of shifts towards improved compliance and internal oversight. To understand context and the social processes, relations and practices of transnational corruption then, enforcement agencies and those interested in researching transnational corporate bribery might aim to develop intervention points in relation to the following processes and characteristics, amongst others, that incorporate both technical and social dimensions and risk assessments (drawing on Levi's (2007: 781) process model of transnational 'serious crimes'):

Table 8.2 Necessary and contingent relations of transnational corporate bribery

Necessary	How are the finances for bribes obtained? For example, how do legitimate corporations channel funds for the creation of slush funds and what are the concealment practices involved (e.g. use of front companies; fake conferences to generate funds; inflated prices)?
	How are bribe payers and receivers recruited (e.g. internal/external, domestic/overseas to the corporation) and how do they develop the expertise/technical ability to develop bribery schemes? Which criteria identify potential intermediaries and bribe receivers (e.g. politicians, state officials)?
	Which corporate mechanisms and tools are utilised and necessary to be able to bribe (e.g. bank accounts in difficult to reach jurisdictions)? How are the proceeds of bribes concealed and converted (i.e. money laundering) from the various domestic and foreign authorities (e.g. law enforcement, tax authorities) and what are the particular legal/structural contexts that enable this?
	Which external and internal actors are required to be complicit for bribery to remain undetected and how are these relations developed over time (e.g. external accountants, high-level management)?
	How might bribe givers neutralise law enforcement responses and/or 'capable guardians'?
Contingent	Which jurisdictions, which industries/sectors (e.g. construction, pharmaceutical, manufacturing) and which corporate employees (e.g. sales agents, middle-level managers) are at highest risk of bribery and how can this risk be located within specific geo-historical contexts?
	Which antecedent factors exist to facilitate corruption in the offending contexts? E.g. organisational cultures, levels of transparency and accountability etc.
	To what extent do macro social, economic and political structures shape local commerce and thus the contexts within which bribe givers and receivers can operate?

Understanding the necessary and contingent relations of bribery enables key vulnerabilities in the above processes to be determined for strategic interventions, even if it may not be possible in the short term politically to close off those loopholes. Law enforcement agencies, however, are under pressure to produce 'results', usually in the form of prosecutions, in order to ensure they maintain their existence and function. Shifts towards prevention and disruption reduce the number of measureable results but may also contradict statutory remits, most notably in Germany:

> Prevention is something that the public prosecutor doesn't do. We only operate in terms of repression ... By law we are explicitly a prosecutorial authority. We have no mandate for prevention (German Prosecutor Interview 212).

However, law enforcement agencies must incorporate more innovative intervention strategies beyond traditional reactive enforcement mechanisms of criminal prosecution if the behaviour of corporations is to be changed. 'Hybrid mechanisms' such as self-reporting by corporations and self-cleaning are a key shift in this direction. Other potential practices such as improved whistleblowing provisions (although American-style financial rewards for 'high-quality' tips as with the Dodd-Frank Act may contradict and undermine corporate anti-bribery policies) and certification schemes (providing these do not conflict with the ability to prosecute and sanction corporations) require consideration but such mechanisms are shaped within the constraints of legal cultures and jurisdictional boundaries. There is, however, much scope for innovation at the multi-jurisdictional, transnational level – coordinated risk-based intervention strategies between anti-corruption agencies and actors in different jurisdictions offers much potential but remains politically and legally difficult. Intergovernmental organisations such as the GRECO, the OECD and the UN do generate themed reports across jurisdictions and provide frameworks for coordinated approaches but joint prevention/proactive exercises are not institutionally possible except via industry initiatives. For example, UK and German authorities could in coordination target high-risk sectors (such as manufacturing or defence) or high-risk jurisdictions (such as corporations operating in a particular country where corruption remains problematic) in raids, but there is currently no obvious prevention mechanism or legislative powers for so doing in advance of criminal complaints.

A variety of methodologies and data sources would be useful for understanding these issues. For example, primary data may be generated through script analysis of those cases that come to the attention of the authorities, victimisation surveys, self-report studies, perceptions studies, interviews with offenders, while secondary data collected by corporations, enforcement agencies, business and sector-specific trade associations and bodies, international organisations and development banks as well as court records, police notification schemes could also inform understandings of the bribery problem.

Conclusion

This chapter has instigated a debate over how we might go about determining how adequate bribery enforcement is, or how active responsible regulatory and enforcement agencies are. The key issue to recognise is that adequacy is dependent upon what we know or could plausibly know about levels of offending behaviour: without a valid indication of the levels and organisation of such crimes or 'public bads', our understanding of the relative impact of enforcement is partial and subjective. Various sources produce data on narrow indices such as prosecution or investigation numbers, but without contextual understanding of how important these cases are or without 'good enough' measurement of the scale of the offending, these data are rendered largely meaningless. This is a problem at the national and even more so at the transnational level where available data on enforcement practices and harms are difficult to obtain.

To address this problem, data sources were considered that have the potential to 'fill the gaps' and provide more valid understandings of prevalence, extent and scope. Collating and analysing data emanating from public, private and third sector sources across local, national and supranational levels provides proxies for these missing data. But better informing our quantitative understandings of the extent of the problem has much more meaning when supplemented by qualitative understandings of how such crimes are organised domestically and transnationally. Once we know more about the size and distribution of the 'criminal markets', a major challenge remains in linking different models of enforcement to changes in those actual as well as formal enforcement changes. There is no reason to suppose that 'what works' is independent of cultural context and expectations, including but not restricted to the independence of regulators, prosecutors and the courts. It seems plausible that where compliance is linked to expectations of how others are complying, more can be achieved with a lighter 'nudge' than where offending is or is believed to be commonplace.

In the light of this, the key argument is that understandings of the *organisation* of transnational corporate bribery offers an alternative means by which enforcement levels can be measured and policing strategies informed. To this end, some key questions to explore the necessary and contingent relations of such activities and the contexts within which they occur were identified. Such thought processes and research questions are transferable to all white-collar and corporate crimes, and provide empirical research frameworks that may be considered useful to reasoned assessments that go beyond the normal claims of advocacy organisations.

However, the assumption here is that enforcement agencies might have an interest in intervention, prevention and reduction. As discussed in Chapter 1, the socio-economic harms of corruption and bribery have led concerned parties at the national and international levels to focus on criminal justice responses, primarily in the form of prosecution, and analysis of the levels of enforcement in this chapter have reflected these aims. Philosophically, however, the aims of enforcement may need readjusting in a move beyond a focus on criminal justice (for example, aiming for the prosecution of individuals and corporations) to also incorporate social justice (for example, fair treatment of conventional and white-collar/corporate crimes; addressing wider, underlying social issues), restorative justice (for example, victim centred repatriation and so on) and risk assessment (for example, targeting high-risk sectors and businesses). Some suggestions to do this have been made in this chapter but until understandings of the effectiveness of these responses and aims is evidenced and understood, how adequate enforcement responses are is difficult to determine.

Chapter 9
The 'Default Position': Accommodating Transnational Corporate Bribery

> Accommodation and collusion reflects the fact that all regulatory agencies possess inadequate resources to pursue policies of full enforcement. An inevitable consequence of their selection of priorities (however this is done) is that much illegal trading and regulation-avoidance occurs without any regulatory response (Edwards and Gill, 2002: 213).

Introduction

This book has been about the regulation of corporations that use bribery in international business transactions in order to win or maintain business contracts in overseas jurisdictions. Regulatory agencies, restricted by their powers of enforcement, accommodate a certain level of corporate bribery either through their inability to do otherwise or as a result of their decisions to prioritise or focus on other issues. Accommodation occurs not only due to practical limitations but also in respect of political and economic ideologies. The purpose of this final chapter is to draw together conclusions on the overriding argument of this book by elaborating how accommodation, as described in the quote above, rather than enforcement or self-regulation, is the normal policy response around which theoretically comparable jurisdictions such as Germany and the UK are converging.

Factors Leading to the 'Default Position' of Accommodation

Throughout this book a series of obstacles to the policy responses of the UK and Germany have emerged. These cannot all be repeated here but in order to demonstrate the 'default position' of accommodation some of these will be revisited. For example, there are substantial difficulties in *criminally* prosecuting corporations which has led to the use of civil settlements (and the introduction of deferred prosecution agreements though issues remain), negotiation and persuasion for the crimes of corporations, there are pressures to use resources 'effectively', there are obstacles in terms of the evidential burdens of transnational investigations and the impacts of self-regulatory practices remain anecdotal and unsubstantiated. In other words, notable structural, legal, procedural, evidential and financial obstacles underpinned by varying levels of political influence are encountered by responsible authorities aiming to regulate transnational corporate bribery. These issues, even more so in times of austerity, inhibit the policy responses of the UK and Germany to address transnational corporate bribery:

> [W]hat you don't want to do is create a climate of affordable risk because once you have a climate of affordable risk it's the enemy of deterrent, if you believe that detection, punishment, adverse publicity is a deterrent ... if you do subscribe to that view then you have to ask yourself how much of a deterrent is it if you can guarantee that if you are caught ... the worst thing that is going to happen to you is that you are going to have to pay some court fine. If there is no kind of debarment, exclusion or disqualification or even any civil forfeiture is that going to be much of a deterrent? (UK Lawyer Interview 121).

Reinforcing this is the insufficient or unequal distribution of resources (which reflects political will and local interests). This creates a landscape that leads to the inevitable accommodation of much transnational bribery. The SFO's 'acceptance criteria' (see Chapter 5), for example, makes clear that only large, complex cases will be investigated, meaning smaller bribery cases may be accommodated. (Though the obstacles faced with even the large cases that are prioritised hinders prosecution.) The same can be said of facilitation payments, which although prohibited in UK law are unlikely to be investigated if small and one-off. Not investigating small facilitation payments caters for those corporations operating in countries where such payments are required to enter the market.

Similar accommodation exists in Germany where unevenly distributed funding and expertise results in some *Bundesländer* being 'less enthusiastic' than others in relation to bribery enforcement or being unable to sufficiently engage in bribery enforcement even where there is a strong will to do so. As one German prosecutor summarised:

> It is, I believe, not so much the difference between *Bundesländer*, but the difference between the public prosecutor's offices ... There is a very unequal prosecutorial intensity or prosecutorial will. What I always notice is that when we approach other *Bundesländer* with a case there is overall actually a strong will with colleagues, with the police. The possibilities are different because the allocation of personnel varies – some have more people at their disposal but there are just very poor *Bundesländer* and very rich *Bundesländer* where the police simply have more money. You have to take that into consideration. Yes, it doesn't always work but there is always the will to cooperate ... There are public prosecutor's offices that place less emphasis on it and have less will to initiate proceedings. But that also depends on the cooperation of the public prosecutor's offices (German Police Investigator Interview 231).

Accommodation, even where the will to enforce the law is high, may be a significant part of all control responses in relation to all forms of criminality. In this case, it is more important to understand how discretion is applied, how resources are allocated and how intelligence is used (for example, prioritisation and disruption) to address certain aspects of any given form of criminality. In other words, what do (or should) 'accommodation' and 'non-accommodation' look like and how can they be systematically analysed? This is not a binary distinction but ought to be understood linearly as issues such as political will (for example, resource starvation or resource abundance but directed elsewhere), case prioritisation, international cooperation and assistance, enforcement levels and so on can take many forms.

In some cases, there is the prospect of the relationships between the regulator and the regulated becoming too intertwined due to shared ideologies and/or personnel, rewards and/or threats – in such scenarios, the regulator may be captured and subsequently ensure non-enforcement (Gill, 2002: 537). As Dorn (2010: 34) notes, this can be understood from two perspectives. From a perspective favourable to public regulation, initially independent regulatory agencies risk becoming the captive of those they are supposed to regulate, through repeated interactions with them. From a deregulatory perspective (Thatcher – Reagan), regulatory ineffectiveness arises from regulatory over-reach: the markets know best. In either case, regulation may be fated to fail. The former conception of 'capture' here reflects occurrences in the anti-corruption landscape in both the UK and Germany where 'regulators', or the state, have adopted the interests of business. For example, following business lobbying, the UK government revised the UK Bribery Act guidance in relation to the circumstances within which an overseas company is considered to be conducting business in the UK which reflected the concerns of business. As one UK investigator/prosecutor stated:

> I certainly don't think we live in a country where you get routine political interference with the Criminal Justice System but sometimes cases of overseas corruption can have an impact on issues like national security and certainly what was said when we dropped the Saudi case so it might happen without there necessarily being anything constitutionally improper (UK Investigator/Prosecutor Interview 111).

The BAE Systems case that involved a government-to-government arms contract between the UK and Saudi Arabia but enlisted BAE Systems as the arms producer and provider in this deal is a prime example of this – governments understand the importance of large corporations to a country's economic and national security interests that are shaped by transnational business agreements (for example, UK – Saudi Arabia). Simultaneously, however, they have a legal obligation to enforce the law (following ratification of key international conventions) and must also manage criticism from intergovernmental/non-governmental organisations which appears only possible through increasing enforcement 'successes'. Notable tensions exist. In addition, the lack of transparency in relation to the frequent and informal dialogue between the SFO and corporations raises further concerns.

The German government has also refrained from revising legal frameworks in relation to 'corporate criminal liability' ensuring German corporations remain free from criminal prosecution. As one expert stated:

> They [the enforcement authorities] mostly have no desire because they view themselves as overstrained. They don't have that many personnel for it [overseas corruption] as when they investigate it becomes very personnel-intensive and that costs years-long work and the polity frequently doesn't want that ... Then there are also political influences ... because they [large corporations] are commonly fellow political party members, and in turn have connections with ministers and political parties (German Country Expert Interview 241).

Thus, with such practices there is a risk that 'the regulated system comes to be operated in the interest of the regulated firms rather than the more general public interest' (Ricketts, 2006: 38). If, for example, the substantial benefits, for wealth creation and tax yield, of under-regulated transnational financial markets remain desired, then certain levels of corruption and bribery become accepted as 'necessary evils'.

Furthermore, in some extreme cases, the 'regulators' may share in the profitability of the market, for example if a regulator was to hold shares in a regulated company (Gill, 2002: 537). The 'revolving door' phenomenon between regulators and business demonstrates this 'grey' area. This term refers to 'the movement of individuals between positions of public office and jobs in the private sector, in either direction' (TI, 2011b: 2). One related example of this is that of BAE Systems and Britain's former envoy to Saudi Arabia, Sir Sherard Cowper-Coles.[1] Sir Sherard Cowper-Coles left the Foreign Office in October 2010, but played a central role in pressurising the SFO to drop the investigation into BAE Systems in relation to the al-Yamamah arms deal with Saudi Arabia. Controversially, he was then hired by BAE Systems in February 2011 as the international business development director, focusing on the Middle East and Southeast Asia. This move raised questions over the relationship between BAE Systems and the UK Government, and the circumstances surrounding the closure of the SFO case into the deal. As one former UK investigator/prosecutor commented:

> The problem is the BAE case is highly politicised. It arguably involves people in the Ministry of Defence at the time the al-Yamamah contract was agreed and some of these people have moved between BAE, Defence and back again. There are other people floating around who years ago had something to do with it and they have been spread across Whitehall because of passage of time (Former UK Investigator/Prosecutor Interview 113).

---

1 See *Guardian*: '*BAE Systems hire Britain's former envoy to Saudi Arabia*', 18/02/2011, available at: http://www.guardian.co.uk/business/2011/feb/18/envoy-saudi-bae-systems <Accessed 10/11/2013>.

The reasons for concern over such public-private and private-public movements relate to the potential for 'conflict of interests' that can occur before, after or during a role in government. As the TI report (2011b: 3) states: public officials might allow the agenda of their previous private sector employer to influence their government work; public officials might abuse their power while in office to favour a certain company, with a view to ingratiating themselves and gaining future employment; former public officials who accept jobs in business might influence their former government colleagues to make decisions in a way that favours their new employer; and former public officials may use confidential information to benefit their new employers, for example during procurement procedures. Alternatively, the revolving door phenomenon may be viewed positively as those with expert knowledge of bribery and corruption and their control may have increased influence in changing the behaviour of corporations that are more difficult to reach when employed by the state.

The SFO is a prime example of such revolving door practices. Keith McCarthy, who was the Head of Anti-Corruption and subsequently Chief Investigator and Executive Board member, left to take up a position beginning January 2012 with PricewaterhouseCoopers' Forensics team.[2] In January 2011, Robert Amaee, the then Head of the SFO's Anti-Corruption Domain, left to join US legal firm Covington and Burling at their London office to advise and assist clients on the UK Bribery Act and other anti-corruption issues.[3] Also in January 2011, Charlie Montieth, the SFO's Head of Assurance and key figure in the drafting of the UK Bribery Act, left to join US legal firm White and Case at their London office.[4] The SFO's General Counsel, Vivian Robinson QC, also left the organisation in 2011 to join international law firm McGuireWoods in their London office.[5] As part of his new role, Robinson has been advising clients on the UK Bribery Act and fraud and corruption more generally. Interestingly, all three of these examples demonstrate how key regulatory actors have moved on to assist and advise those they previously regulated on the specific criminality that they assisted in prosecuting during their time with the SFO. The movement of key individuals out of the SFO raises questions over available resources (although the SFO will never be able to match private sector wages), capability to investigate and prosecute (loss of valuable expertise and experience) and therefore the legitimacy of the organisation as an anti-corruption authority.

2 See PwC press release, 11/10/2011, available at: http://www.ukmediacentre.pwc.com/News-Releases/PwC-appoints-Keith-McCarthy-to-its-Forensics-practice-1115.aspx <Accessed 15/12/2011>.

3 See Covington and Burling press release, 17/01/2011, available at: http://www.cov.com/news/detail.aspx?news=1593. <Accessed 10/11/2013>.

4 See White and Case press release, 17/01/2011, available at: http://www.whitecase.com/press-01172011–1/ <Accessed 10/11/2013>.

5 See publication by McGuireWoods from *Bribery Library*: '*The SFO's Vivian Robinson to join McGuireWoods*', 27/04/2011, available at: http://www.briberylibrary.com/fcpa/sfos-vivian-robinson-to-join-mcguirewoods/ <Accessed 10/11/2013>.

The enhancement of links between the SFO and private practice, whilst potentially productive, requires transparency given the blurring of public-private boundaries in relation to close relationship of regulators and regulatees.

In any case, of course, there are some procedures in place to regulate this phenomenon. Ministers and senior crown servants must seek advice from the Advisory Committee on Business Appointments (ACOBA) before taking private sector employment but ACOBA does not have the resources to assess specific risks in individual cases or to monitor compliance. Some changes have been evident, with initiatives to ban former public officials from engaging in lobbying for two years after leaving office, but the TI report argues this is not enough.

Concluding Thoughts

In short, national authorities are pressured to respond to transnational corporate bribery using inter-national frameworks for enforcement but in doing so face significant difficulties in controlling complexly organised transnational, multi-jurisdictional corporate bribery. Exemplary instances, such as the Siemens and Innospec cases discussed in Chapter 2, demonstrate this complex organisation where responsible anti-corruption authorities are limited by their national jurisdictional boundaries as well as procedural, evidential, legal, structural and financial obstacles (see Chapters 5, 6 and 7). Much concern has been expressed in international conventions and discourse but in these official narratives as well as those of criminological theory on corporate and white-collar crime, the problem of controlling transnationally organised corporate bribery has not been sufficiently analysed.

This book addressed this analytical gap by drawing on the broader research literature on regulation to complement criminological insights which have largely been concerned with problems of corporate crimes *within*, rather than *across*, nation-states. More specifically, regulation theory has tended to be based on empirical findings within specific industrial sectors (for example, the pharmaceutical industry), on easily detectable and measureable forms of harm (for example, health and safety crimes, environmental waste, and so on) or on areas already under formal regulation (for example, financial services). Transnational corporate bribery, in contrast to these examples, is a problem of all corporations and businesses that operate internationally and is therefore not limited to any one jurisdiction, sector or regulator. Instead, a multi-agency/departmental approach to controlling corporate bribery is in existence in the UK and Germany but these traditional 'policing' authorities are adopting regulatory techniques and approaches traditionally associated with those of industry regulators.

Key themes promoted in regulation theory remain fundamental to the approach analysed in this book. The need for a varied set of sanctions and strategies including both enforcement and self-regulatory mechanisms; the necessity of 'negotiated relationships' between the regulators and regulatees; the accomplishment of compliance; the reflexivity, responsiveness and agency of the regulators; and the involvement of non-state actors and agencies albeit within varying degrees of state intervention. All these principles emerged as significant in this research. The difficulty for current regulation theory, however, lies with the transnationality of the problem. Transnational corporate bribery is inherently a market phenomenon whereby specific undesired corrupt practices occur within otherwise legal commerce and business transactions.

With this in mind, a framework for understanding the negotiation of regulation through a mixture of enforcement and self-regulatory mechanisms has been presented. This framework from Edwards and Gill (2002) foregrounded the regulation of behaviour in market societies as being *a*, but arguably *the*, principal context of modern policing in 'the West' (Gill, 2002). In this context, regulation is considered a negotiated, social relationship between regulators and regulatees in legal and illegal markets with analytical focus shifted onto the regulation of 'populations' rather than a preoccupation with 'individuals' (see Gill, 2000, 2002; Edwards and Gill, 2002; Edwards, 2010). Using a broad and inclusive definition of regulation, it is possible to understand how behaviour in market societies can be regulated by a diverse mixture of state and non-state 'regulatory' actors involved directly and indirectly in negotiating regulation. Compliance outcomes and behaviour changes are accomplished and negotiated through the interactions of such 'regulators' and 'regulatees' (that is, MNCs) over time. In this sense, there is no preoccupation with formal regulatory institutions and their regulatory strategies, though such social actors are of course key in regulation. By focusing on the market, analytical attention is placed on the regulation of populations of corporations rather than individual corporations per se. This enables analysis of the mixture of enforcement mechanisms (such as criminal prosecution and civil settlements), hybrid mechanisms (such as self-reporting and self-cleaning) and (enforced) self-regulatory mechanisms of a more organic or manufactured nature (see Chapters 5, 6 and 7) that are regulating the behaviour of corporations operating in international markets in relation to transnational corporate bribery.

However, there is an assumption that these mechanisms provide sufficient means for dealing with transnational corporate bribery. In reality, this is unlikely to be the case. Much corporate bribery currently goes undetected and is therefore unknown beyond the direct parties. Investigators and prosecutors in the UK and Germany have no comprehensive plausible estimations of the scope and the extent of the transnational corporate bribery problem – the enforcement authorities are only aware of those cases that come to their attention. These cases are centrally recorded in both the UK and Germany and represent the scope and extent of the problem as understood by the enforcement authorities – the true scale of the problem can be presumed to be much greater. However, such knowledge of bribery cases reflects only the extent of the resources invested into detection or the extent to which other parties are willing or able to notify the authorities. The key issue, however, is that even these (relatively conservative) estimations outweigh the UK's and Germany's capacities for enforcement.

Intergovernmental organisations such as the OECD as well as international organisations such as TI collate data on the number of investigations, prosecutions and sanctions as part requirements of the OECD Anti-Bribery Convention. These data provide the most wide-ranging understanding of the extent and scope of transnational corporate bribery but provide no credible insights into the *proportion* of estimated cases dealt with by comparable jurisdictions – only an understanding of the proportion of cases responded to through enforcement mechanisms can provide insights into *levels* of enforcement, in particular when comparing jurisdictions. Yet these data are often used to rank how 'active' nation-states are in enforcing the law. Attempts have been made to better measure the extent and scope of corruption but there remains a preoccupation with perception studies that are of course beset by various methodological problems.

Establishing how much regulation these enforcement, hybrid and self-regulatory mechanisms achieve is difficult as there are little valid 'before and after' data on their impacts. Some level of regulation is achievable but without reliable data difficulties in determining 'what works' become evident. Significant differences are evident in the enforcement responses of the UK and Germany (for example, centralised (UK) or decentralised (Germany) systems, existence of corporate criminal liability (UK) or not (Germany), varying legal cultures such as in relation to formal (UK) or informal (Germany) uses of discretion). The principle argument is that despite these differences, responsible authorities in both the UK and Germany (i) face similar difficulties in enforcement as they are limited by their national jurisdictional boundaries and face several procedural, evidential, legal, financial and structural obstacles and (ii) are converging towards similar prosecution policies (for example, the negotiation of civil settlements for corporations that commit criminal acts). This emerging landscape, characterised by the enforcement, self-regulatory and hybrid mechanisms analysed throughout this book, does provide some level of regulation as we have seen in the increasing numbers of cases being investigated, prosecuted and sanctioned. However, while these mechanisms are aiding the response, the issues discussed throughout this book indicate they are likely to be insufficient, leading to (iii) the default position of accommodation by state agencies, even where the will to enforce the law is high.

The existence of transnational corporate bribery is known but its full extent is not. It is worthwhile, therefore, to shift the analytical focus away from 'how much' of a problem it is (relative to the capacity for enforcement approaches) to how known bribery is organised and how such knowledge and analysis can aid reduction and prevention (see Chapter 6). Rather than evaluating the outcomes of enforcement mechanisms, analysing the vulnerabilities inherent in corporate bribery can aid the reduction of opportunities to commit such acts. By questioning current regulation and criminological theory in relation to the control of transnational corporate bribery, the under-researched and under-theorised area of transnational corporate bribery can be placed on the criminological agenda, shifting the phenomenon from the margins where it may currently be located under the framework of white-collar and corporate crimes. This book has made an initial step in developing criminological understandings of transnational corporate bribery and with further research these understandings may be further illuminated.

Bibliography

Abbott, K. and Snidal, D. (2006) *The Governance Triangle: Regulatory Standards Institutions and the Shadow of the State*. Working Paper, Global Governance Project, Oxford University.

Abbott, K. and Snidal, D. (2009) 'Strengthening International Regulation through Transnational New Governance: Overcoming the Orchestration Deficit', *Vanderbilt Journal of Transnational Law*, 42: 501–78.

Abbott, K. and Snidal, D. (2013) 'Taking Responsive Regulation Transnational: Strategies for International Organizations', *Regulation and Governance* 7(1): 95–113.

Almond, P. (2013) Corporate Manslaughter and Regulatory Reform. *Crime Prevention and Security Management*. Basingstoke, Palgrave Macmillan.

Annan, K. (2004) 'Foreword' to UN Convention against Corruption, available at: http://www.unodc.org/documents/treaties/UNCAC/Publications/Convention/08–50026_E.pdf <Accessed 10/11/2013>.

Arrowsmith, S., Priess, H-P. and Friton, P. (2009) 'Self-cleaning as a Defence to Exclusions for Misconduct: An Emerging Concept in EC Public Procurement Law?' *Public Procurement Law Review*, 6: 257–82.

Ayres, I. and Braithwaite, J. (1992) *Responsive Regulation: Transcending the Deregulation Debate*. New York: Oxford University Press.

Baldwin, R., Scott, C. and Hood, C. (1998) (eds) *A Reader on Regulation*. Oxford: Oxford University Press.

Baldwin, R. and Cave, M. (1999) *Understanding Regulation. Theory, Strategy, and Practice*. Oxford: Oxford University Press.

Bardhan, P. (2006) 'The Economist's Approach to the Problem of Corruption', *World Development*, 34(2): 341–8.

Beare, M.E. and Naylor, R.T. (1999) *Major Issues Relating to Organized Crime: within the Context of Economic Relationships*. Prepared for Law Commission of Canada, available at: https://www.ncjrs.gov/nathanson/organized.html <Accessed 10/11/2013>.

Becker, H.S. (1973) *Outsiders: Studies in the Sociology of Deviance*. New York: The Free Press.

Benson, M.L. and Simpson S.S. (2009) *White-collar Crime: An Opportunity Perspective*. Abingdon, Oxfordshire: Routledge.

Benson, M.L., Madensen, T.D. and Eck, J.E. (2009) 'White-collar Crime from an Opportunity Perspective', in S.S. Simpson and D. Weisburd (eds), *The Criminology of White-Collar Crime*. New York: Springer.

Bernstein, S. and Cashore, B. (2007) 'Can Non-state Global Governance be Legitimate? An Analytical Framework', *Regulation and Governance*, 1: 347–71.

Black, J. and Baldwin, R. (2010) 'Really Responsive Risk-based Regulation', *Law and Policy*, 32(2): 181–213.

Bottoms, A. and Tankebe, J. (2012) 'Beyond Procedural Justice: A Dialogic Approach to Legitimacy in Criminal Justice', *The Journal of Criminal Law and Criminology*, 102(1): 119–170

Braithwaite, J. (2000) *Regulation, Crime, Freedom*. Aldershot: Dartmouth Publishing Company Limited.

Braithwaite, J. (2008) *Regulatory Capitalism: How It Works, Ideas for Making It Work Better*. Cheltenham: Edward Elgar.

Braithwaite, J. and Drahos, P. (2000) *Global Business Regulation*. Cambridge: Cambridge University Press.

Braithwaite, V. (2010) 'Criminal Prosecution within Responsive Regulatory Practice', *Criminology and Public Policy*, 9(3): 515–23.

Cadot, O. (1987) 'Corruption as a Gamble', *Journal of Public Economics*, 33: 233–44.

Chayes, A., Chayes, A.H. and Mitchell, R.B. (1998) 'Managing Compliance: A Comparative Perspective', in E. Brown Weiss and H.K. Jacobson (eds), *Engaging Countries: Strengthening Compliance with International Environmental Accords*. Cambridge, MA: MIT Press.

Choi, J.P. and Thum, M. (2005) 'Corruption and the Shadow Economy', *International Economic Review*, 46(3): 817–36.

Christie, N. (2000) *Crime Control as Industry: Towards Gulags, Western Style*. 3rd ed., London: Routledge.

Clarke, M. (1990) *Business Crime. Its Nature and Control*. Oxford: Polity Press.

Council of Europe (1999a) *Criminal Law Convention on Corruption*. Council of Europe, available at: http://conventions.coe.int/Treaty/en/Treaties/Html/173.htm <Accessed 10/11/2013>.

Council of Europe (1999b) *Civil Law Convention on Corruption*. Council of Europe, available at: http://conventions.coe.int/treaty/en/Treaties/Html/174.htm <Accessed 10/11/2013>.

Cragg, A.W. (1998) 'Business, Globalization, and the Logic and Ethics of Corruption', *International Journal*, 53: 643–60.

Croall, H. (2001) *Understanding White-collar Crime*. Buckingham: Open University Press.

Çule, M. and Fulton, M. (2005) 'Some Implications of the Unofficial Economy-Bureaucratic Corruption Relationship in Transition Countries', *Economic Letters*, 89: 207–11.

Davies, P., Francis, P. and Jupp, V. (1999) 'The Features of Invisible Crimes', in P. Davies, P. Francis and V. Jupp (eds), *Invisible Crimes: Their Victims and their Regulation*. Basingstoke: Palgrave Macmillan.

Deflem, M. (1995) 'Corruption, Law, and Justice: A Conceptual Clarification', *Journal of Criminal Justice*, 23(3): 243–58.

Delaney, P.X. (2007) 'Transnational Corruption: Regulation Across Borders', *Virginia Journal of International Law*, 47(2): 413–61.

Dixon, D. (1997) *Law in Policing: Legal Regulation and Police Practices*. Oxford: Clarendon Press.

Djelic, M-L. and Sahlin-Andersson, K. (2006) *Transnational Governance: Institutional Dynamics of Regulation*. Cambridge: Cambridge University Press.

Doig, A. (1984) *Corruption and Misconduct in Contemporary British Politics*. Harmondsworth: Penguin Books.

Doig, A. (2003) 'Political Corruption in the United Kingdom', in M.J. Bull and J.L. Newell (eds), *Corruption in Contemporary Politics*. Basingstoke: Palgrave Macmillan.

Doig, A. (2006) *Fraud*. Cullompton, UK: Willan Publishing.

Doig, A. and Theobald, R. (eds) (1999) *Corruption and Democratisation*. London: Frank Cass.

Dorn, N. (2010) 'The Governance of Securities: Ponzi Finance, Regulatory Convergence, Credit Crunch', *British Journal of Criminology*, 50: 23–45.

Edwards, A. (2010) 'Evaluation of the Cardiff Night-Time Economy Co-ordinator (NTEC) Post'. Working Paper 133, School of Social Sciences (SOCSI), Cardiff University, available at: http://www.cardiff.ac.uk/socsi/resources/wp133.pdf <Accessed 10/11/2013>.

Edwards, A. and Gill, P. (2002) 'Crime as Enterprise? The Case of "transnational organised crime"', *Crime, Law and Social Change*, 37: 203–23.

Edwards, A. and Hughes, G. (2005) 'Comparing the Governance of Safety in Europe: A Geo-historical Approach', *Theoretical Criminology*, 9(3): 345–63.

Edwards, A. and Levi, M. (2008) 'Researching the Organisation of Serious Crimes', *Criminology and Criminal Justice*, 8(4): 363–88.

Ekblom, P. (1999) 'Can We Make Crime Prevention Adaptive by Learning from Other Evolutionary Struggles?' *Studies on Crime and Crime Prevention*, 8(1): 27–51.

Elliot, L. (2009) 'Combating Transnational Environmental Crime: "joined up" Thinking about Transnational Networks', in K. Kangaspunta and I.H. Marshall (eds), *Eco-Crime and Justice: Essays on Environmental Crime*. Turin, Italy: Public Information Department UNICRI.

Foster, J.E., Horowitz, A.W. and Méndez, F. (2009) 'An Axiomatic Approach to the Measurement of Corruption: Theory and Applications'. OPHI Working Paper No. 29, available at: http://www.ophi.org.uk/wp-content/uploads/OPHI-wp29.pdf <Accessed 10/11/2013>.

Foucault, M. (1991) 'Governmentality', in G. Burchell, C. Gordon and P. Miller (eds), *The Foucault Effect: Studies in Governmentality*. Hemel Hempstead: Harvester Wheatsheaf, 87–104.

Fraud Trials Committee Report (1986) (Roskill Report) London: HM Stationery Office.

Freckmann, A. and Wegerich, T. (1999) *The German Legal System*. London: Sweet and Maxwell.

Garland, D. (1996) 'The Limits of the Sovereign State: Strategies of Crime Control in Contemporary Society', *British Journal of Criminology*, 36(4): 445–71.

Garland, D. (2001) *The Culture of Control: Crime and Social Order in Contemporary Society*. Oxford: Oxford University Press.

George, B.C., Lacey, K.A. and Birmele, J. (2000) 'The 1998 OECD Convention: An Impetus for Worldwide Changes in Attitudes Toward Corruption in Business Transactions', *American Business Law Review*, 37(3): 485–525.

Gerring, J. and Thacker, S.C. (2004) 'Political Institutions and Corruption: The Role of Unitarianism and Parliamentarism', *British Journal of Political Science*, 34: 295–330.

Gibbs, C., McGarrell, E.F. and Axelrod, M. (2010) 'Transnational White-collar Crime and Risk: Lessons from the Global Trade in Electronic Waste', *Criminology and Public Policy*, 9(3): 543–60.

Gill, P. (2000) *Rounding Up the Usual suspects? Developments in Contemporary Law Enforcement Intelligence*. Aldershot: Ashgate Publishing Ltd.

Gill, P. (2002) 'Policing and Regulation: What is the difference?' *Social and Legal Studies*, 11: 523.

Gobert, J. (2011) 'Squaring the Circle. The Relationship between Individual and Organizational Fault', in J. Gobert and A-M. Pascal (eds), *European Developments in Corporate Criminal Liability*. London: Routledge.

Gobert, J. and Punch, M. (2003) *Rethinking Corporate Crime*. London: Butterworths.

Goodin, R.E. (2010) 'Perverting the Course of Politics', *British Journal of Political Science*, 40(4): 725–39.

Goldstein, J. (1960) 'Police Discretion not to Invoke the Criminal Process: Low Visibility Decisions in the Administration of Justice', *Yale Law Journal*, 69: 543–94.

Grabosky, P. (2013) 'Beyond Responsive Regulation: The Expanding Role of Non-state Actors in the Regulatory Process', *Regulation and Governance*, 7: 114–23.

Grabosky, P. and Braithwaite, J. (1986) *Of Manners Gentle: Enforcement Strategies of Australian Business Regulatory Agencies*. Melbourne: Oxford University Press.

GRECO (2001) *First Evaluation Round. Evaluation Report on the United Kingdom*. Council of Europe, available at: http://www.coe.int/t/dghl/monitoring/greco/evaluations/round1/GrecoEval1%282001%298_UnitedKingdom_EN.pdf <Accessed 10/11/2013>.

GRECO (2009) *Third Evaluation Round. Evaluation Report on Germany on Incriminations (ETS 173 and 191, GPC 2)*. Council of Europe, available at: http://www.coe.int/t/dghl/monitoring/greco/evaluations/round3/GrecoEval3%282009%293_Germany_One_EN.pdf <Accessed 10/11/2013>.

Gunningham, N. and Grabosky, P. (1998) *Smart Regulation: Designing Environmental Policy*. Oxford: Clarendon Press.

Haines, F. (2011) 'Addressing the Risk, Reading the Landscape: The Role of Agency in Regulation', *Regulation and Governance*, 5(1): 118–44.

Haufler, V. (2006) 'Global Governance and the Private Sector', in C. May (ed.), *Global Corporate Power*. Boulder, CO: Lynne Rienner.

Hawkins, K. (1998) *Law as Last Resort: Prosecution Decision-making in a Regulatory Agency*. Oxford: Oxford University Press.

Hefendehl, R. (2001) 'Corporate Criminal Liability: Model Penal Code Section 2.07 and the Development in Western Legal Systems', *Buffalo Criminal Law Review*, 4(1): 283–300.

Home Office (2012) Crime Against Businesses: Headline Findings from the 2012 Commercial Victimisation Survey, Home Office, available at: https://www.gov.uk/government/uploads/system/uploads/attachment_data/file/147935/crime-business-prem-2012-pdf.pdf <Accessed 10/11/2013>.

Judiciary of England and Wales (2010) R -v- Innospec Limited. Crown Court at Southwark Sentencing Remarks, available at: http://www.judiciary.gov.uk/Resources/JCO/Documents/Judgments/sentencing-remarks-thomas-lj-innospec.pdf <Accessed 10/11/2013>.

Juy-Birmann, (2002) 'The German System', in M. Delmas-Marty and J.R. Spencer (eds), *European Criminal Procedures*. Cambridge: Cambridge University Press.

Kagan, R.A. (1984) 'On Regulatory Inspectorates and Police', in K. Hawkins and J.M. Thomas (eds), *Enforcing Regulation*. Boston: Kluwer-Nijhoff.

Karstedt, S. (2007) 'Creating Institutions: Linking the "local" and the "global" in the Travel of Crime Policies', *Police Practice and Research*, 8(2): 145–58.

Karstedt, S. and Farrall, S. (2006) 'The Moral Economy of Everyday Crime. Markets, Consumers and Citizens', *British Journal of Criminology*, 46: 1011–36.

Kaufmann, D., Kraay, A. and Mastruzzi, M. (2007) 'Measuring Corruption: Myths and Realities', in Transparency International (TI) *Global Corruption Report 2007*, available at: http://archive.transparency.org/publications/gcr/gcr_2007 <Accessed 10/11/2013>.

Khanna, V.S. (2004) 'Corporate Crime Legislation: A Political Economy Analysis', *Washington University Law Quarterly*, 82: 95–141.

Kooiman, J. (1993) 'Findings, Speculations and Recommendations', in J. Kooiman (ed.), *Modern Governance: New Government-Society Interactions*. London: Sage.

KPMG (2010) *Blessing in Disguise: How the UK Bribery Act Creates Opportunities for Better Corporate Culture and Control*, KPMG, available at: http://www.kpmg.com/UK/en/IssuesAndInsights/ArticlesPublications/Documents/PDF/Advisory/251554%20BID_Accessible1_new%20brand.pdf <Accessed 10/11/2013>.

Krygier, M. (1999) 'Ethical Positivism and the Liberalism of Fear', *Australian Journal of Legal Philosophy*, 24: 65–94.

Lambsdorff, J. Graf (2007) *The New Institutional Economics of Corruption and Reform: Theory, Evidence and Policy*. Cambridge: Cambridge University Press.

Lange, B. (1999) 'Compliance Construction in the Context of Environmental Regulation', *Social and Legal Studies*, 8(4): 549–67.

Leighton, P. (2010) 'Fairness Matters – More than Deterrence: Class Bias and the Limits of Deterrence', *Criminology and Public Policy*, 9(3): 525–33.

Levi, M. (1986) 'Fraud in the Courts: Roskill in Context', *British Journal of Criminology*, 26(4): 394–401.

Levi, M. (1987) *Regulating Fraud*. London: Tavistock.

Levi, M. (2007) 'Organized Crime and Terrorism', in M. Maguire, R. Morgan and R. Reiner (eds), *The Oxford Handbook of Criminology*. Oxford: Oxford University Press.

Levi, M. (2010) 'Serious Tax Fraud and Noncompliance: A Review of Evidence on the Differential Impact of Criminal and Noncriminal Proceedings', *Criminology and Public Policy*, 9(3): 493–513.

Levi, M. (2011) 'Assessing the Costs of Frauds', in D. Gadd, S. Karstedt and S. Messner (eds), *The SAGE Handbook of Criminological Research Methods*. London: Sage.

Levi, M. (2013) 'Legitimacy, Crimes and Compliance in "the city": *De Maximis non Curat Lex?*' in J. Tankebe and Liebling, A. (eds), *Legitimacy and Criminal Justice: An International Exploration*. Oxford: Oxford University Press.

Levi, M. and Lord, N. (2011) 'Links between Corruption and Organised Crime and Research Gaps', in D. Thelesklaf and P. Gomes Pereira (eds), *Non-State Actors in Asset Recovery*. Bern: Peter Lang.

Levi, M. and Maguire, M. (2004) 'Reducing and Preventing Organised Crime: An Evidence-based Critique', *Crime, Law and Social Change*, 41(5): 397–469.

Mascini, P. (2013) 'Why was the Enforcement Pyramid so Influential? And what Prices was Paid?' *Regulation and Governance*, 7: 48–60.

Mauro, P. (1997) 'Why Worry About Corruption?', *Economic Issues 6*. International Monetary Fund.

Mayntz, R. (1993) 'Governing Failures and the Problem of Governability', in J. Kooiman (ed.), *Modern Governance: New Government-Society Interactions*. London: Sage.

Michalowski, R. and Bitten, K. (2005) 'Transnational Environmental Crime', in P. Reichel (ed.), *Handbook of Transnational Crime and Justice*. Thousand Oaks, CA: Sage.

Ministry of Justice (2010) *The Bribery Act 2010. Guidance about Procedures which Relevant Commercial Organisations can put into Place to Prevent Persons Associated with them from Bribing (section 9 of the Bribery Act 2010)*. Ministry of Justice, available at: http://www.justice.gov.uk/downloads/legislation/bribery-act-2010-guidance.pdf <Accessed 10/1/2013>.

Montinola, G.R. and Jackman, R.W. (2002) 'Sources of Corruption: A Cross-Country Study', *British Journal of Political Science*, 32: 147–70.

Moran, M. (2001) 'The Rise of the Regulatory State in Britain', *Parliamentary Affairs*, 54: 19–34.

Nelken, D. (2012) 'Comparing Criminal Justice', in M. Maguire, R. Morgan and R. Reiner (eds), *The Oxford Handbook of Criminology*. 5th ed. Oxford: Oxford University Press.

Nichols, P.M. (2000) 'The Myth of Anti-bribery Laws as Transnational Intrusion', *Cornell International Law Journal*, 33: 627–56.

Nye, J.S. (1967) 'Corruption and Political Development: A Cost-Benefit Analysis', *American Political Science Review*, 61(2): 417–27.

OECD (2007a) *United Kingdom Phase 2. Follow-up Report in the Implementation of the Phase 2 Recommendations*. OECD Publishing, available at: http://www.oecd.org/investment/anti-bribery/anti-briberyconvention/38962457.pdf <Accessed 10/11/2013>.

OECD (2008a) *Corruption: A Glossary of International Criminal Standards*, available at: http://www.oecd.org/daf/anti-bribery/41194428.pdf <Accessed 10/11/2013>.

OECD (2008) *United Kingdom: Phase 2bis Report on the Application of the Convention on Combating Bribery of Foreign Public Officials in International Business Transactions and the 1997 Recommendation on Combating Bribery in International Business Transactions*. OECD Publishing, available at: http://www.oecd.org/investment/anti-bribery/anti-briberyconvention/41515077.pdf <Accessed 10/11/2013>.

OECD (2009) *Recommendation of the Council for Further Combating Bribery of Foreign Public Officials in International Business Transactions*. OECD Publishing, available at: http://www.oecd.org/investment/anti-bribery/anti-briberyconvention/44176910.pdf <Accessed 10/11/2013>.

OECD (2011a) *Convention on Combating Bribery of Foreign Public Officials in International Business Transactions and Related Documents*. OECD Publishing, available at: http://www.oecd.org/daf/anti-bribery/ConvCombatBribery_ENG.pdf <Accessed 10/11/2013>.

OECD (2011b) *Phase 3 Report on Implementing the OECD Anti-Bribery Convention in Germany*. OECD Publishing, available at: http://www.oecd.org/germany/Germanyphase3reportEN.pdf <Accessed 10/11/2013>.

Ogus, A.I. (1994) *Regulation: Legal Form and Economic Theory*. Oxford: Clarendon Press.

O'Malley, P. (1992) 'Risk, Power and Crime Prevention', *Economy and Society*, 21: 252–75.

O'Malley, P. and Palmer, D. (1996) 'Post-Keynsian Policing', *Economy and Society*, 25(2): 137–55.

Parker, C. (2002) *The Open Corporation: Self-regulation and Corporate Citizenship*. Melbourne: Cambridge University Press.

Parker, C. (2013) 'Twenty Years of Responsive Regulation: An Appreciation and Appraisal', *Regulation and Governance*, 7: 2–13.

Passas, N. (1999) 'Globalization, Criminogenic Asymmetries and Economic Crime', *European Journal of Law Reform*, 1(4): 399–423.

Passas, N. (2002) 'Cross-border Crime and the Interface between Illegal and Illegal Actors', in P.C. van Duyne, K. von Lampe and N. Passas (eds), *Upperworld and Underworld in Cross-border Crime*. Mijmegen, the Netherlands: Wolf Legal.

PBS Frontline Documentary (2009) *Black Money*, available online at: http://www.pbs.org/wgbh/pages/frontline/blackmoney/view/ <Accessed 10/11/2013>.

Pearce, F. and Tombs, S (1998) *Toxic Capitalism: Corporate Crime and the Chemical Industry*. Aldershot: Ashgate.

PricewaterhouseCoopers (2010) *Will You Act Now or Pay Later?* PwC, available at: http://www.pwc.co.uk/en_UK/uk/assets/pdf/act-now-pay-later-workshop.pdf <Accessed on 10/11/2013>.

PricewaterhouseCoopers (Germany) (2010) *Compliance und Unternehmenskultur*, PwC, available at: http://www.pwc.de/de/risiko-management/assets/studie_Compliance-und-Unternehmenskultur.pdf <Accessed 10/11/2013>.

Punch, M. (2011) 'The Organizational Component in Corporate Crime', in J. Gobert and A-M. Pascal (eds), *European Developments in Corporate Criminal Liability*. London: Routledge.

Reiner, R. (2010) *The Politics of the Police*. 4th ed. Oxford: Oxford University Press.

Reinikka, R. and Svensson, J. (2006) 'Using Micro-surveys to Measure and Explain Corruption', *World Development*, 34(2): 359–70.

Reiss, A. (1984) 'Consequences of Compliance and Deterrence Models of Law Enforcement for the Exercise of Police Discretion', *Law and Contemporary Problems*, 47(4): 83–122.

Ricketts, M. (2006) 'Economic Regulation: Principles, History and Methods', in M. Crew and D. Parker (eds), *International Handbook on Economic Regulation*. Edward Elgar: Cheltenham.

Rogall, K. (2011) 'Country Report: Germany', in J. Gobert and A-M. Pascal (eds), *European Developments in Corporate Criminal Liability*. London: Routledge.

Rose-Ackerman, S. (1997) 'The Political Economy of Corruption', in K.A. Elliot (ed.), *Corruption and the Global Economy*. Washington, DC: Institute for International Economics.

Rose-Ackerman, S. (1999) *Corruption and Government. Causes, Consequences and Reform*. Cambridge: Cambridge University Press.

Rothe, D.L. (2010) 'Global E-waste Trade: The Need for Formal Regulation and Accountability beyond the Organization', *Criminology and Public Policy*, 9(3): 561–7.

Scott, C. (2001) 'Analysing Regulatory Space: Fragmented Resources and Institutional Design', *Public Law*, Summer: 329–53.

Seligson, M.A. (2006) 'The Measurement and Impact of Corruption Victimization: Survey Evidence from Latin America', *World Development*, 34(2): 381–404.

Shihata, I.F.I. (1997) 'Corruption – A General Review with an Emphasis on the Role of the World Bank', *Dickinson Journal of International Law*, 15(3): 451–85.

Shover, N. and Hochstetler, A. (2006) *Choosing White-collar Crime*. Cambridge: Cambridge University Press.

Silbey, S.S., Huising, R. and Coslovsky, S. (2009) 'The Sociological Citizen: Recognizing Relational Interdependence in Law and Organizations', *L'Année Sociologique*, 59: 201–29.

Silbey, S.S. (2011) 'The Sociological Citizen: Pragmatic and Relational Regulation in Law and Organizations', *Regulation and Governance*, 5(1): 1–13.

Slapper, G. and Tombs, S. (1999) *Corporate Crime*. London: Longman.

Smarzynska, B.K. and Wei, S-J. (2000) 'Corruption and the Composition of Foreign Direct Investment: Firm-Level Evidence', *Policy Research Working Paper 2360*, The World Bank.

Snider, L. and Bittle, S. (2011) 'The Challenges of Regulating Powerful Economic Actors', in J. Gobert and A-M. Pascal (eds), *European Developments in Corporate Criminal Liability*. London: Routledge.

Sparrow, M.K. (2008) *The Character of Harms. Operational Challenges in Control*. Cambridge: Cambridge University Press.

Spencer, J.R. (2002) 'The English system', in M. Delmas-Marty and J.R. Spencer (eds), *European Criminal Procedures*. Cambridge: Cambridge University Press.

Straw, J. (2009) 'Foreword' to Ministry of Justice's *Bribery: Draft Legislation*, available at: http://www.justice.gov.uk/downloads/legislation/bribery-act-2010-guidance.pdf <Accessed 10/1/2013>.

Sutherland, E. (1983) *White-collar Crime: The Uncut Version*. New Haven, CT: Yale University Press.

Tankebe, J. and Liebling, A. (2013) 'Legitimacy and Criminal Justice: An Introduction' in J. Tankebe and A. Liebling (eds), *Legitimacy and Criminal Justice: An International Exploration*. Oxford: OUP.

Tanzi, V. and Davoodi, H. (1998) 'Roads to Nowhere: How Corruption in Public Investment Hurst Growth', *Economic Issues 12*, International Monetary Fund.

Teubner, G. (1998) 'Juridification: Concepts, Aspects, Limits, Solutions', in R. Baldwin, C. Scott and C. Hood (eds), *A Reader on Regulation*. Oxford: Oxford University Press.

Tombs, S. (2011) 'State Complicity in the Production of Corporate Crime', in J. Gobert and A-M. Pascal (eds), *European Developments in Corporate Criminal Liability*. London: Routledge.

Tombs, S. and Whyte, D. (2007) *Safety Crimes*. Cullompton: Willan Publishing.

Tombs, S. and Whyte, D. (2013) 'Transcending the Deregulation Debate? Regulation, Risk, and the Enforcement of Health and Safety Law in the UK', *Regulation and Governance*, 7: 61–79.

Transparency International (2009a) *Progress Report 2009: Enforcement of the OECD Convention on Combating Bribery of Foreign Public Officials in International Business Transactions*. Transparency International, available at: http://archive.transparency.org/publications/publications/conventions/oecd_report_2009 <Accessed 10/11/2013>.

Transparency International (2009b) 'The Anti-corruption Plain Language Guide', available at: http://www.transparency.am/misc_docs/TI_Plain_Language_Guide_280709.pdf <Accessed 10/11/2013>.

Transparency International (2011a) *Bribe Payers Index 2011*. Transparency International, available at: http://bpi.transparency.org/bpi2011/results/ <Accessed 10/11/2013>.

Transparency International (2011b) *Cabs For Hire? Fixing the Revolving Door between Government and Business*. Transparency International, available at: http://www.transparency.org.uk/our-work/publications/10-publications/132-cabs-for-hire-fixing-the-revolving-door-between-government-and-business <Accessed 10/11/2013>.

Transparency International (2012) *Enforcing Corruption? Country Enforcement of the OECD Anti-Bribery Convention Progress Report 2012*. Transparency Internal, available at: http://www.transparency.org/whatwedo/pub/exporting_corruption_country_enforcement_of_the_oecd_anti_bribery_conventio <Accessed 10/11/2013>.

Transparency International (2013) *Exporting Corruption: Progress Report 2013: Assessing Enforcement of the OECD Convention on Combating Foreign Bribery*. Transparency International, available at: http://www.transparency.org/whatwedo/pub/exporting_corruption_progress_report_2013_assessing_enforcement_of_the_oecd <Accessed 10/11/2013>.

United Nations (2003) *United Nations Convention against Corruption*, UN, available at: http://www.unodc.org/pdf/crime/convention_corruption/signing/Convention-e.pdf <Accessed 10/11/2013>.

United Nations (2009) *Technical Guide to the United Nations Convention against Corruption*, UN, available at: http://www.unodc.org/documents/corruption/Technical_Guide_UNCAC.pdf <Accessed 10/11/2013>.

Vogel, D. (2010) 'The Private Regulation of Global Corporate Conduct. Achievements and Limitations', *Business and Society*, 49(1): 68–87.

Wells, C. (2011) 'Containing Corporate Crime. Civil or Criminal Controls?' in J. Gobert and A-M. Pascal (eds), *European Developments in Corporate Criminal Liability*. London: Routledge.

Whyte, D. (2007) 'The Crimes of Neo-Liberal Rule in Occupied Iraq', *British Journal of Criminology*, 47(2): 177–95.

Williams, S. (2006) 'The Mandatory Exclusions for Corruption in the New EC Procurement Directives', *European Law Review*, 31(5): 711–34.

Windsor, D. and Getz, K.A. (2000) 'Multilateral Cooperation to Combat Corruption: Normative Regimes Despite Mixed Motives and Diverse Values', *Cornell International Law Journal*, 33: 731–72.

Wolf, S. (2006) 'Modernization of the German Anti-corruption Criminal Law by International Legal Provisions', *German Law Journal*, 7(9): 785–92.

Zimring, F.E. and Johnson, D.T. (2005) 'On the Comparative Study of Corruption', *British Journal of Criminology*, 45(6): 793–809.

Index

CPSIA information can be obtained
at www.ICGtesting.com
Printed in the USA
BVHW041759141118
533056BV00006B/99/P

9 781138 637702